FRANCIS FRITH'S

EAST DEVON

PHOTOGRAPHIC MEMORIES

JOHN BAINBRIDGE was born in Staffordshire and now lives in Devon, where he works both as a freelance writer and chief executive of a conservation charity. He has spent much of his life exploring our countryside and towns on foot, and has written and broadcast widely about the topography, history, natural history and environment of the British Isles.

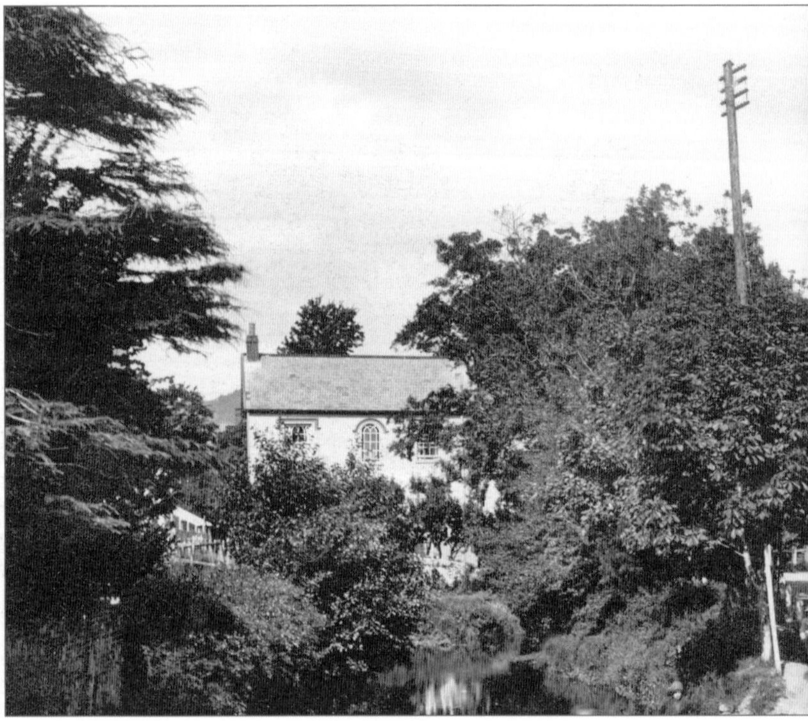

FRANCIS FRITH'S
PHOTOGRAPHIC MEMORIES

EAST DEVON

PHOTOGRAPHIC MEMORIES

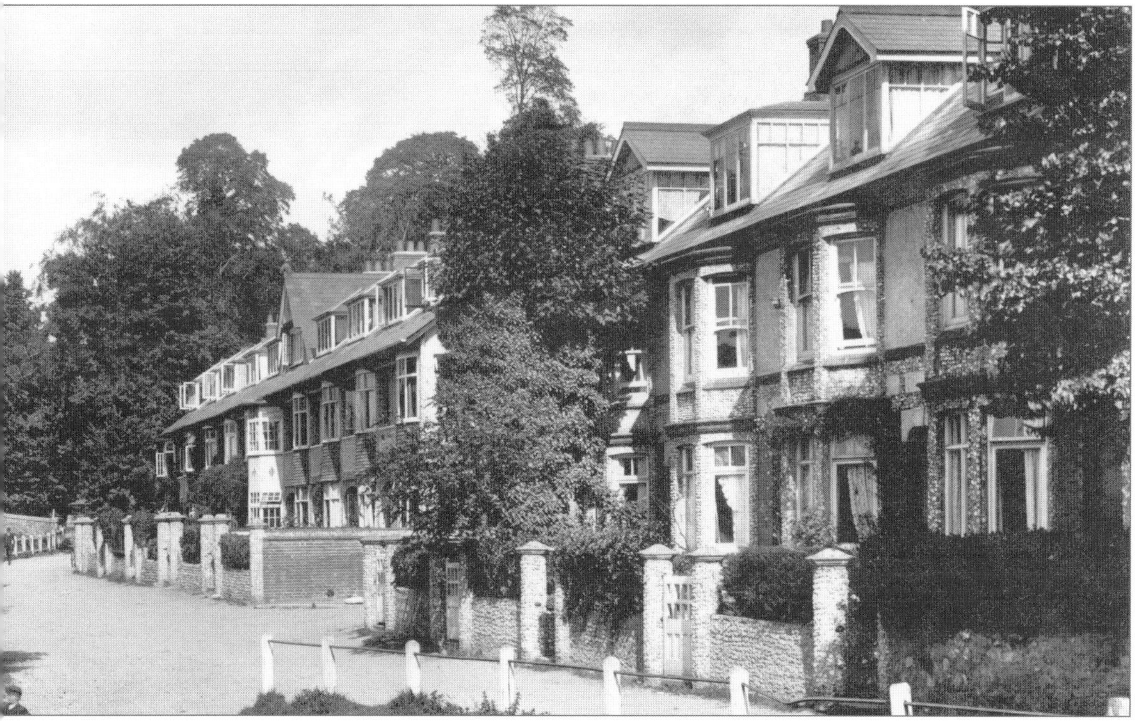

JOHN BAINBRIDGE

First published in the United Kingdom in 2004 by
Frith Book Company Ltd

Paperback Edition 2004
ISBN 1-85937-803-X

British Library Cataloguing in Publication Data

Francis Frith's East Devon - Photographic Memories
John Bainbridge
ISBN 1-85937-803-X

Frith Book Company Ltd
Frith's Barn, Teffont,
Salisbury, Wiltshire SP3 5QP
Tel: +44 (0) 1722 716 376
Email: info@francisfrith.co.uk
www.francisfrith.co.uk

Printed and bound in Great Britain

Front Cover: **SIDMOUTH,** *York Terrace 1924* 76352
Frontispiece: **SIDMOUTH,** *Milford Road 1918* 68750

The colour-tinting is for illustrative purposes only, and is not intended to be historically accurate

AS WITH ANY HISTORICAL DATABASE THE FRITH ARCHIVE IS CONSTANTLY BEING CORRECTED AND IMPROVED AND THE PUBLISHERS WOULD WELCOME INFORMATION ON OMISSIONS OR INACCURACIES

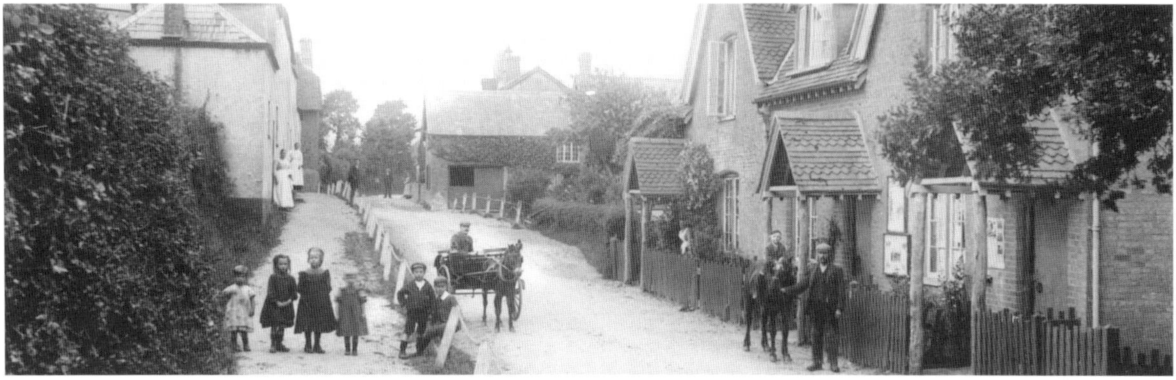

CONTENTS

FRANCIS FRITH: VICTORIAN PIONEER 7

EAST DEVON - AN INTRODUCTION 10

EAST OF THE EXE 14

THE VALE OF THE OTTER 40

THE LONELY COAST 62

A PASTORAL LAND 92

INDEX 115

Free Mounted Print Voucher 119

FRANCIS FRITH

VICTORIAN PIONEER

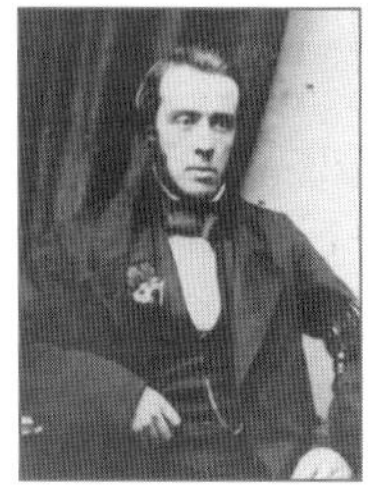

FRANCIS FRITH, founder of the world-famous photographic archive, was a complex and multi-talented man. A devout Quaker and a highly successful Victorian businessman, he was philosophical by nature and pioneering in outlook.

By 1855 he had already established a wholesale grocery business in Liverpool, and sold it for the astonishing sum of £200,000, which is the equivalent today of over £15,000,000. Now a very rich man, he was able to indulge his passion for travel. As a child he had pored over travel books written by early explorers, and his fancy and imagination had been stirred by family holidays to the sublime mountain regions of Wales and Scotland. 'What lands of spirit-stirring and enriching scenes and places!' he had written. He was to return to these scenes of grandeur in later years to 'recapture the thousands of vivid and tender memories', but with a different purpose. Now in his thirties, and captivated by the new science of photography, Frith set out on a series of pioneering journeys up the Nile and to the Near East that occupied him from 1856 until 1860.

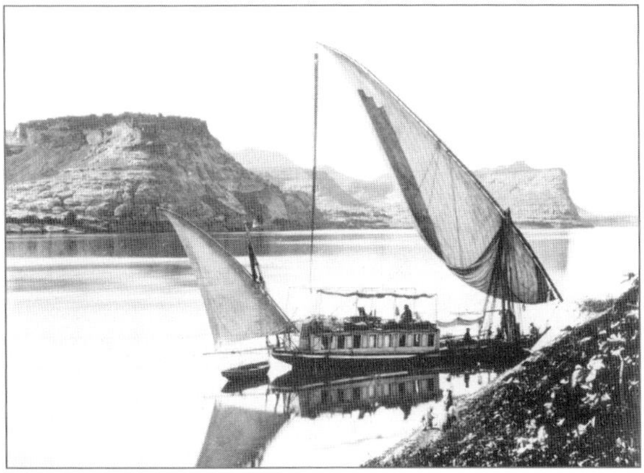

INTRIGUE AND EXPLORATION

These far-flung journeys were packed with intrigue and adventure. In his life story, written when he was sixty-three, Frith tells of being held captive by bandits, and of fighting 'an awful midnight battle to the very point of surrender with a deadly pack of hungry, wild dogs'. Wearing flowing Arab costume, Frith arrived at Akaba by camel sixty years before Lawrence of Arabia, where he encountered 'desert princes and rival sheikhs, blazing with jewel-hilted swords'.

He was the first photographer to venture beyond the sixth cataract of the Nile. Africa was still the mysterious 'Dark Continent', and Stanley and Livingstone's historic meeting was a decade into the future. The conditions for picture taking confound belief. He laboured for hours in his wicker dark-room in the sweltering heat of the desert, while the volatile chemicals fizzed dangerously in their trays. Back in London he exhibited his photographs and was 'rapturously cheered' by members of the Royal Society. His reputation as a photographer was made overnight.

VENTURE OF A LIFE-TIME

Characteristically, Frith quickly spotted the opportunity to create a new business as a specialist publisher of photographs. He lived in an era of immense and sometimes violent change.

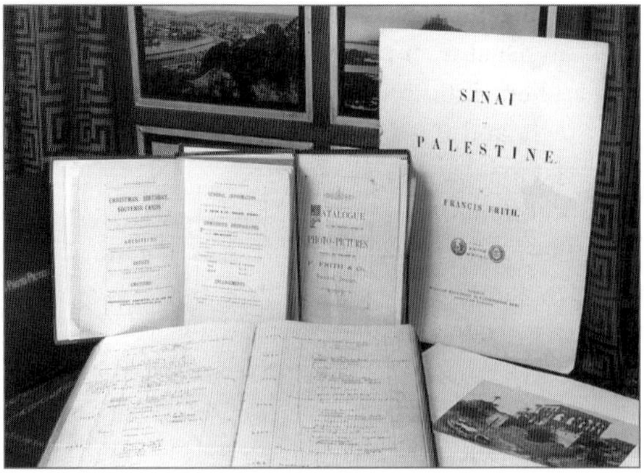

For the poor in the early part of Victoria's reign work was exhausting and the hours long, and people had precious little free time to enjoy themselves. Most had no transport other than a cart or gig at their disposal, and rarely travelled far beyond the boundaries of their own town or village. However, by the 1870s the railways had threaded their way across the country, and Bank Holidays and half-day Saturdays had been made obligatory by Act of Parliament. All of a sudden the working man and his family were able to enjoy days out and see a little more of the world.

With typical business acumen, Francis Frith foresaw that these new tourists would enjoy having souvenirs to commemorate their days out. In 1860 he married Mary Ann Rosling and set out on a new career: his aim was to photograph every city, town and village in Britain. For the next thirty years he travelled the country by train and by pony and trap, producing fine photographs of seaside resorts and beauty spots that were keenly bought by millions of Victorians. These prints were painstakingly pasted into family albums and pored over during the dark nights of winter, rekindling precious memories of summer excursions.

THE RISE OF FRITH & CO

Frith's studio was soon supplying retail shops all over the country. To meet the demand he gathered about him a small team of photographers, and published the work of independent artist-photographers of the calibre of Roger Fenton and Francis Bedford. In order to gain some understanding of the scale of Frith's business one only has to look at the catalogue issued by Frith & Co in 1886: it runs to some 670 pages, listing not only many thousands of views of the British Isles but also many photographs of most European countries, and China, Japan, the USA and Canada - note the sample page shown on page 9 from the hand-written Frith & Co ledgers recording the pictures. By 1890 Frith had created the greatest specialist photographic publishing company in the world, with over 2,000 sales outlets - more than the combined number that Boots and WH Smith have today! The picture on the next page shows the Frith & Co display board at Ingleton in the Yorkshire Dales (left of window). Beautifully constructed with a mahogany frame and gilt inserts, it could display up to a dozen local scenes.

POSTCARD BONANZA

The ever-popular holiday postcard we know today took many years to develop. In 1870 the Post Office issued the first plain cards, with a pre-printed stamp on one face. In 1894 they allowed other publishers' cards to be sent through the mail with an attached adhesive halfpenny stamp. Demand grew rapidly, and in 1895 a new size of postcard was permitted called the court card, but there was little room for illustration. In 1899, a year after Frith's death, a new card measuring 5.5 x 3.5 inches became the standard format, but it was not until 1902 that the divided back came into being, so that the address and message could be on one face and a full-size illustration on the other. Frith & Co were in the vanguard of postcard development: Frith's sons Eustace and Cyril continued their father's monumental task, expanding the number of views offered to the public and recording more and more places in Britain, as the

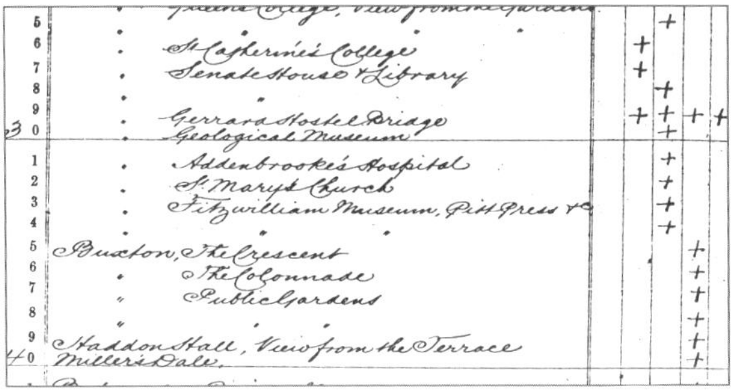
St Catherine's College
Senate House & Library
Gerrard Hostel Bridge
Geological Museum
Addenbrooke's Hospital
St Mary's Church
Fitzwilliam Museum, Pitt Press &c
Buxton, The Crescent
The Colonnade
Public Gardens
Haddon Hall, View from the Terrace
Miller's Dale

coasts and countryside were opened up to mass travel.

Francis Frith had died in 1898 at his villa in Cannes, his great project still growing. The archive he created continued in business for another seventy years. By 1970 it contained over a third of a million pictures showing 7,000 British towns and villages.

FRANCIS FRITH'S LEGACY

Frith's legacy to us today is of immense significance and value, for the magnificent archive of evocative photographs he created provides a unique record of change in the cities, towns and villages throughout Britain over a century and more. Frith and his fellow studio photographers revisited locations many times down the years to update their views, compiling for us an enthralling and colourful pageant of British life and character.

We are fortunate that Frith was dedicated to recording the minutiae of everyday life. For it is this sheer wealth of visual data, the painstaking chronicle of changes in dress, transport, street layouts, buildings, housing, engineering and landscape that captivates us so much today. His remarkable images offer us a powerful link with the past and with the lives of our ancestors.

THE VALUE OF THE ARCHIVE TODAY

Computers have now made it possible for Frith's many thousands of images to be accessed almost instantly. Frith's images are increasingly used as visual resources, by social historians, by researchers into genealogy and ancestry, by architects and town planners, and by teachers involved in local history projects.

In addition, the archive offers every one of us an opportunity to examine the places where we and our families have lived and worked down the years. Highly successful in Frith's own era, the archive is now, a century and more on, entering a new phase of popularity. Historians consider the Francis Frith Collection to be of prime national importance. It is the only archive of its kind remaining in private ownership. Francis Frith's archive is now housed in an historic timber barn in the beautiful village of Teffont in Wiltshire. Its founder would not recognize the archive office as it is today. In place of the many thousands of dusty boxes containing glass plate negatives and an all-pervading odour of photographic chemicals, there are now ranks of computer screens. He would be amazed to watch his images travelling round the world at unimaginable speeds through internet lines.

The archive's future is both bright and exciting. Francis Frith, with his unshakeable belief in making photographs available to the greatest number of people, would undoubtedly approve of what is being done today with his lifetime's work. His photographs depicting our shared past are now bringing pleasure and enlightenment to millions around the world a century and more after his death.

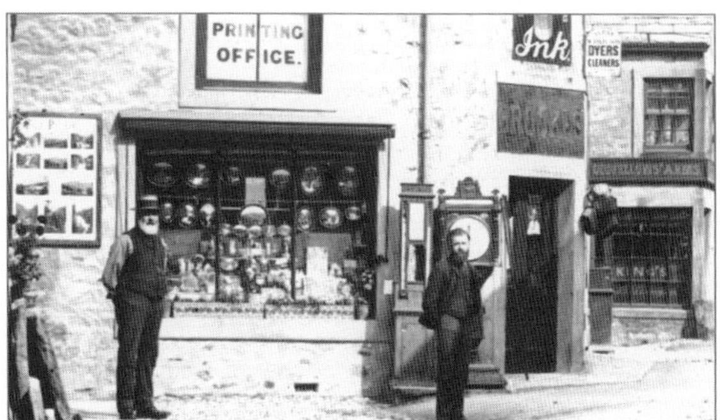

EAST DEVON
AN INTRODUCTION

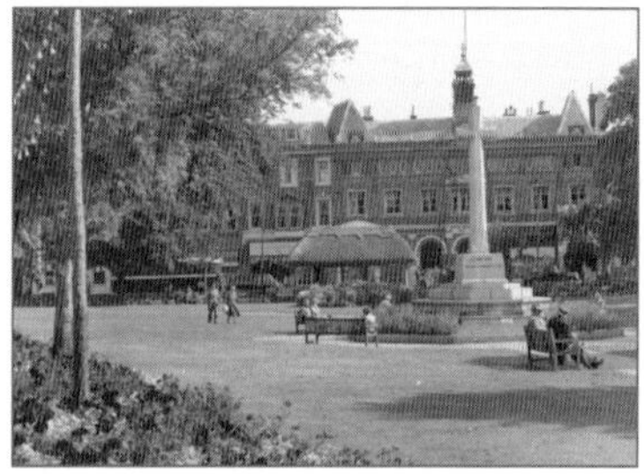

BETWEEN the Exe estuary and the Dorset border is a beautiful stretch of pastoral countryside, wild, unspoiled and timeless, surprisingly unchanged since the earliest of these photographs was taken in Queen Victoria's reign. East Devon is a land where you may still walk for a day and scarcely see a soul, where fields are farmed much as they were generations ago, and where long views look across broad river valleys, hilly ridges, heathlands and one of Britain's most dramatic coastlines.

In East Devon the divisions between past and present seem less rigid than in most of modern England, for this part of the county seems to breathe history. Towards the highest point of the rolling heaths just inland from Exmouth and Budleigh Salterton is the Iron Age hill-fort of Woodbury Castle, wooded now and bisected by a road. Three thousand years ago it was bare and fortified, dominating the landscape as a demonstration of the status of some chieftain of the Dumnonii, the Celtic tribe which occupied much of Devon. Within a few hours' walk are a dozen other great forts, guarding the land for a society we barely understand - the forts still hold the landscape today, for it is impossible to ignore their mighty presence.

East Devon's countryside has its history writ large for all to see. The fields worked by today's farmers are much the same as when they were farmed by their Saxon and medieval forebears. The hedgerows which create the patchwork quilt effect of colourful little meadows are centuries old, filled with wild flowers each spring, their banks tumbled by badgers. Many of the villages and farms bear Saxon names, and the parish churches would be recognisable to the Normans who endowed them, despite the excesses of Victorian restorers. The cottages illustrated in some of these photographs have been lived in for generations, and in some cases are little changed.

This is a land where we walk in the footsteps of our own history. Raiding Vikings sailed their longships up the estuaries of the Exe and Axe; the latter may even be the setting of the Battle of Brunanburgh, King Athelstan's great victory over the Danes, Picts and Scots which created modern England. Tales are told of many a Civil War skirmish in what are now peaceful pastures. Local men flocked to the Duke of Monmouth's banner in 1685, and a great number died at the Battle of Sedgemoor or faced transportation or execution after Judge Jeffries' Bloody Assizes.

But the more peaceful past is visible too. A walk around any East Devon churchyard will reveal the names and history of those who trod these lanes and paths before you: villagers, landlords, fishermen, country gentlemen and ladies - those otherwise anonymous folk who knew the lie of this land and left their subtle marks on its fields, homes, parklands and forests.

To understand the true beauty of East Devon, you really do need to explore its ancient pathways, quiet country lanes, and dramatic coastline on foot as past generations did. The area is blessed with a wonderful network of footpaths and bridleways, and within a little distance the noise and cares of the 21st century are left behind. The quietness of this countryside is beyond belief; often you will hear just the wind soughing through the trees, the mewing of a buzzard and the yelp of a fox. One delightful noise on Sunday mornings is the pealing of church bells, centuries old, their tolling lifting up to the ridge tops and down to the river valleys. It is a sound that would have been so familiar to the people captured for ever on film by the Frith photographers, and to those who went before and now rest in a score of village churchyards. It is a strange feeling to listen to a sound that our forebears would have recognised.

A number of long ridges run from inland towards the sea, divided from one another by the area's rivers, the Otter, the Sid, the Branscombe and Beer Brooks, and the Axe. East Devon's long ridgeway paths date from at least the Iron Age; most run in the general direction of the sea, suggesting that they were routes to collect salt for the preservation of meat. Some ridge paths may even have been ceremonial, or ways of the dead, for on the high ground around Broad Down and Farway is a Bronze Age necropolis, or burial ground, the largest in Devon outside Dartmoor.

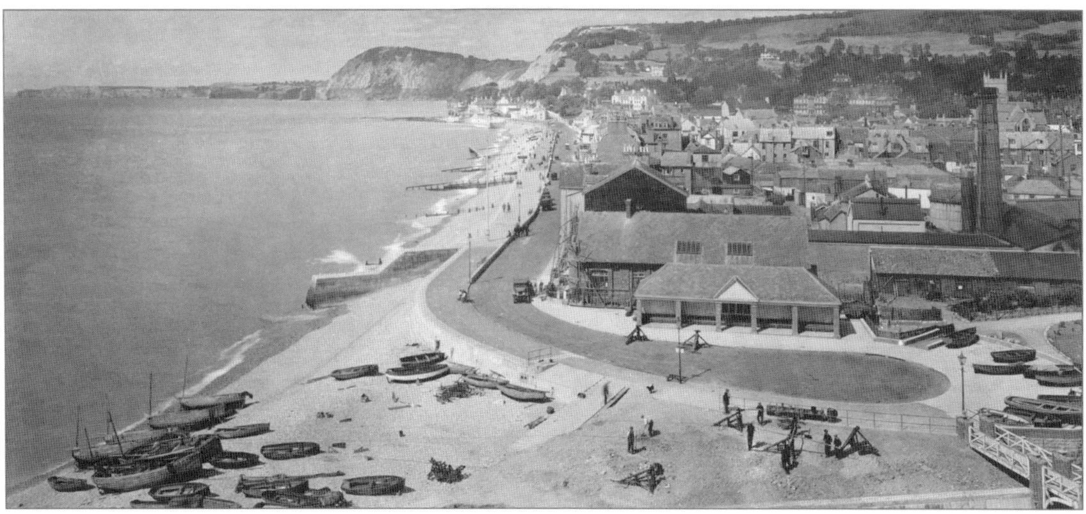

SIDMOUTH, *From Salcombe Hill 1931* 84078

These early residents of East Devon held the land to be sacred, living in tune with its seasons and harmonies. A day alone walking in their steps can give a hint of such feelings to the modern-day explorer, but leave your watch at home and take your time from the swing of the sun over the earth.

The valley field paths indicate ways followed by parishioners on their way to church. Coastal footpaths - now part of the South West Way National Trail - came into being as coastguards paced their length attempting to deter the landing of smugglers' contraband.

Some of the inland paths form the route of the East Devon Way from Exmouth to Lyme Regis, which passes through many of the towns and villages illustrated in this book, and through the wilder countryside as well. This waymarked route is an excellent introduction to East Devon; it can be walked in a long weekend, or why not add a few more days and return to Exmouth along the coastal footpath?

The resorts along this coast developed earlier than most, receiving a boost to their fortunes when Napoleon closed the Continent to British visitors. Exmouth is Devon's oldest resort. It has managed to retain the air of dignity that attracted such Georgian luminaries as Lady Nelson and Lady Byron, who gave added status to an already well-established watering place. Sidmouth is a delightful Regency town, and has its place in history. In 1819 George III's spendthrift son the Duke of Kent hid here from his creditors, bringing with him his baby daughter Alexandrina Victoria. In fact, our history might have been very different, for a local on a shooting expedition very nearly dispatched the future Queen of England with a badly aimed shot that missed the royal cot by inches!

Budleigh Salterton is so genteel that it almost defines the word. Here we can see the sea wall where Sir John Everett Millais painted his much-reproduced work *The Boyhood of Raleigh*. This is an appropriate subject and setting too, for the young Raleigh almost certainly sat on this sea front listening to yarns from old sailors and fishermen. The town's beach comprises millions of round stones or 'pobbles', and there are few more evocative sounds than the waves crashing down on them on stormy days, followed by a noise like a sigh as the water runs back into the sea. On the coastal headlands around Sidmouth it is possible to look in either direction at most of East Devon's coastline, which is red sandstone to the west and chalk to the east. The deep combes running towards the sea were transport routes for smugglers such as the notorious Jack Rattenbury. Rattenbury knew well those little fishing villages, such as Beer and Branscombe, now modest resorts for those who favour a seaside holiday with the emphasis on coastal walking, seeking out rock pools, or browsing in antique shops.

The market towns of East Devon, such as Honiton and Axminster, are best visited on their market days, when colourful stalls fill the streets and the country dwellers of East Devon throng the shops. There is a cheerful chaos about such occasions, as pedestrians weave in and out of the pavements and motor cars take second place. There is something wonderfully medieval about the whole procedure – the atmosphere is carnival-like and anarchic. At Axminster Fair the Lord of the Manor opens the festivities on

Minster Green by handing to the town crier a glove to the declamation of the ancient rhyme: 'The glove is up, the fair's begun, let no man be arrested till glove be down, God Save the Queen!' In Honiton, the Mayor throws hot pennies into the crowd and the local children scramble to pick them up. These are not just quaint customs, but a real throwback to medieval times, embraced with great joy by the assembled crowds.

On quieter days a walk around the streets of East Devon with these photographs to hand will show how little has changed, even from Victorian times. Some rows of cottages have been demolished, but you will be able to see where they were. Occasionally, a new road has forced itself out on to a main street, or a new development been built, and these Frith photographs are a valuable visual record of what was there before. Such expeditions are best made early in the morning or on quiet summer evenings when the pavements are less crowded and the roads freer of cars. It is easier then to see the buildings as the Frith photographers would have seen them.

The parish churches have changed least of all; they are a direct link to earlier periods of our history. But they are not just museums, but places of worship for today's residents, just as they were for local folk in medieval, Norman, and even Saxon times. Shops have changed the most, though some town businesses featured in this book have survived to this day, occasionally in their original premises. The inns of East Devon feature prominently. In the earliest photographs they would have had a patronage that seldom went beyond the local population. Today, visitors from all over flock to the best of them for the quality of their meals and the fame of their ales.

East Devon remains one of the least spoiled corners of England. We are indeed fortunate not only to have this superb collection of photographs, but also to be able to wander across a land that has changed so little since they were taken.

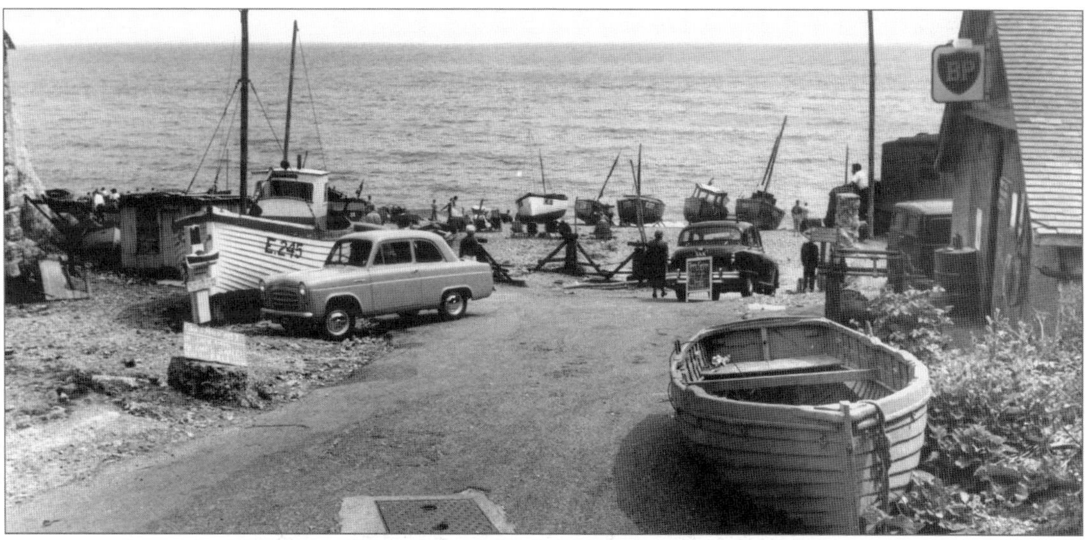

BEER, *Sea Hill c1965* B55060

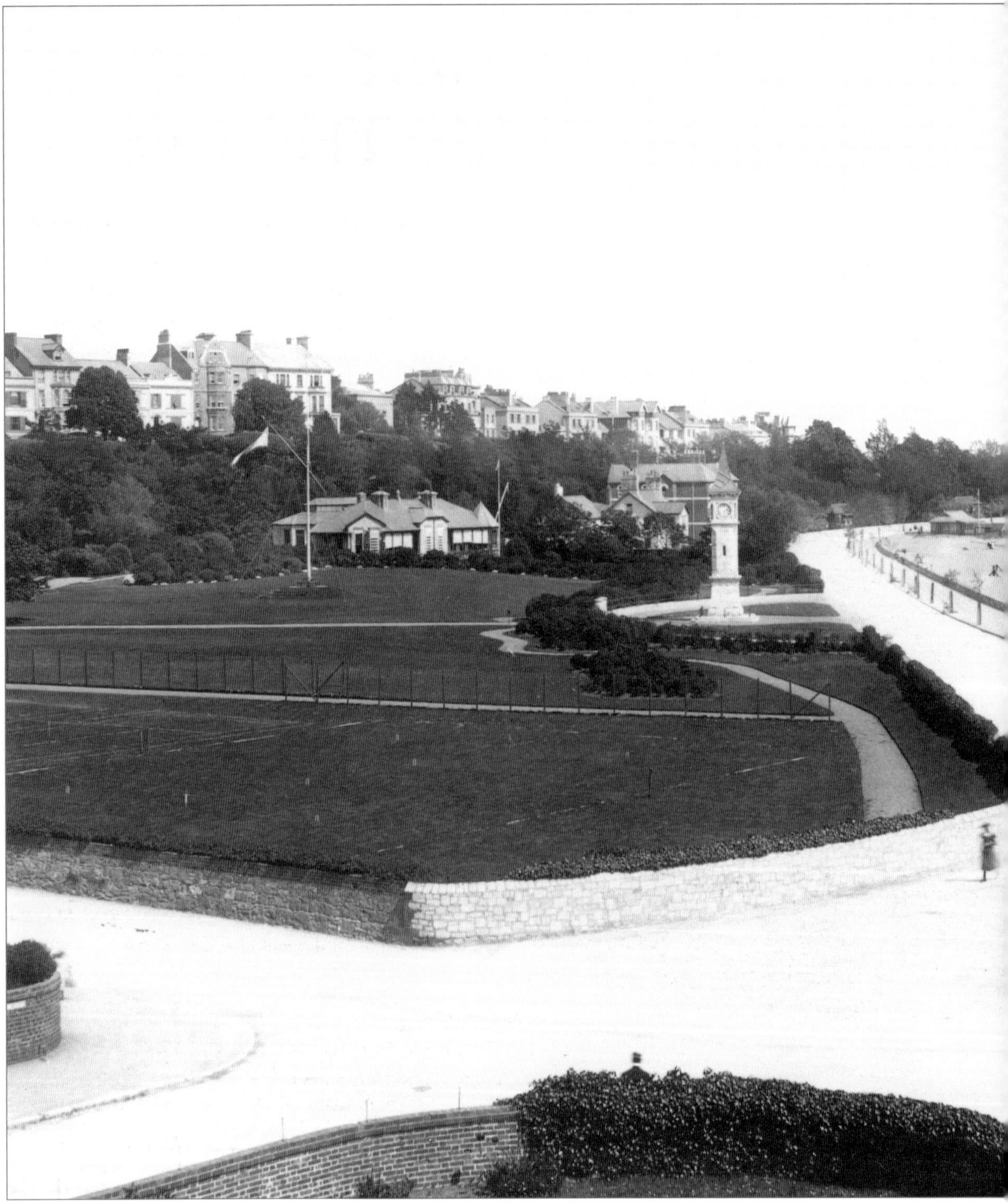

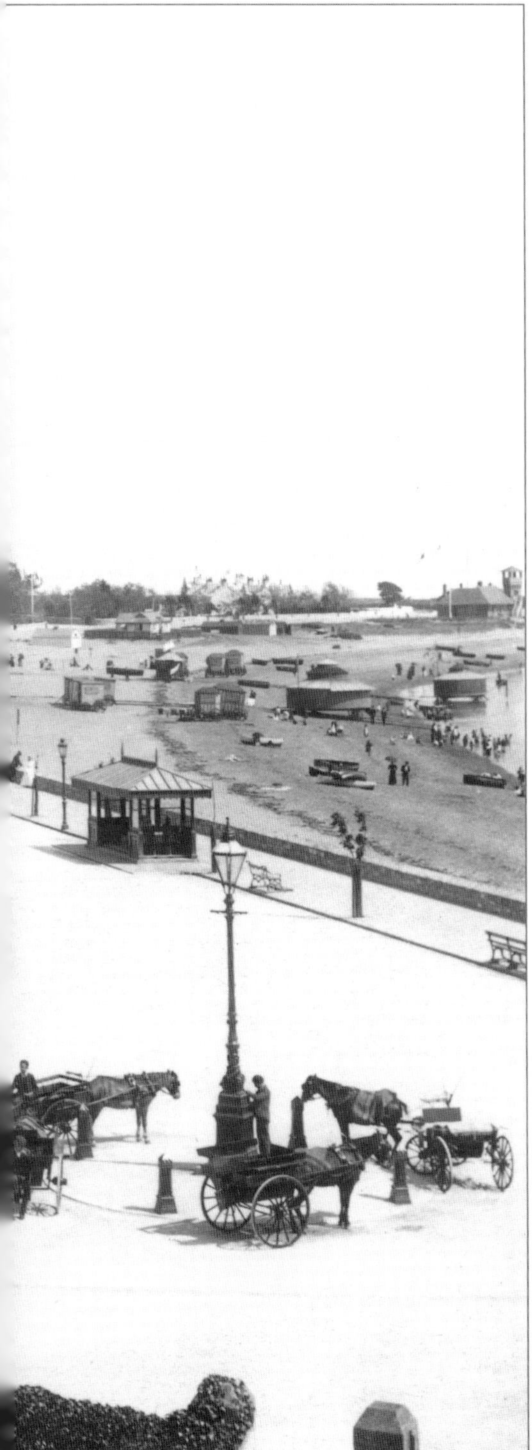

EAST OF THE EXE

THE EXE ESTUARY is one of the finest spots in England for bird watching, with considerable numbers of wildfowl to be seen in the early months of the year. Exmouth, Devon's oldest seaside resort, lines the eastern side of the river mouth, with the sand dunes of Dawlish Warren to the west. Towards Exeter are the fishing ports of Lympstone and Topsham, each a delight for artists and photographers, and settlements from the time that marauding Danes sailed up the broad reaches of the Exe.

The heart of the countryside between the rivers Exe and Otter is wild and rolling heathland; Woodbury, Bicton and Aylesbeare Commons are probably little changed since the great hill-fort of Woodbury Castle was occupied by Iron Age Celts, and are now places to listen for nightjars on long summer evenings.

Exmouth is the largest town in this part of East Devon, and a very popular family resort with miles of long beaches. Here are all the facilities one might expect in a modern seaside town catering for all ages. Budleigh Salterton is more a town that just happens to be by the sea, unspoiled and unpretentious, just the place for a quiet escape from the pressures of 21st-century life. Both resorts are excellent places to begin an exploration of the ancient land East of Exe.

EXMOUTH
The Beach from Moreton Crescent 1896 37620

Exmouth found favour as a holiday resort in the early 18th century, and it prospered when the continent was closed to tourists during the Napoleonic Wars. Away from the mouth of the River Exe, the long sandy beaches provide safe bathing. In this view, looking towards The Beacon, we can see bathing machines on the sands and carriages waiting to take holidaymakers back to their hotels.

EXMOUTH
The Parade 1906
53941

Where better for Edwardian ladies to promenade than on Exmouth's Parade, the long walk above the sea wall? Work began on the Parade in 1780, enclosing marsh and pastureland; a more substantial sea wall was built in the 19th century. Hotels and boarding houses dominated the sea front by King Edward VIII's reign.

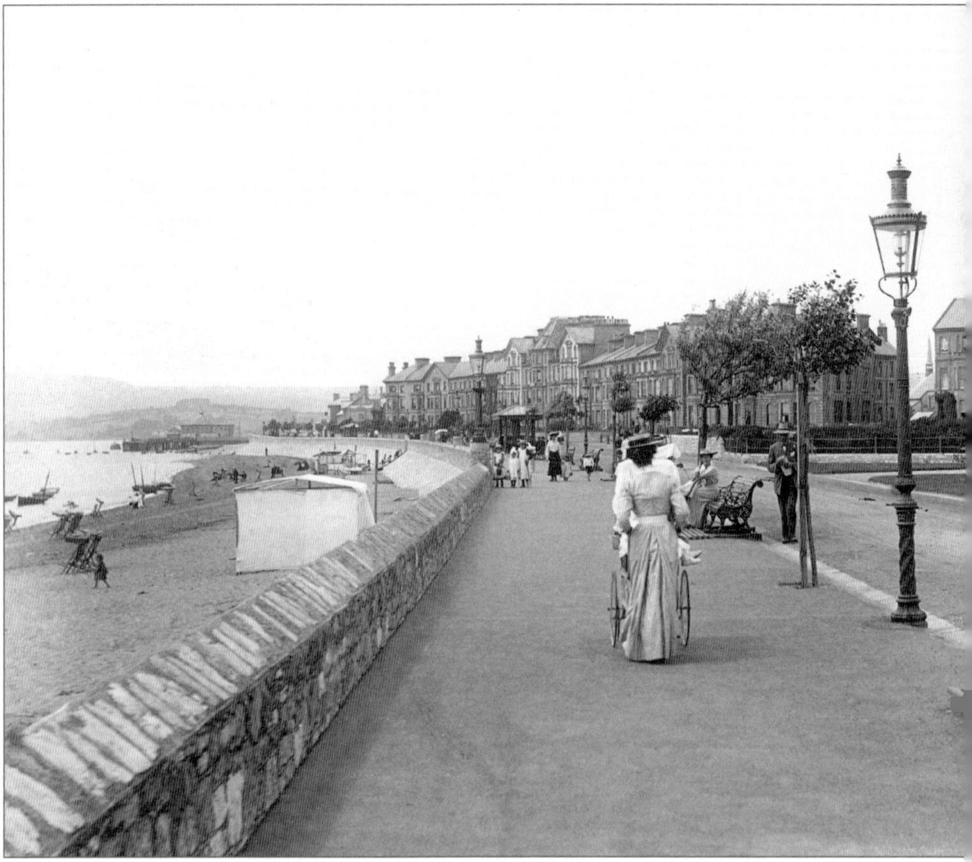

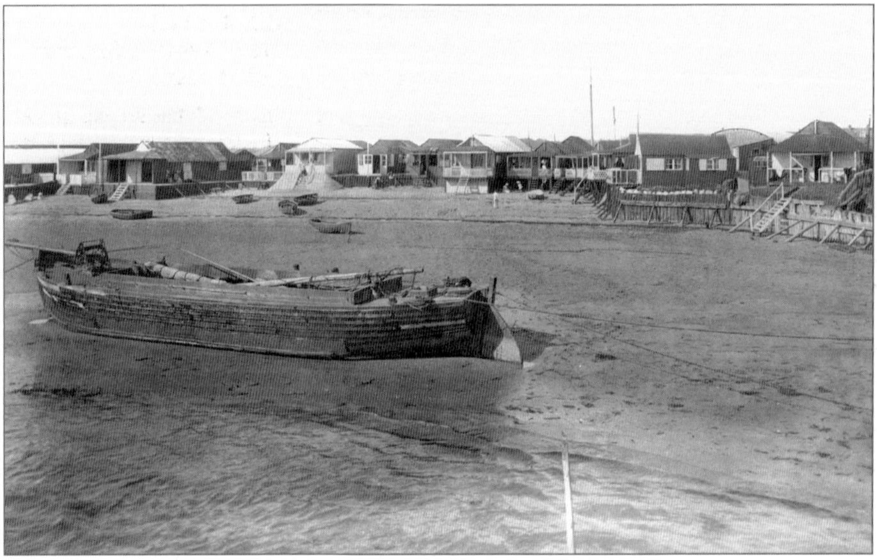

EXMOUTH
The Boathouses 1906
56773

In the mid-19th century, Exmouth gained importance as a shipbuilding centre and fishing port - tons of herring were landed each month. Trains were laid on to rush the fish to the London and Midland markets. By 1906 these industries were in decline, and leisure boats were taking the place of fishing trawlers.

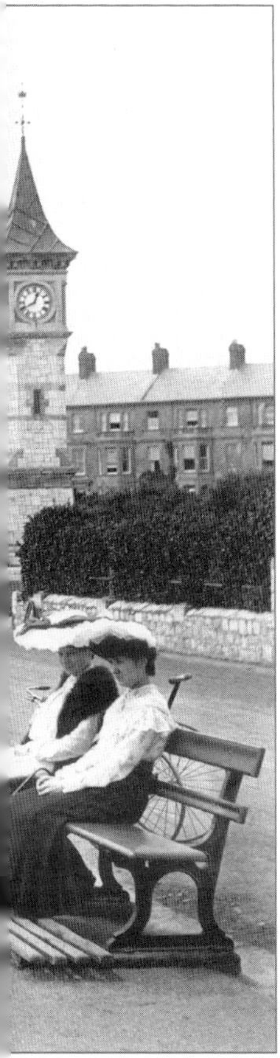

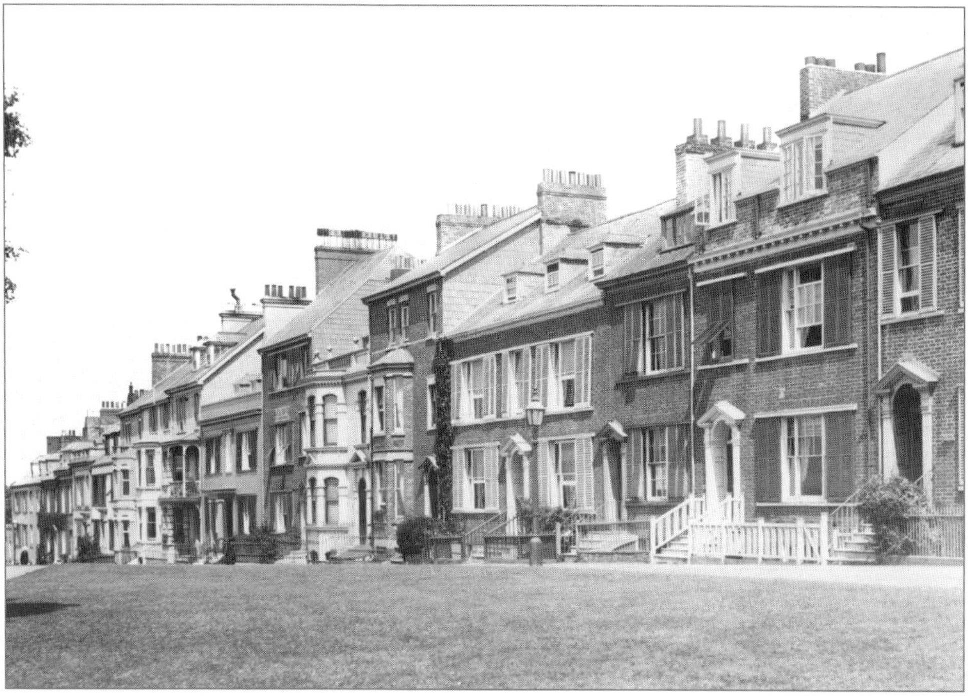

▲ **EXMOUTH,** *Beacon Terrace 1906* 56770

As Exmouth developed, residential streets such as the mostly Georgian Beacon Terrace were built on higher ground overlooking the sea. Many visitors made the town their home, and the population increased markedly as Exmouth entered the 20th century.

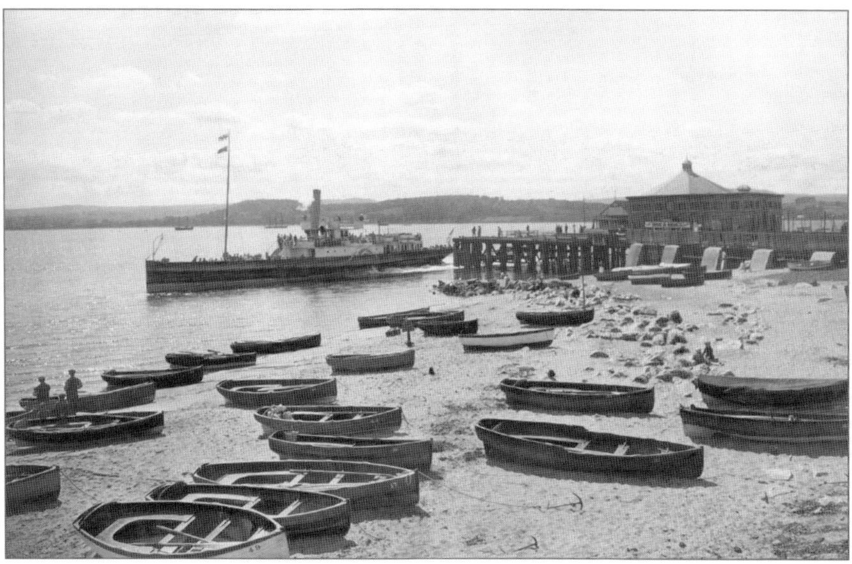

◄ **EXMOUTH**
The Pier and Steamer 1922 72957

Exmouth has no pier in the traditional sense of the word, but this landing stage served as an embarkation point for tourists wishing to take to the water. By 1836 steam packets linked the resort to London, and there was soon a regular shipping route to the Channel Islands. The vessel we see here took trippers along the cost of Lyme Bay, visiting other resorts along the way.

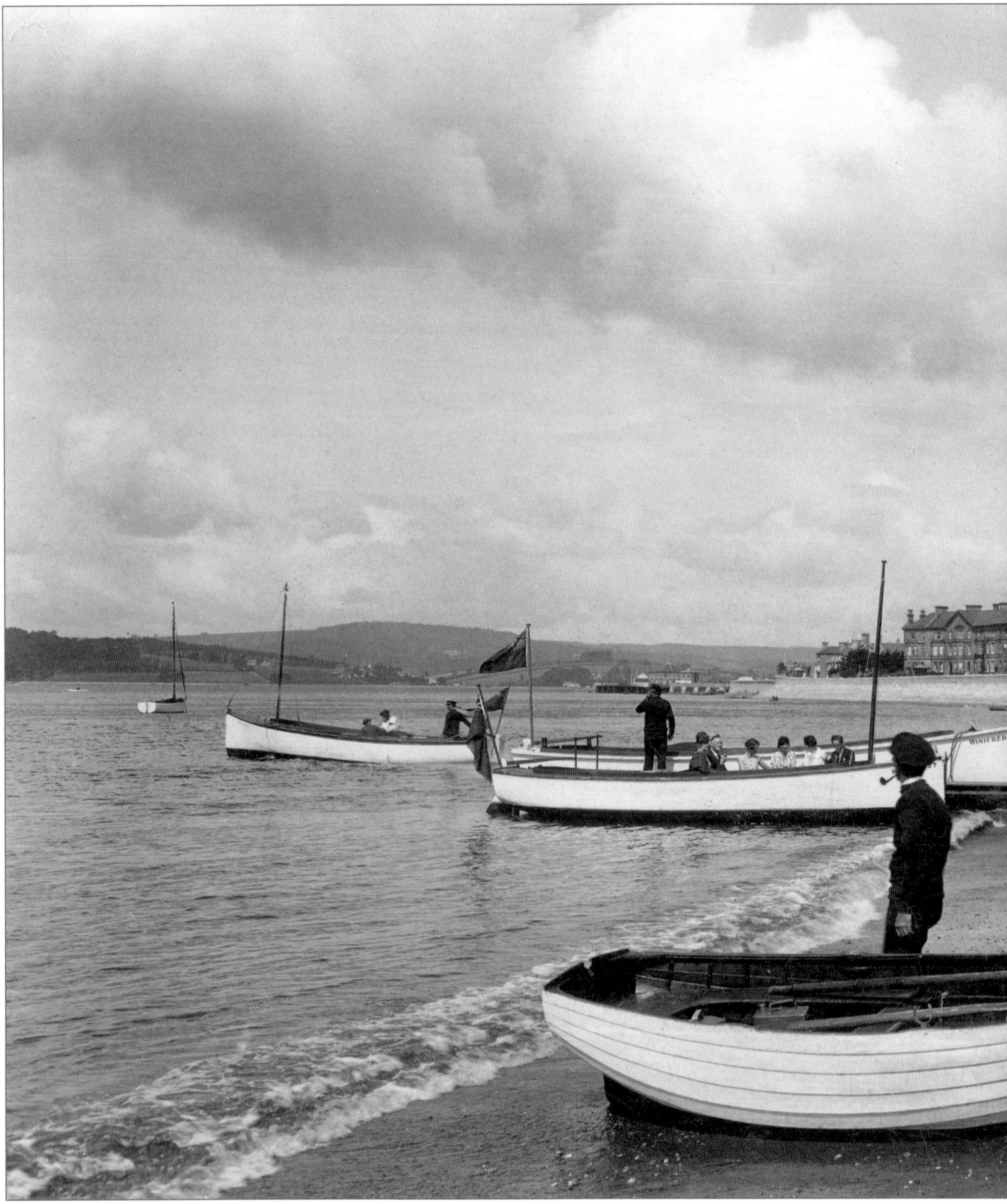
WINIFRED

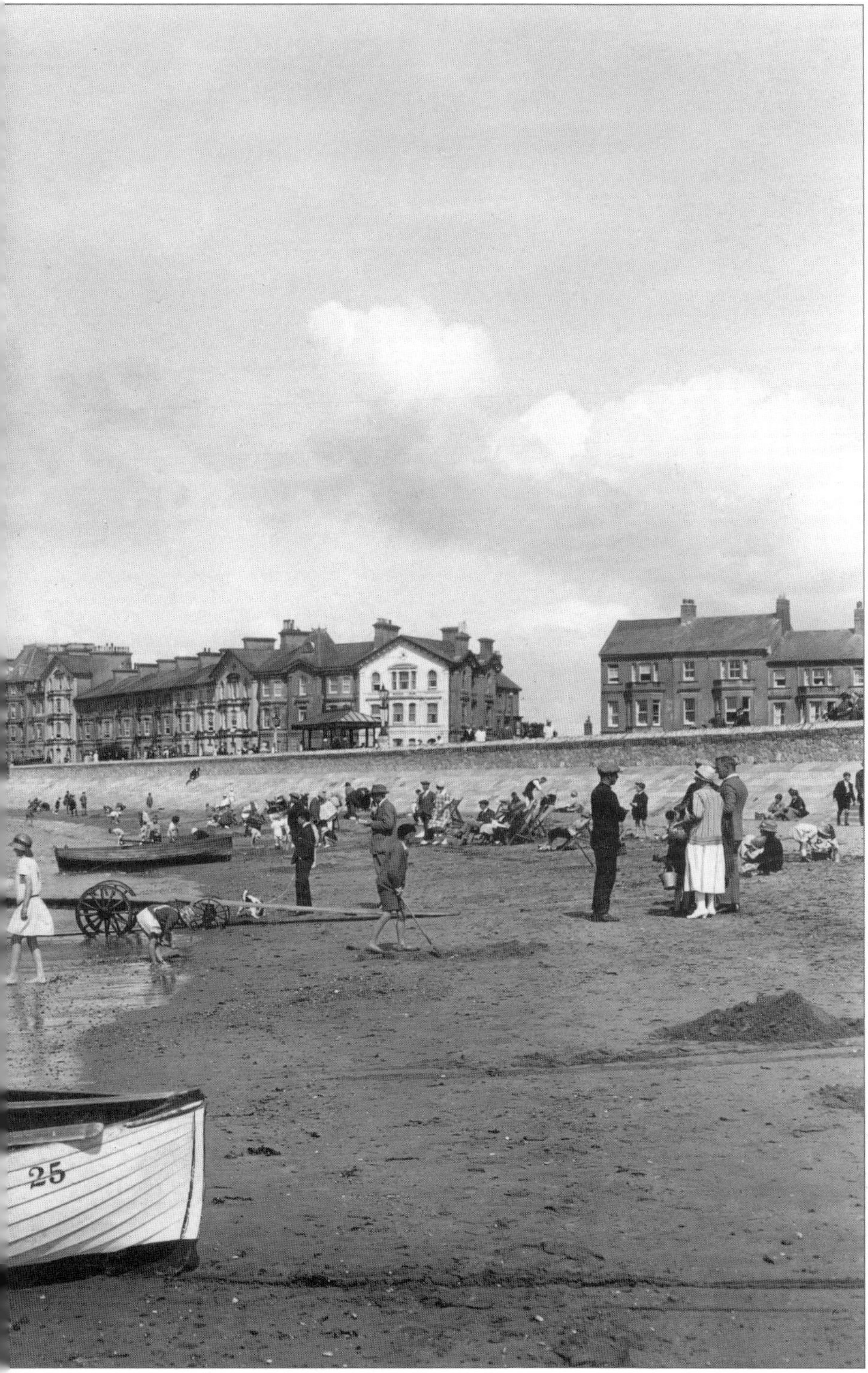

EXMOUTH
The Sands and Boats 1925 78600

Exmouth's long beach offers safe bathing, and its gently shelving sands allow easy access for boats. Here we see local mariners taking passengers out for trips along the coast. The numbered boat in the foreground is one of many for hire.

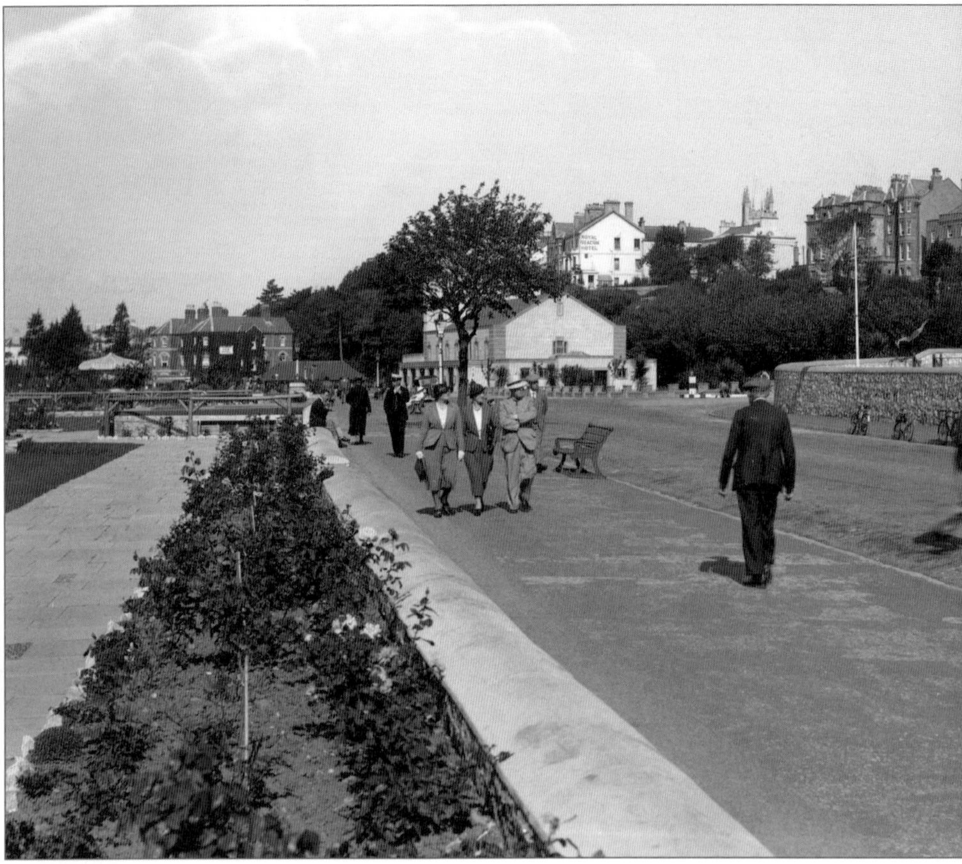

▶ **EXMOUTH**
The Swimming Pool 1938 88618

As Exmouth grew as a resort, new attractions were laid on for visitors, including this swimming pool (right), which used water from the sea. Not far away, bowling greens and tennis courts were laid out, and a 600-seat theatre was built.

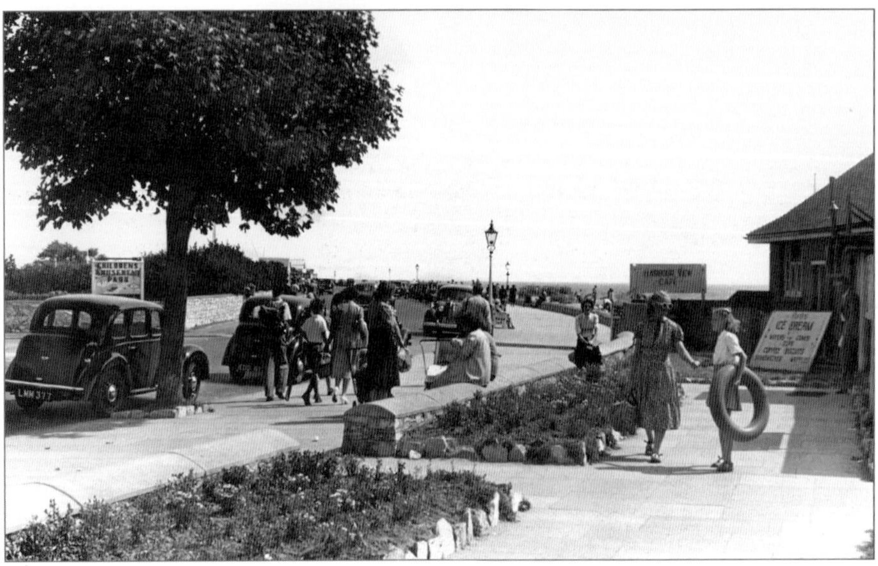

◀ **EXMOUTH**
The Promenade c1955 E52018

In the decade before World War II, most visitors to Exmouth arrived by train. By the more affluent 1950s car ownership had increased, and the resort's long sea front served as a convenient car park. On the right of the photograph is the Harbour View Café, and to the left the children's amusement park.

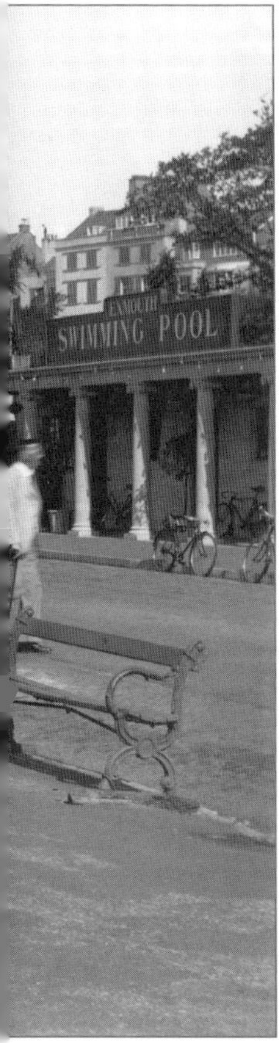

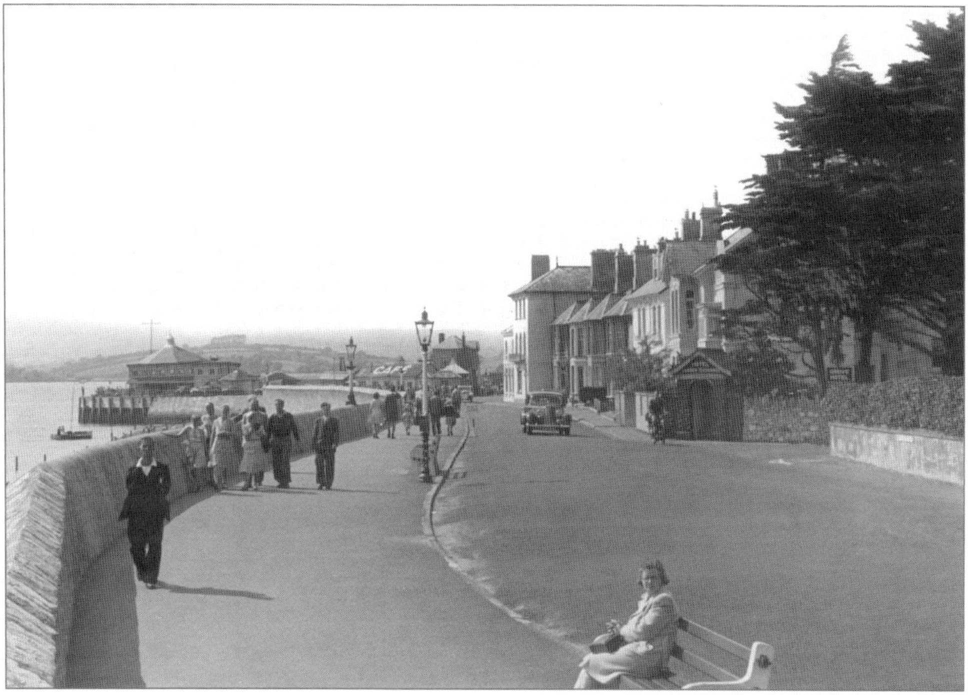

▲ **EXMOUTH,** *The Promenade and the Pier c1955* E52026

Despite an increase in traffic, the Parade remains a pleasant area for a walk or to simply sit and admire the views across to Dawlish Warren and Berry Head. It is interesting to notice how fashions have changed since the 1906 photograph (53941 on page 16), though they are still very formal compared to our modern t-shirted world.

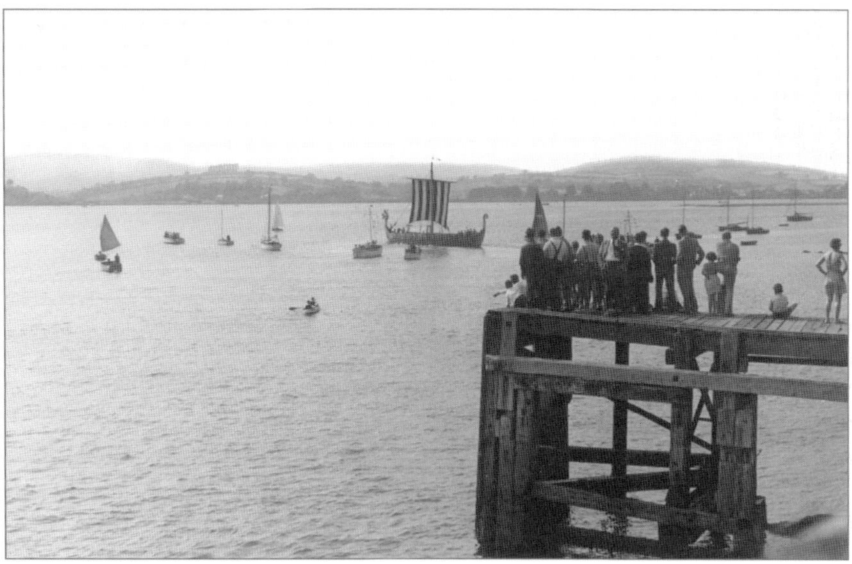

◄ **EXMOUTH**
The Estuary c1955
E52031

In AD1001, Viking raiders under the command of King Sweyn landed in the Exe estuary, raiding and burning the town of Exanmutha before marching on to Exeter. Here we see holidaymakers and residents watching a re-enactment of those troubled times.

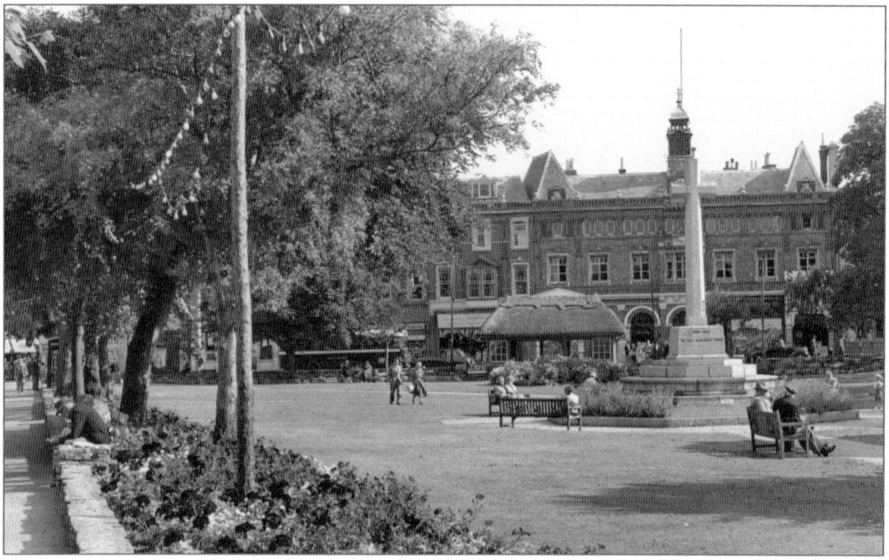

EXMOUTH
The Strand Gardens c1955 E52053

The Strand Gardens are an oasis of green in the very heart of Exmouth, a place to rest whilst shopping and a meeting place for friends. Here too is Exmouth's war memorial.

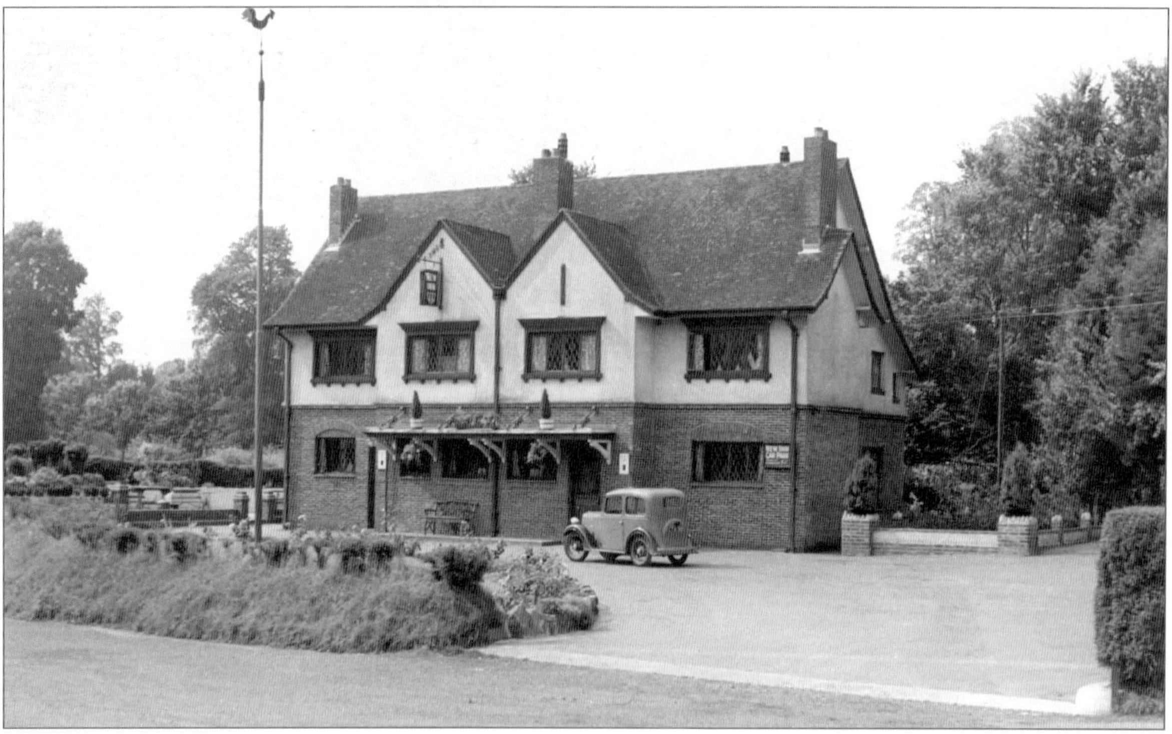

LITTLEHAM, *The New Inn c1955* L57013

Modern-day Exmouth sprawls across the two ancient parishes of Withycombe Raleigh and Littleham. The latter became a suburb of Exmouth in the last decades of the 20th century. The New Inn was built to cater for Littleham's growing population.

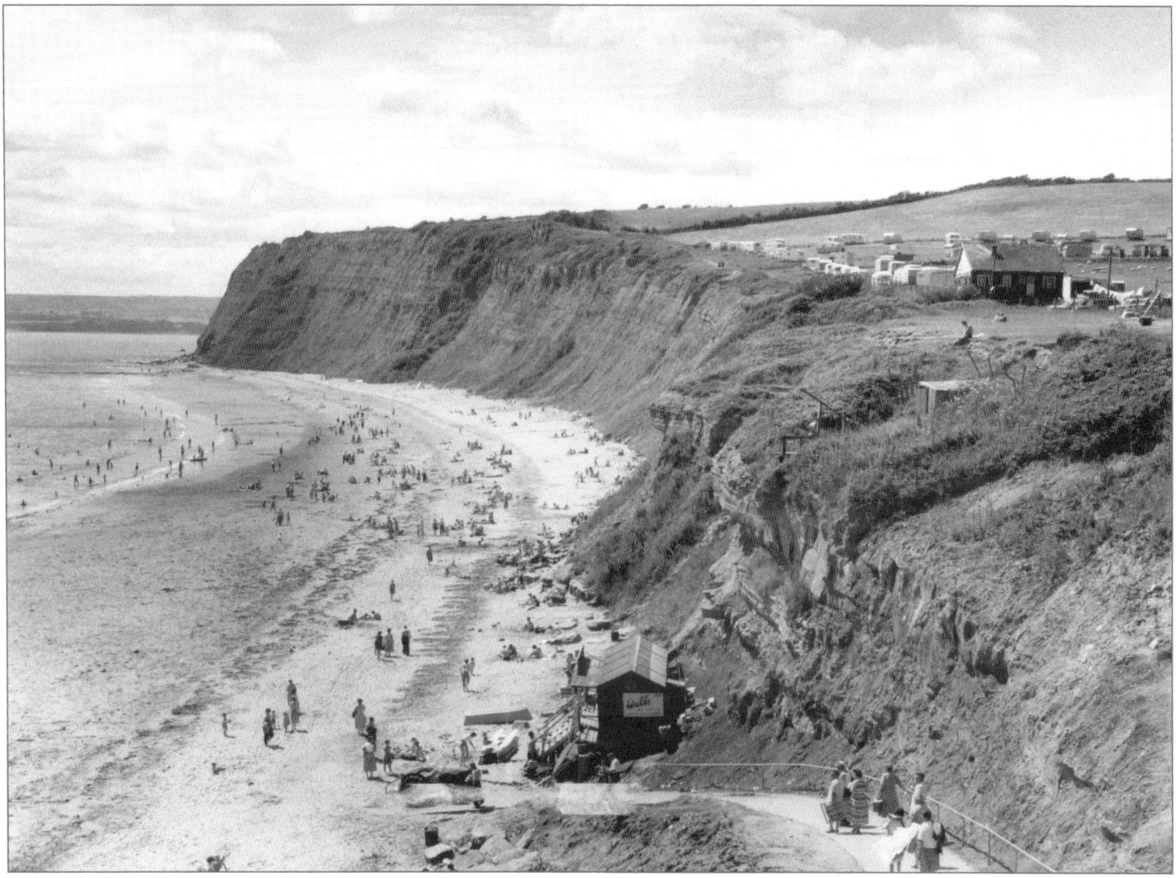

LITTLEHAM, *Sandy Bay Beach c1960* L57056

Sandy Bay is Littleham's beach, offering some of the finest bathing on the East Devon coast. The few scattered caravans on the cliff top mark the site of what has now become a vast 'caravanopolis' with hundreds of caravans, a car park, a restaurant and a shop.

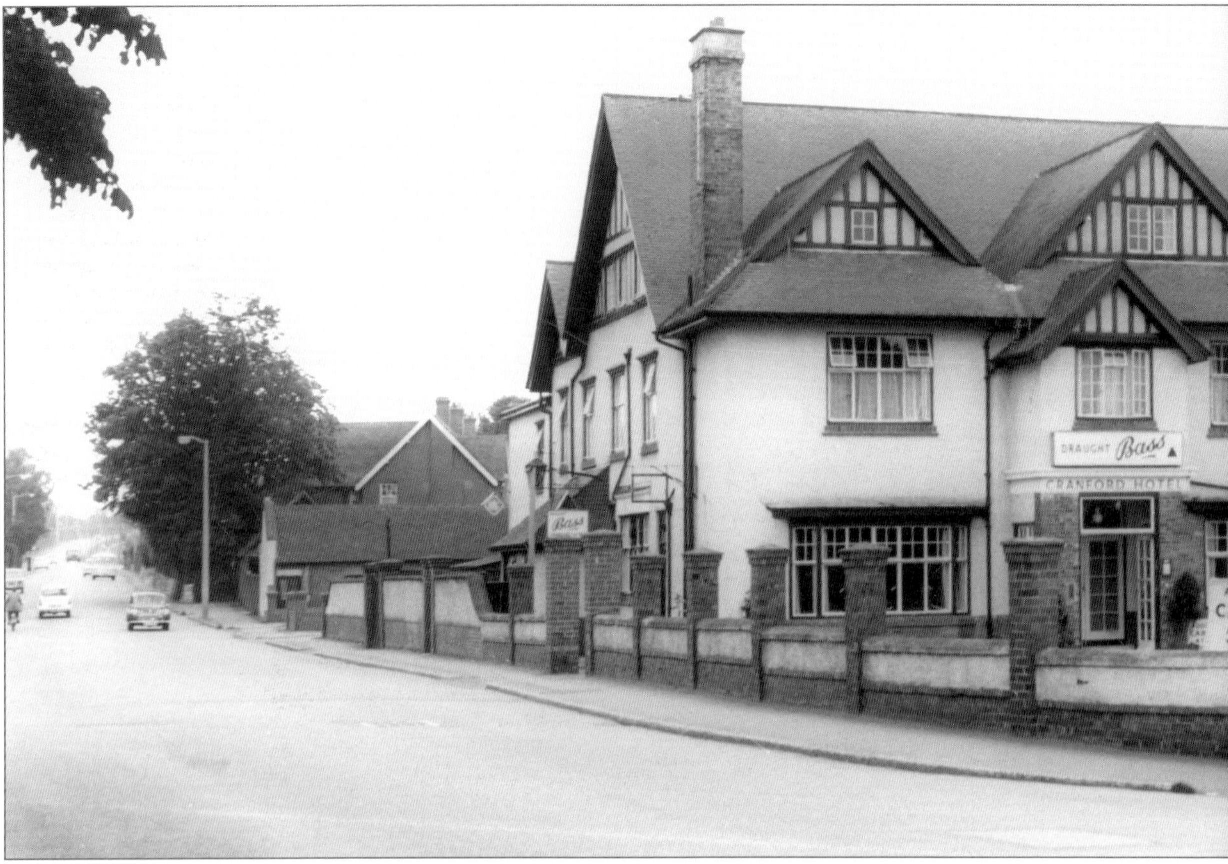

▶ **BUDLEIGH SALTERTON**
From the East 1898
42451

This quiet resort takes its name from the salterns or salt pans used by the monks from the nearby Otterton Priory. Budleigh's long beach is made up of millions of large pebbles, or 'pobbles', as they are known locally. Its lack of sand might be the reason that it did not develop as a traditional family resort, but rather as a refined watering place much loved by residents and visitors, who return year after year.

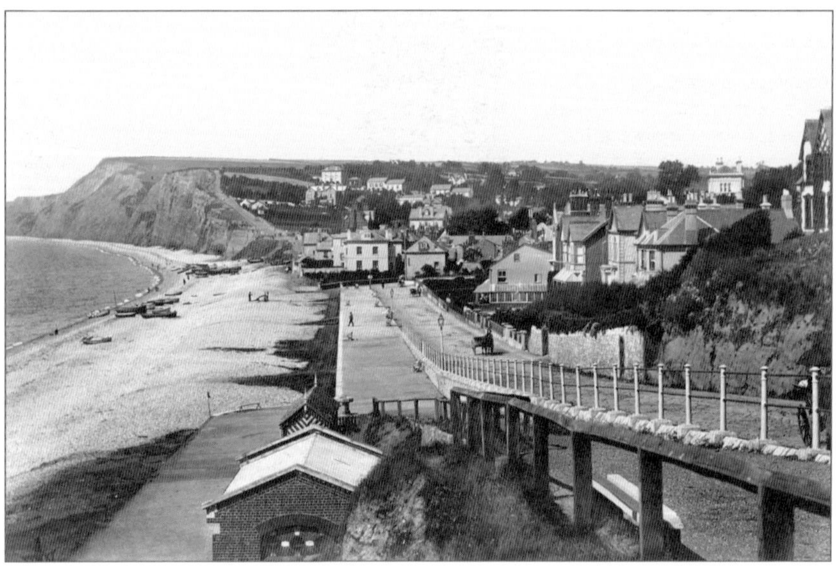

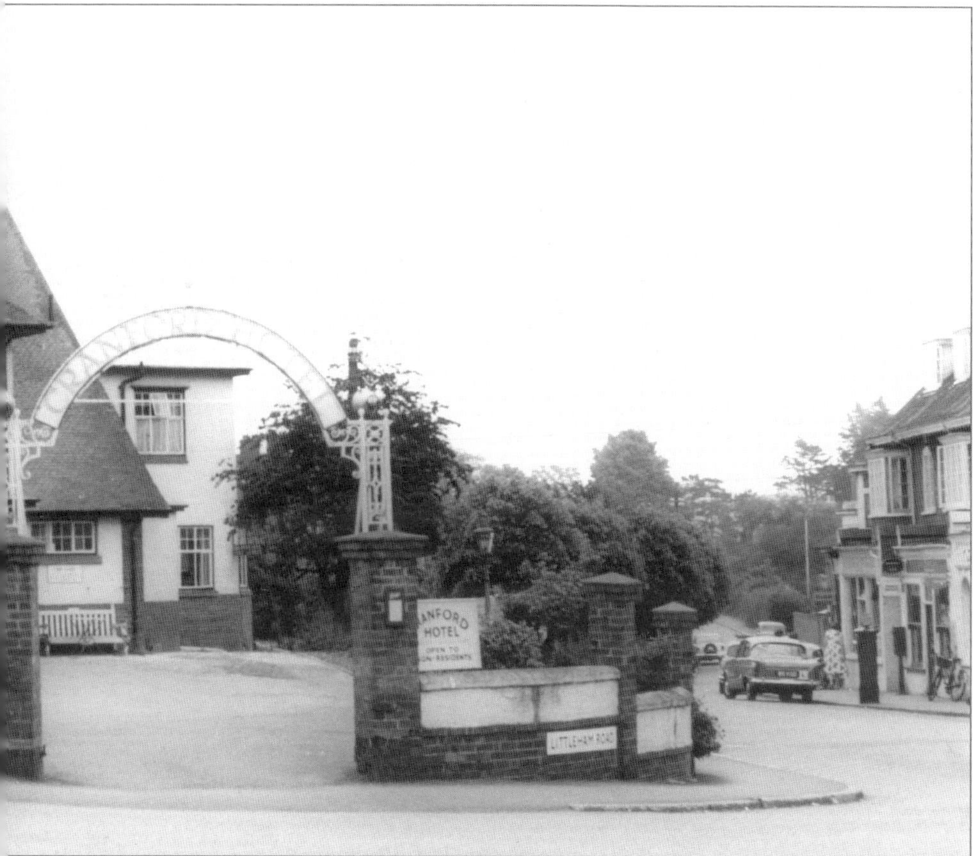

LITTLEHAM
The Cranford Hotel c1960 L57066

Littleham became fashionable during the Georgian period when such notables as Lady Nelson, who was estranged from her naval hero husband, came to live in the village. Lady Nelson now lies beneath the trees of Littleham's churchyard. Legend relates that Sir Walter Raleigh smoked the first tobacco to be brought into England whilst staying in Littleham.

BUDLEIGH SALTERTON
East Terrace 1901 47842

Once just a hamlet of fishermen's cottages, Budleigh grew as a town and watering place in the first half of the 19th century, when a number of well-heeled society figures took up residence. Many new properties were built to cater for the demand of these newcomers, such as these fine terraced houses. The church building seen in the distance has since been demolished.

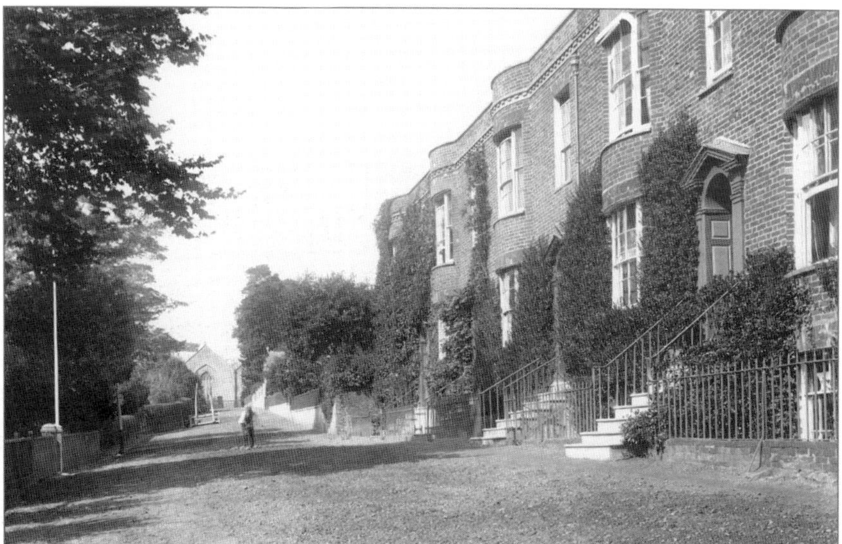

BUDLEIGH SALTERTON
High Street 1918 68727

Budleigh Salterton remains remarkably free of chain stores; its shops remain as individual and refined as the ones in this photograph. To the right we have the local tobacconist, and then Messrs Palmer, upholsterer and undertaker, still in operation today as a funeral director. Beyond is Messrs Pullars of Perth. On the opposite corner is the National Provincial and Union Bank, now the Natwest. Today's residents will envy a time when it was possible to take a careless walk down the middle of the High Street.

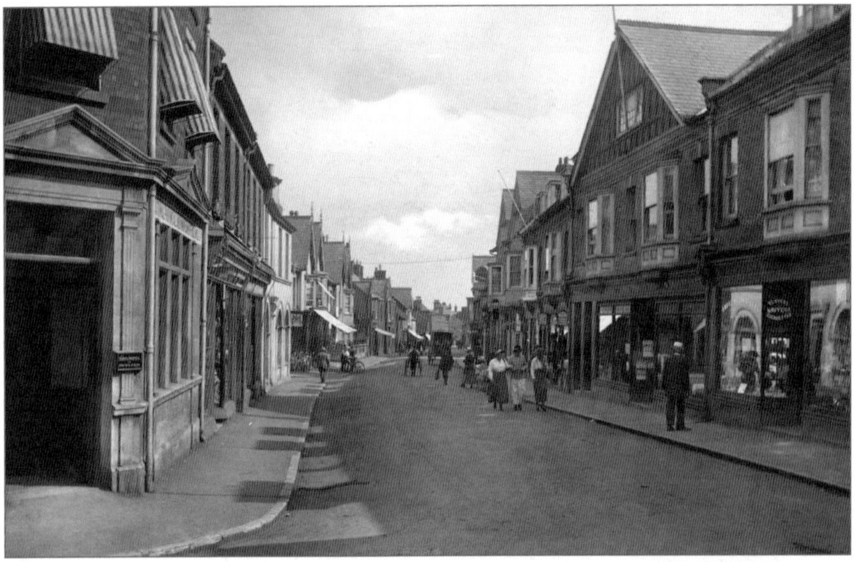

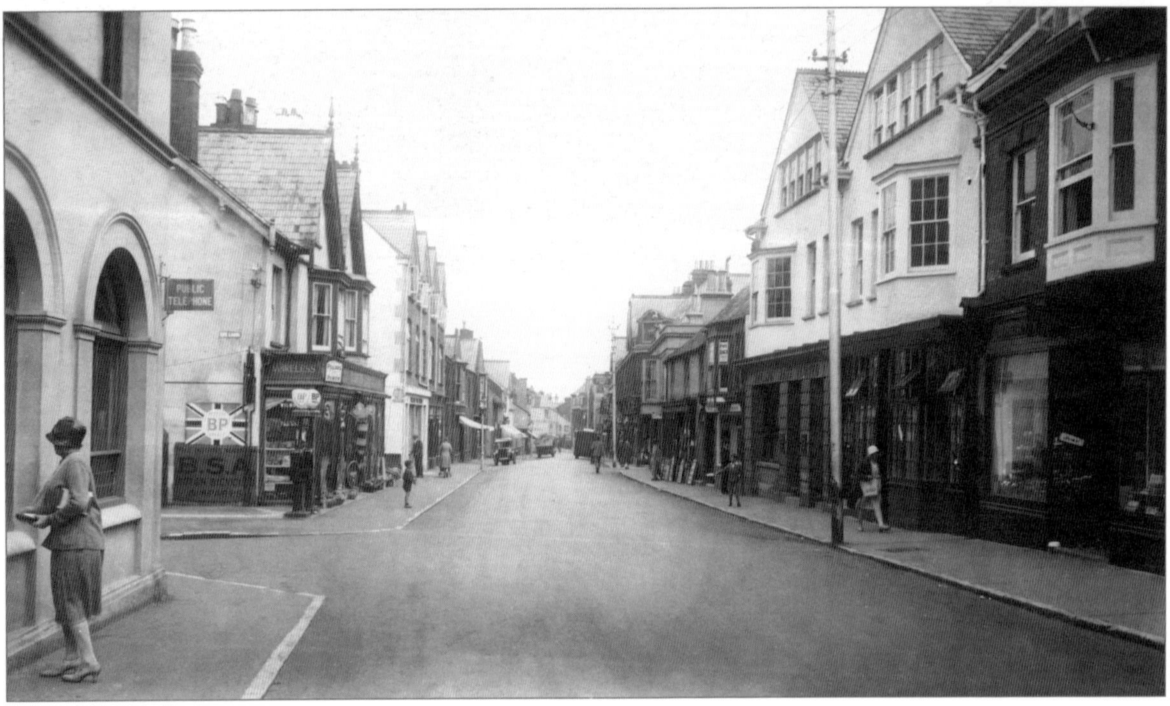

BUDLEIGH SALTERTON, *High Street 1931* 84100

Yet just a dozen years after photograph 68727 (above), the High Street was much busier with traffic - we get a feeling of Budleigh entering our familiar modern world. On the street corner (left) are petrol pumps, an agent for BSA motorcycles and a wireless shop - the latter is an electrical goods shop to this day. The lady on the left is standing outside Budleigh's post office, as we may even today, for it has so far survived on the same site.

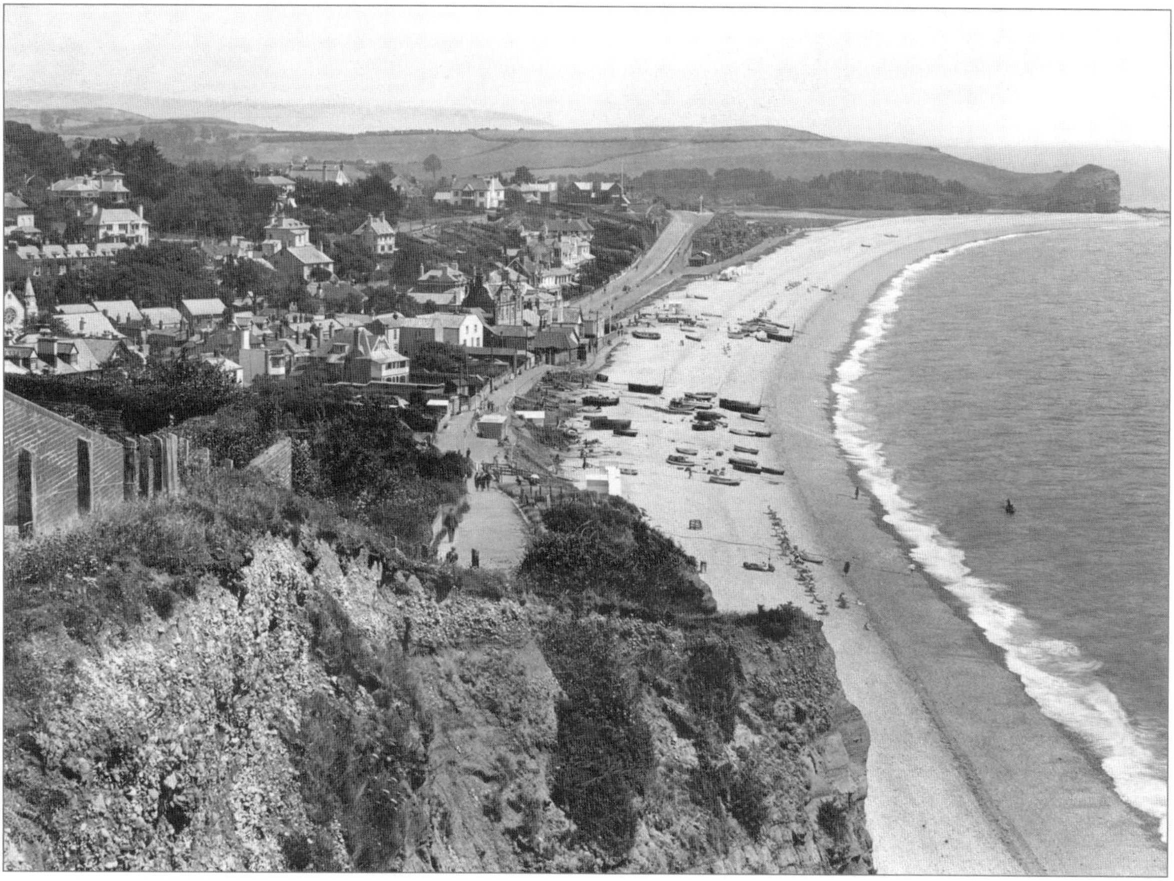

BUDLEIGH SALTERTON, *From the West 1925* 78562

This fine view along Budleigh's strand looks towards the mouth of the River Otter and the bulbous cliff top of Otterton Ledge. Apart from some infilling by more houses, this scene remains relatively unchanged. Budleigh's sea front is mostly a Victorian construction, for a century earlier green meadows sloped down to the edge of the seashore.

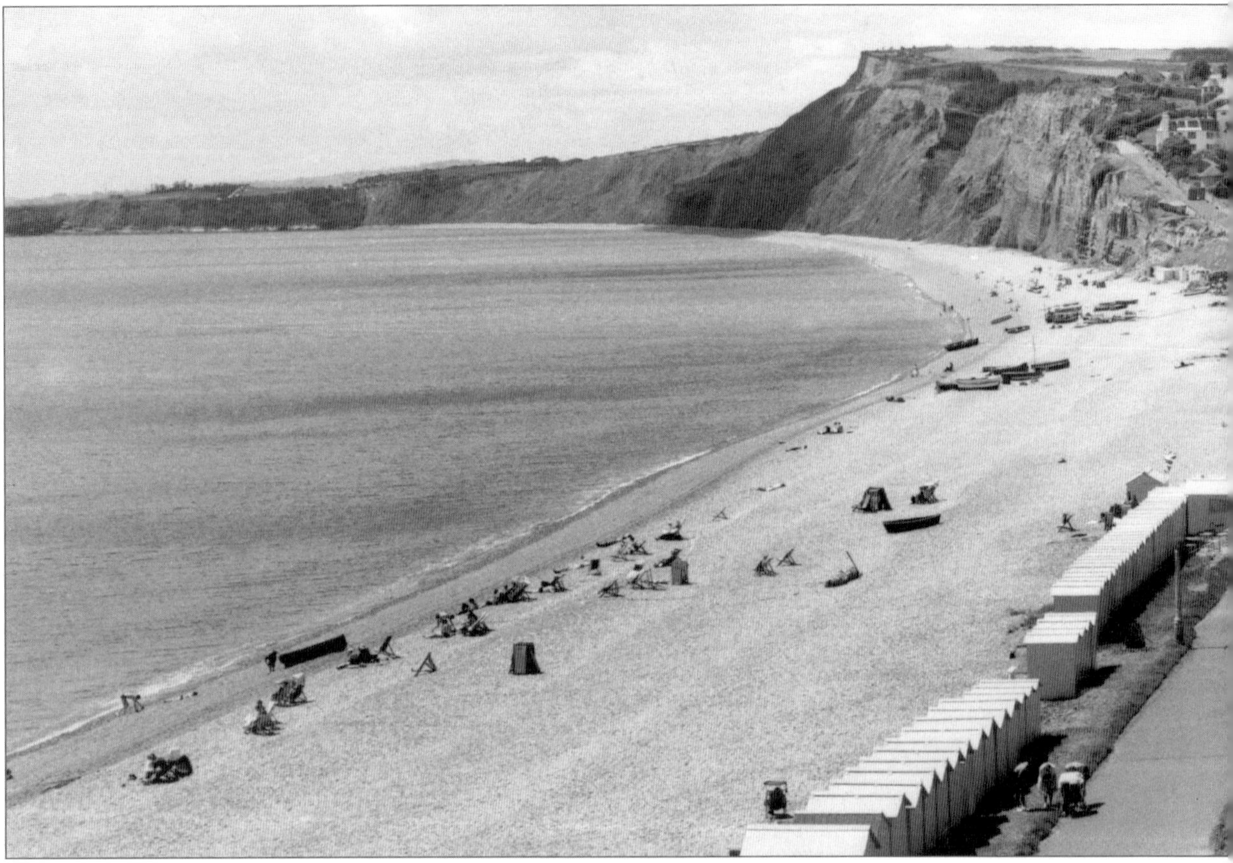

► **LYMPSTONE**
The Village Square 1904 52221

Lympstone is still a secretive little village on the estuary of the River Exe, once a haunt of fishermen and smugglers and now beloved of artists and birdwatchers. It owes its solitude to the fact that the Exeter road bypasses it. It achieved a status as a modest resort in the early years of the 19th century when a number of the cottages we see here were built to accommodate visitors.

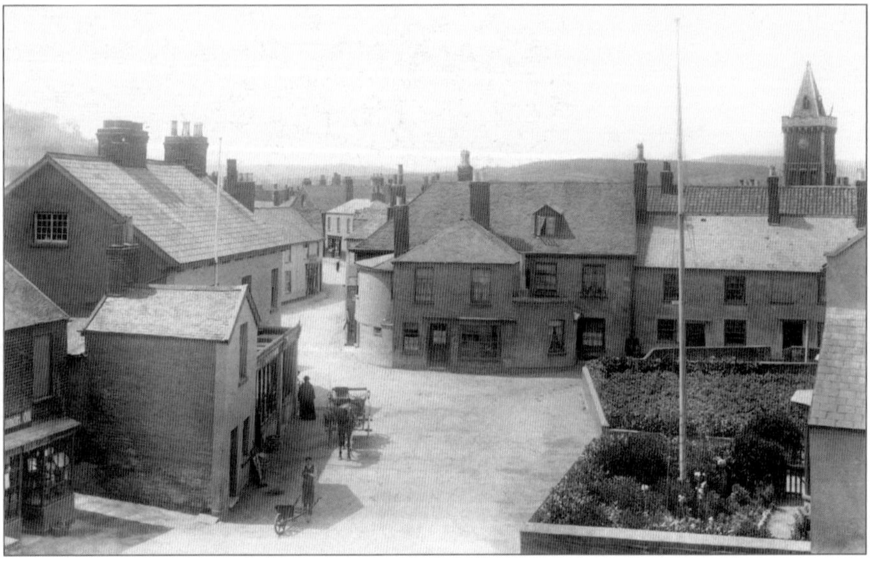

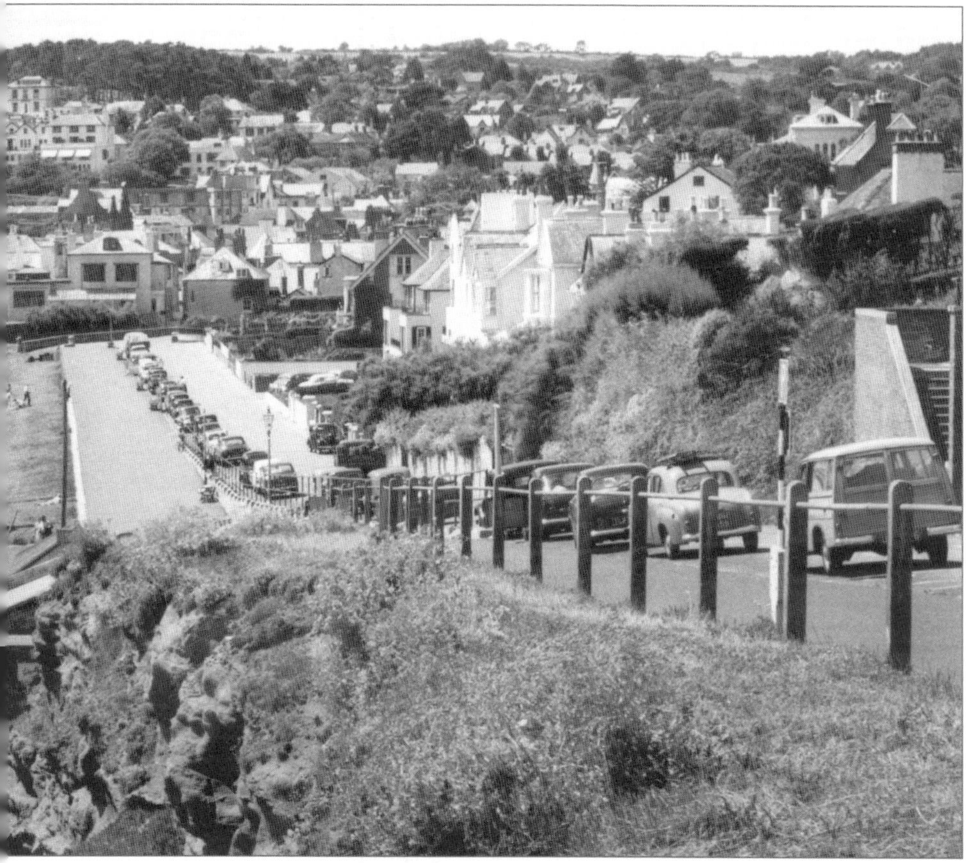

◄ **BUDLEIGH SALTERTON**
The Beach c1960
B243041

At a first glance little seems to have changed since this view was photographed in 1898 (42451 page 24). But notice the parked cars - an increasingly common feature of 20th-century life - and the row of beach huts. In the latter half of the last century, Budleigh grew considerably in size.

► **LYMPSTONE**
Church Street 1904
52219

Lympstone suffered economic depression at the end of the Napoleonic Wars when its shipbuilding yards closed. A number of residents moved to Devonport to continue their trade. The advent of tourism saved Lympstone from terminal decline. Visitors staying in these cottages would enjoy a quiet holiday walking the marshy banks of the estuary and the surrounding heathlands, or boating and fishing.

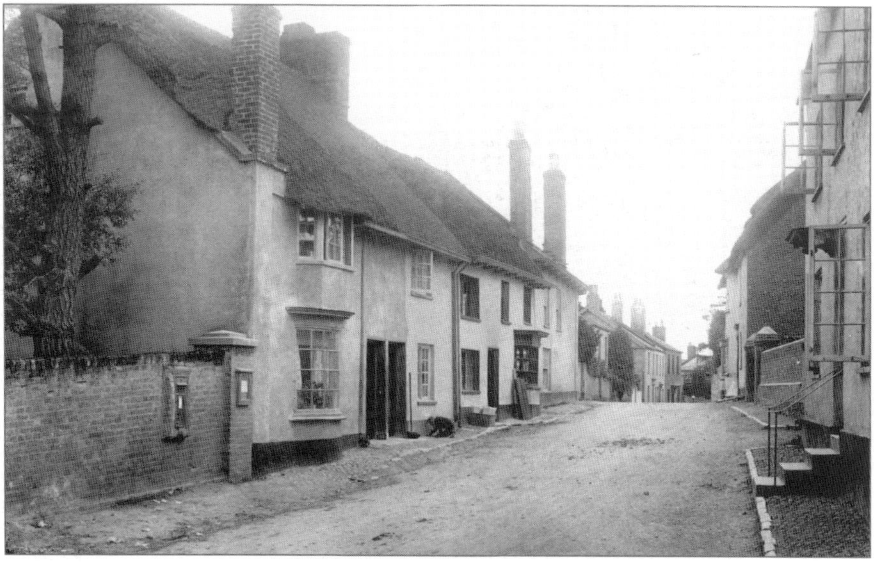

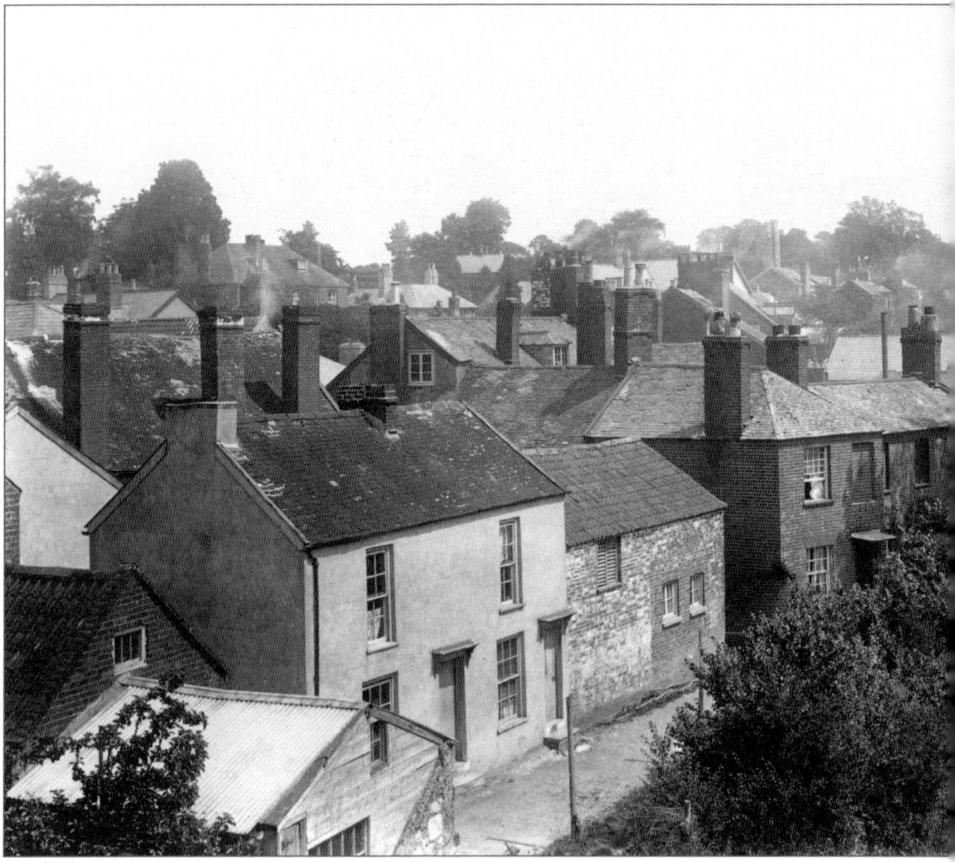

LYMPSTONE
Brookside 1904
52222

The arrival of the railway added to Lympstone's fortunes. The Royal Marine Commando Training Centre was built on nearby fields, and recruits can often be seen yomping through the nearby lanes.

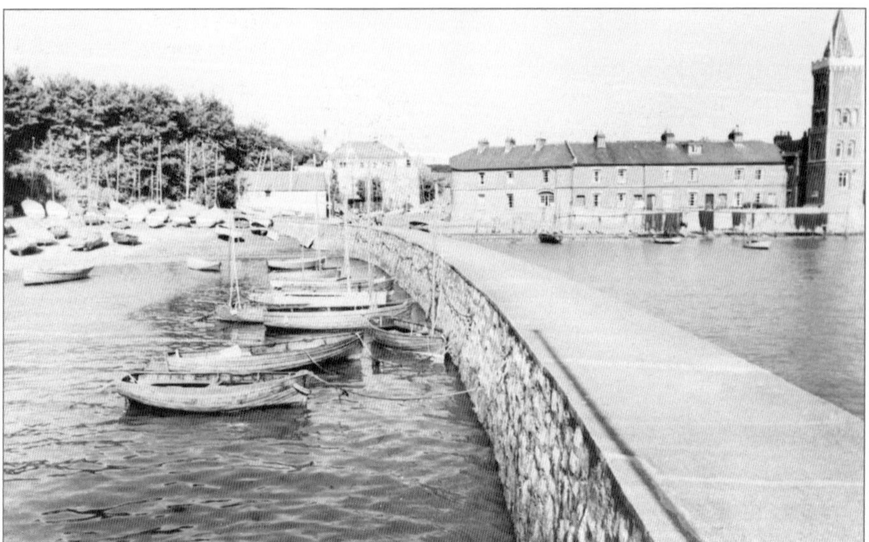

LYMPSTONE
The Harbour c1960
L129012

Lympstone's harbour offers fine views across the River Exe to the long ridge of the Haldon Hills. This haven is now used mostly for leisure yachting, though a century ago fishermen still made a living here. It remains an excellent viewpoint for a glimpse of the Exe's famous wildfowl.

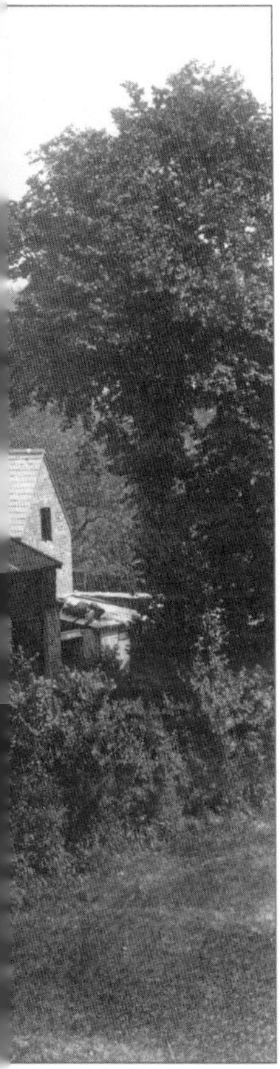

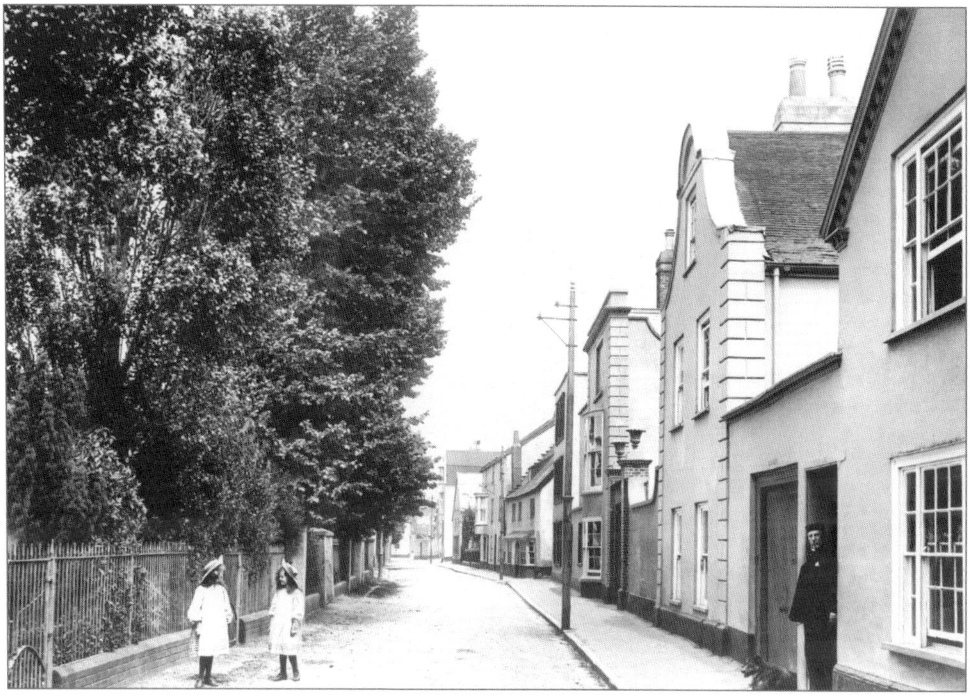

▲ **TOPSHAM,** *The Strand 1906* 53993

Topsham, a delightful little port situated where the Exe estuary narrows, long had trading links with Holland, with the export of cloth and wool and the import of sailcloth and linen. Topsham's merchant adventurers used Dutch brick brought over as ballast in otherwise empty ships to build these gabled houses in the Dutch style.

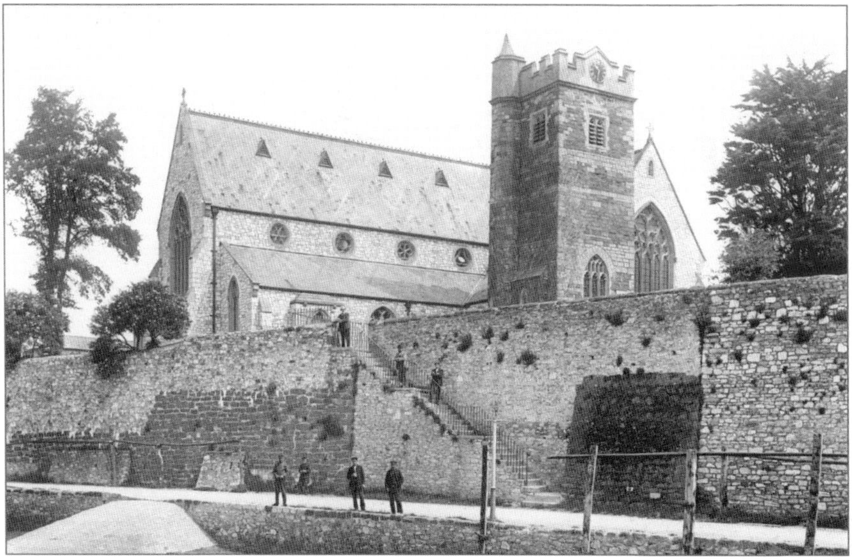

◀ **TOPSHAM**
The Church 1906 53994

The parish church of St Margaret's high position above the Exe makes it a most prominent landmark, and its sandstone tower is a mark for shipping. The 50 steps alongside the wall (centre) lead to a churchyard with one of the finest views in Devon. Inside is a memorial to the Duckworths, father and son, both slain during the war with Napoleon.

TOPSHAM
The Quay 1906 53990

George Gissing, the Victorian novelist and journalist, summed up the atmosphere of Topsham in *The Private Papers of Henry Ryecroft*: 'a long ramble hour after hour entirely enjoyable. It ended at Topsham, where I sat on the little churchyard terrace, and watched the evening tide come up the broad estuary. I have a great liking for Topsham, and that churchyard overlooking what is not quite sea, yet more than river, is one of the most restful spots I know.'

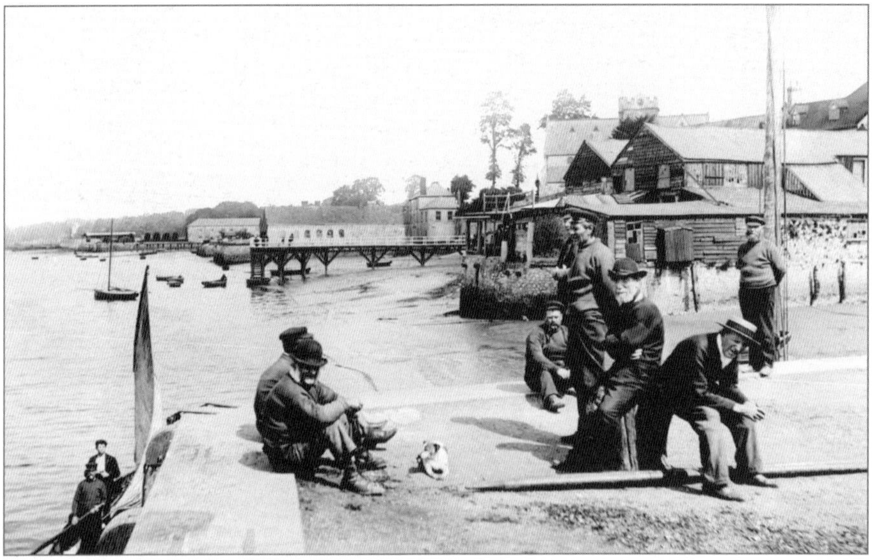

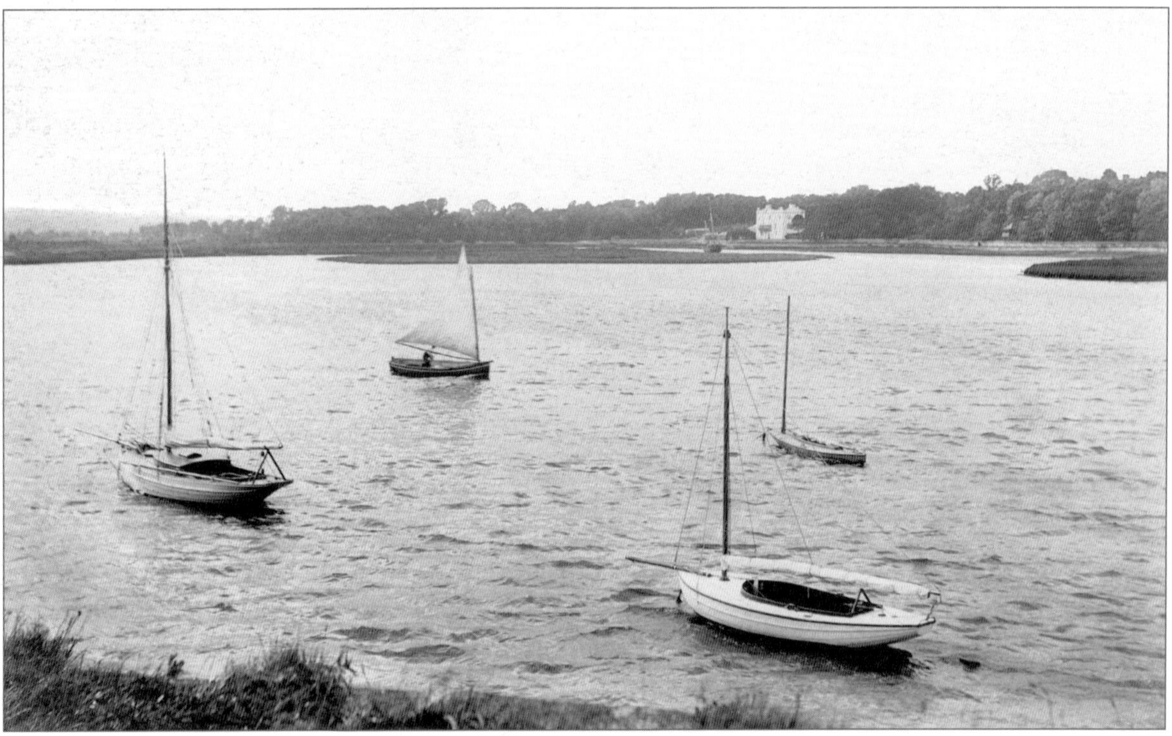

TOPSHAM, *The River Exe 1906* 53992

In 1282, the Countess of Devon, aggrieved with the merchants of Exeter, constructed a weir across the River Exe obstructing access to the city's port. Topsham, downstream from her weir, flourished as a port, as exporters were forced to ship wool from this new centre of commerce.

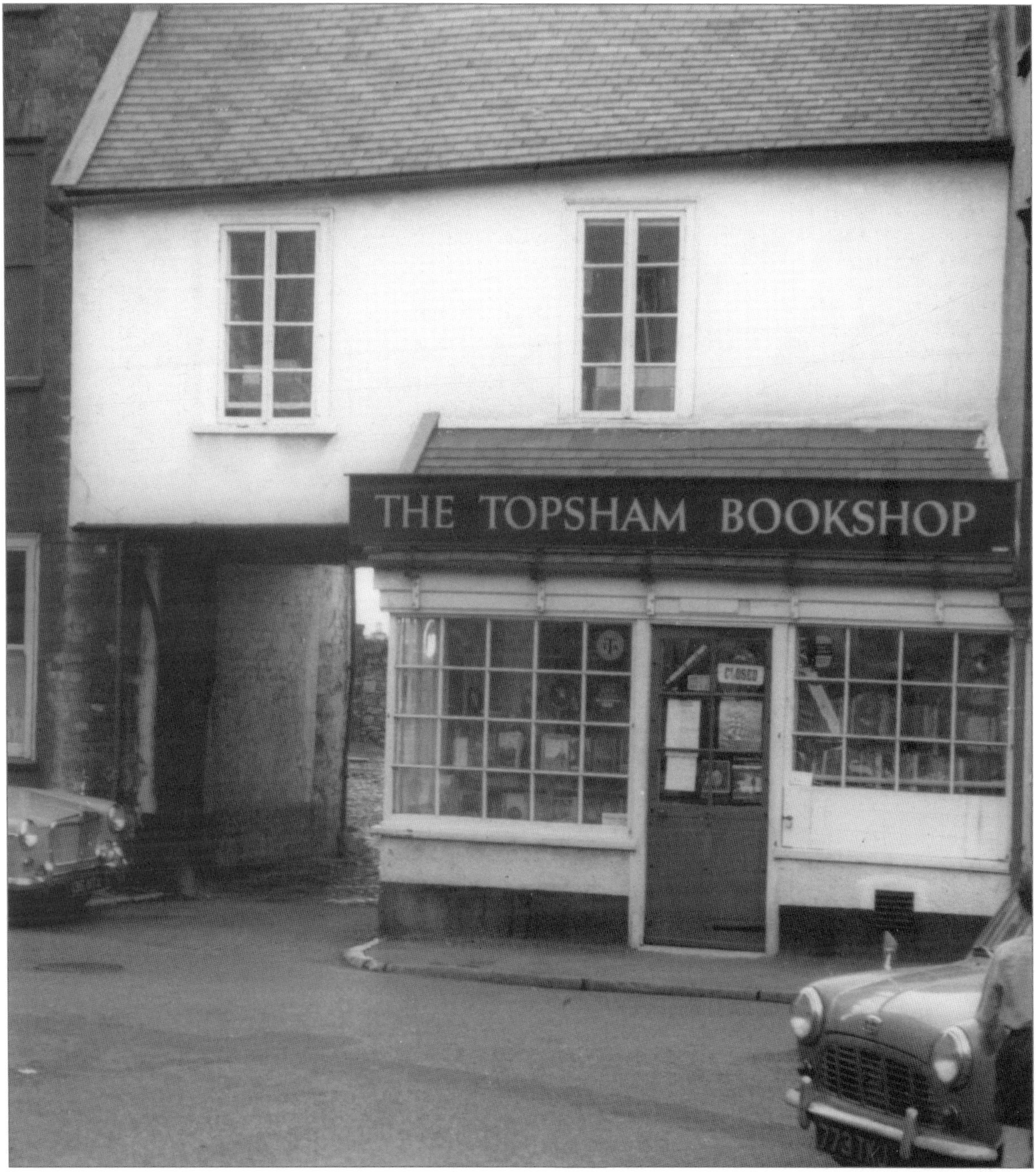

TOPSHAM, *Church House c1965* T59009A

Topsham is a muddle of delightful old buildings, with narrow lanes and alleys diverging from its long, winding main street. The little town has become a centre for the antiques trade, and it is one of Britain's best bird-watching centres.

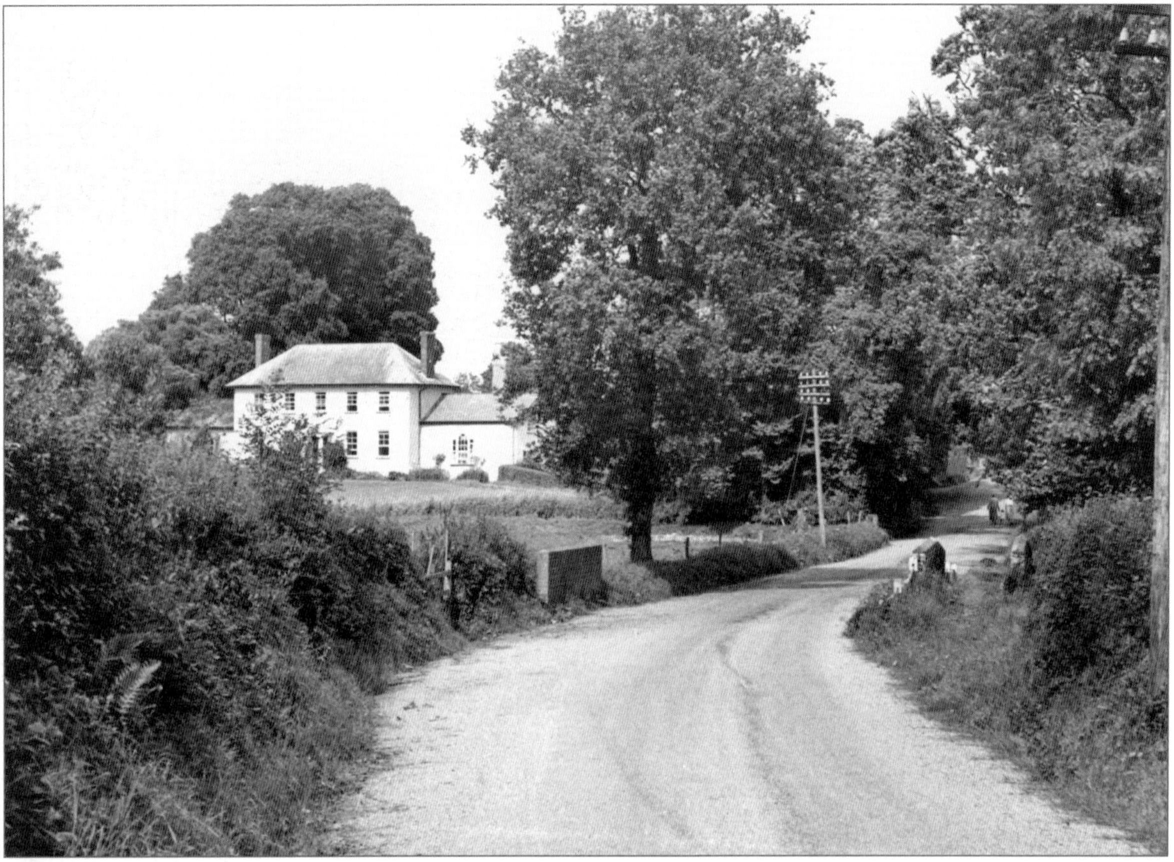

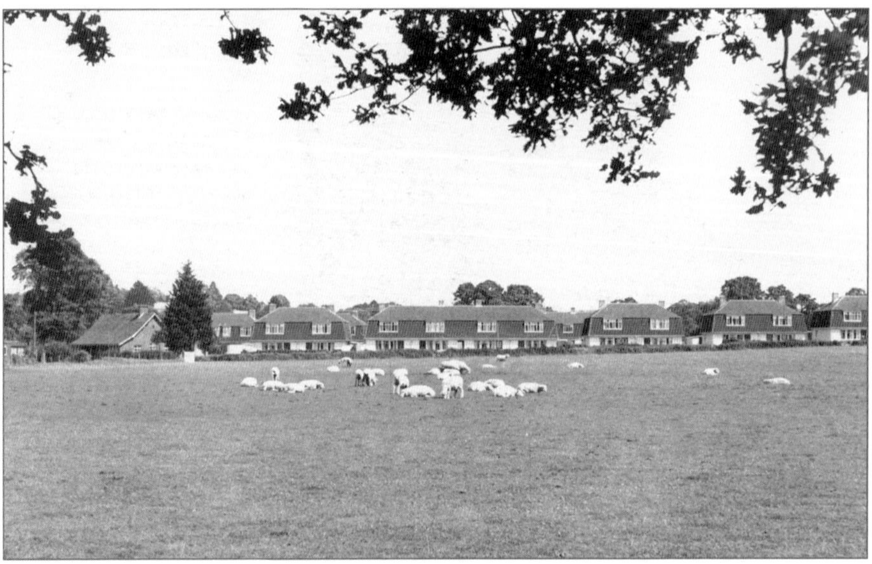

◄ **ROCKBEARE**
Low Brook c1955
R257006

Low Brook was built in the middle of the 20th century as an overspill housing estate just to the south-east of Rockbeare village. Even at the time of its construction, many of its residents would have commuted to Exeter for work.

ROCKBEARE *Gribble Lane c1955* R257011

Rockbeare hides just to the south of the old Exeter to London coaching route, itself originally a Roman road and known to generations of motorists as the 'Rockbeare Straight'. With the construction of the new A30 a mile or two to the south, the parish of Rockbeare has become much quieter, a perfect place of exploration for the rambler and cyclist.

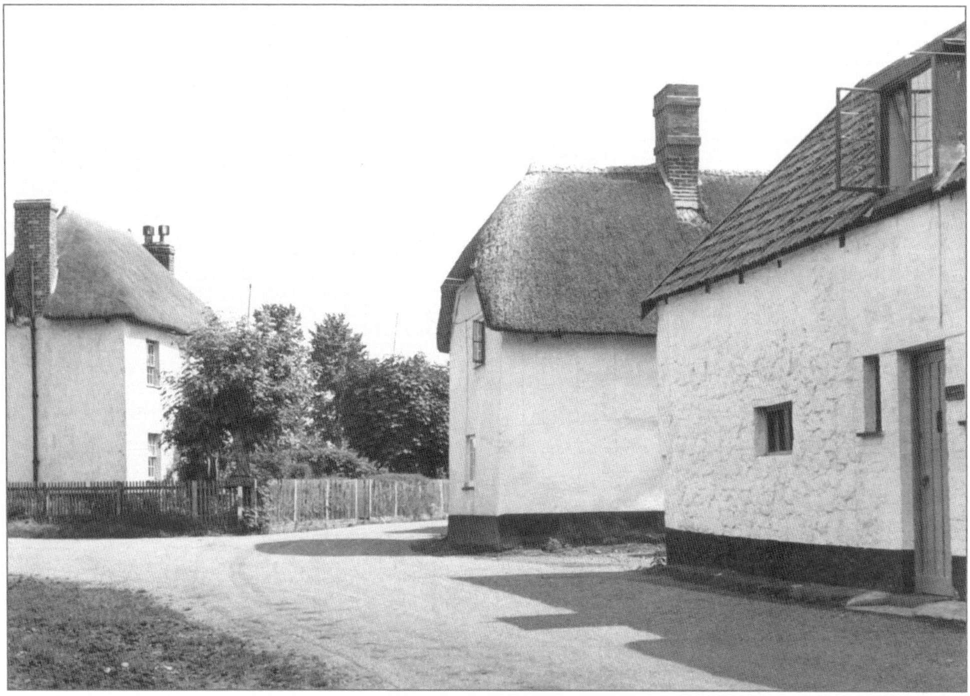

ROCKBEARE, *The Village c1955* R257005

Rockbeare is one of Devon's smaller villages. Even so, it lost 21 men during World War I, whose names are inscribed on the village war memorial; this was probably the greatest catastrophe to befall the village since the Black Death centuries before.

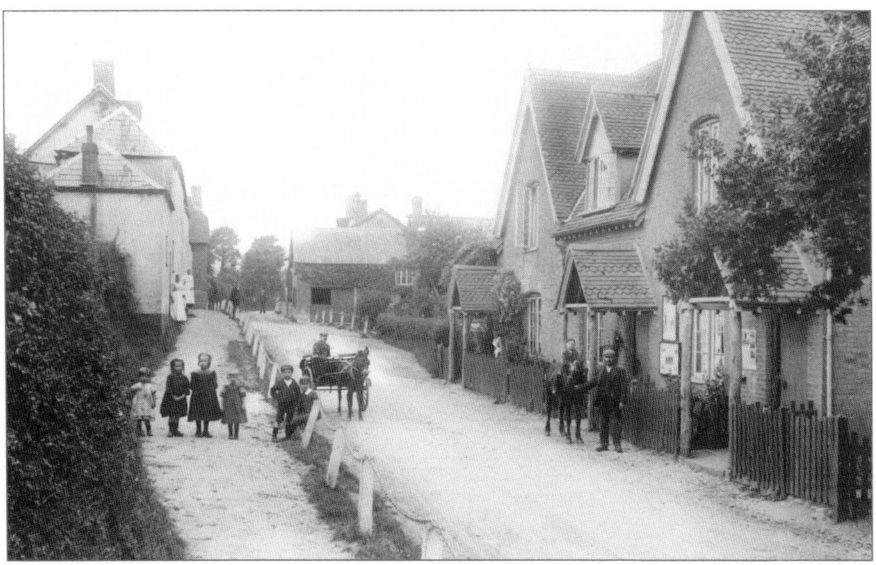

TALATON *The Village 1906* 56675

Talaton is a charming village in the lonely countryside to the north of the Exeter to London coaching route. Far away from the tourist trail, it has changed little since this photograph was taken a century ago. It seems that the Frith photographer has persuaded several local families to come out of doors to pose.

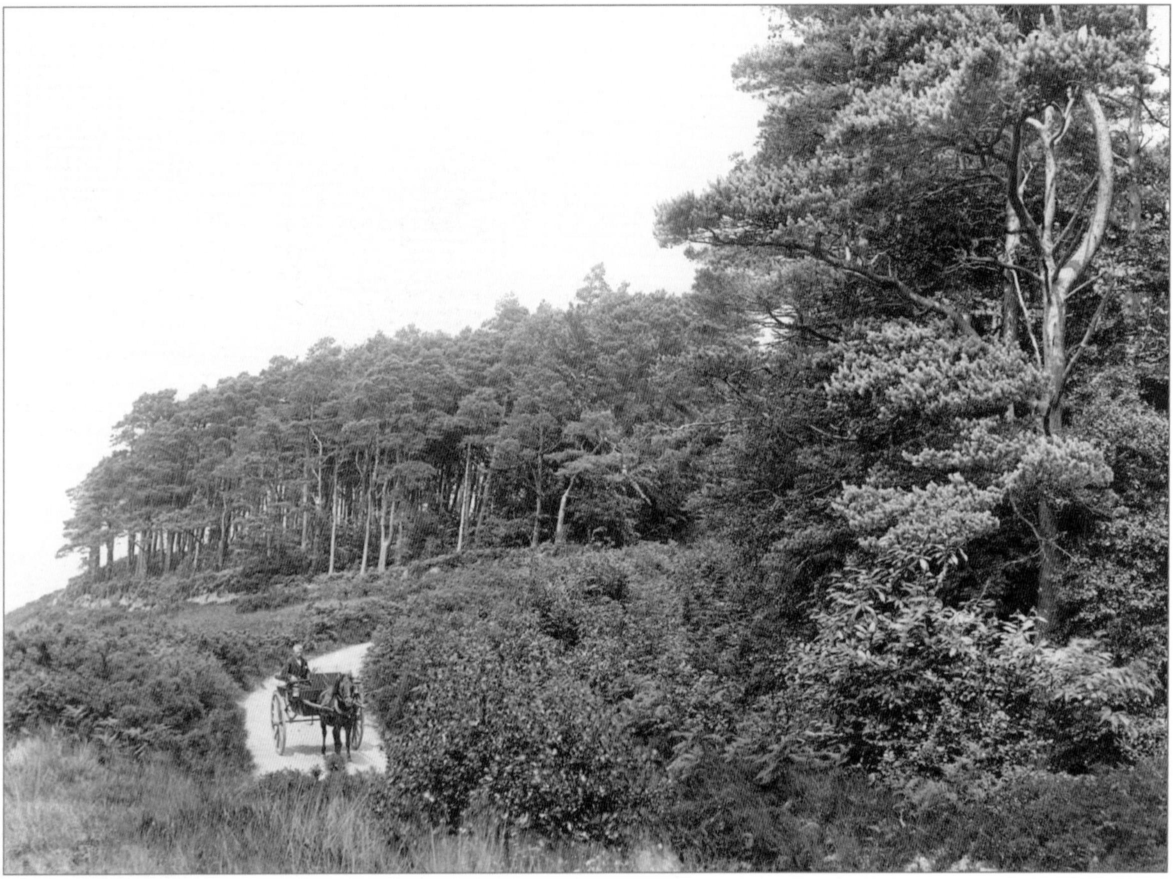

WOODBURY COMMON *1906* 53998

Great heathlands cover much of the countryside east of the Exe, including the commons of Woodbury, Bicton and Aylesbeare. Woodbury Common is crowned by the massive Iron Age hill-fort of Woodbury Castle, visible from miles around and one of the best viewpoints in Devon.

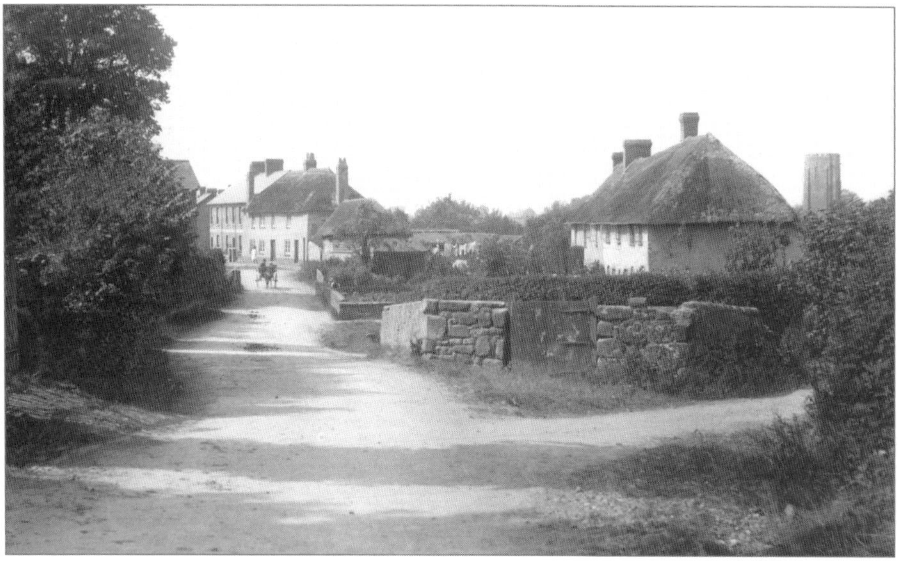

WOODBURY
The Village 1907
57261a

Woodbury was a working agricultural village when this photograph was taken, and journeys into Exeter were an occasion and not a regular event. Woodbury remains a rural parish, though many of its residents now work elsewhere. Despite an increase in motor traffic, the village remains relatively unspoiled.

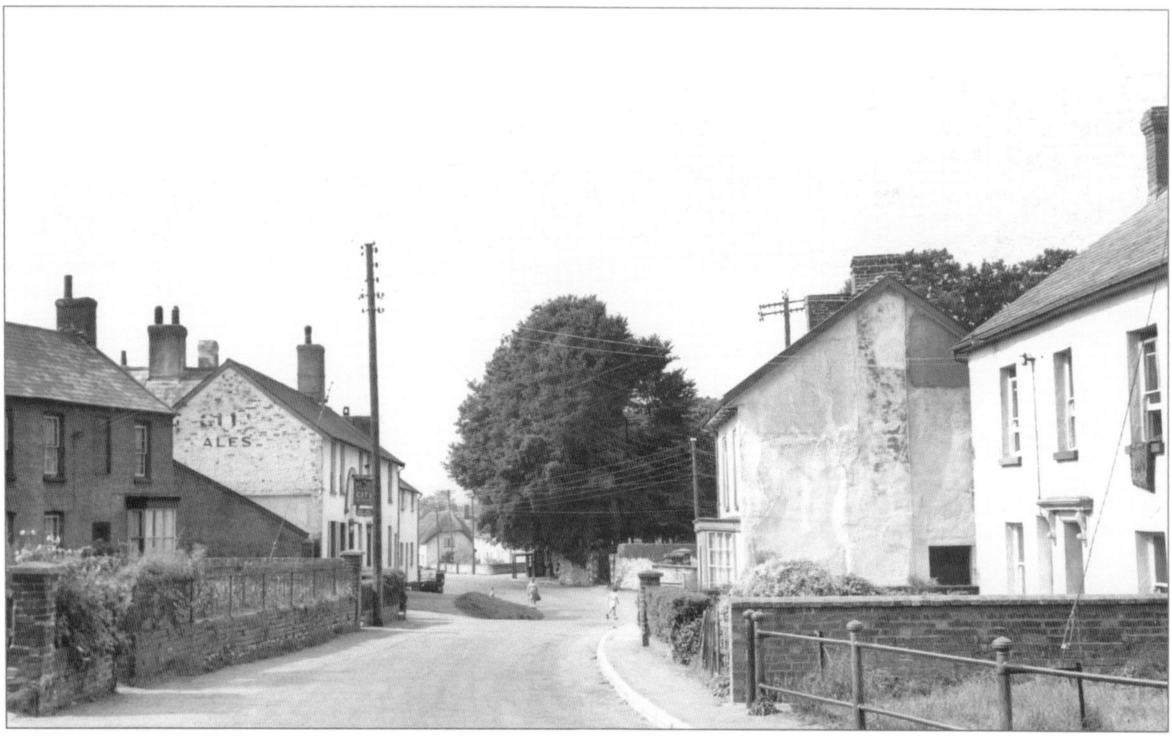

WOODBURY, *The Village c1955* W129007

Woodbury is one of Devon's largest parishes, and it occupies the great vale between Woodbury Common and the flood plains of the Exe. The village, thought to date to Saxon times, takes its name from the nearby hill-fort. On the left here is the Maltsters' Arms, still a thriving public house.

WOODBURY
The Church c1960
W129023

The parish church of St Swithin dates back to 1409, but it was unsympathetically restored by its Victorian parson, the Reverend Loveband Fulford. This clerical gentleman cut through the medieval rood screen so that his parishioners might hear his sermons with better clarity.

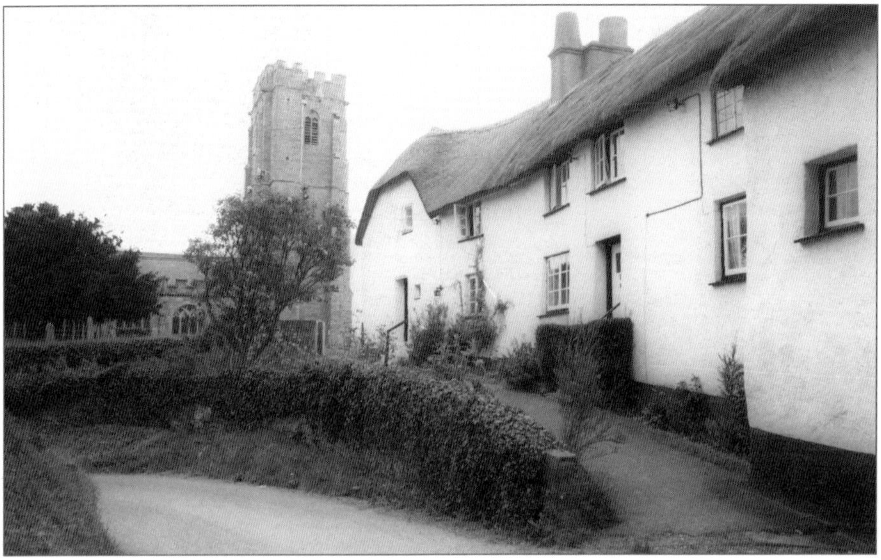

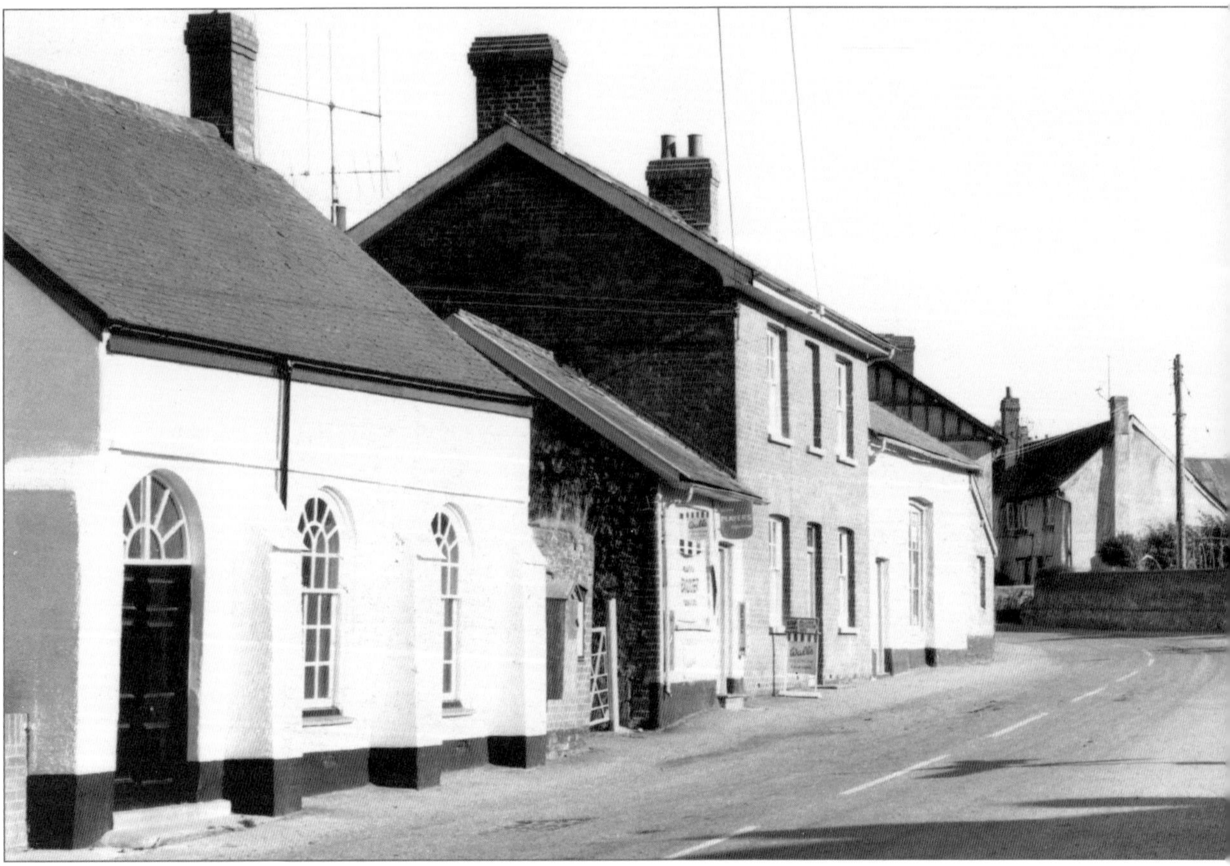

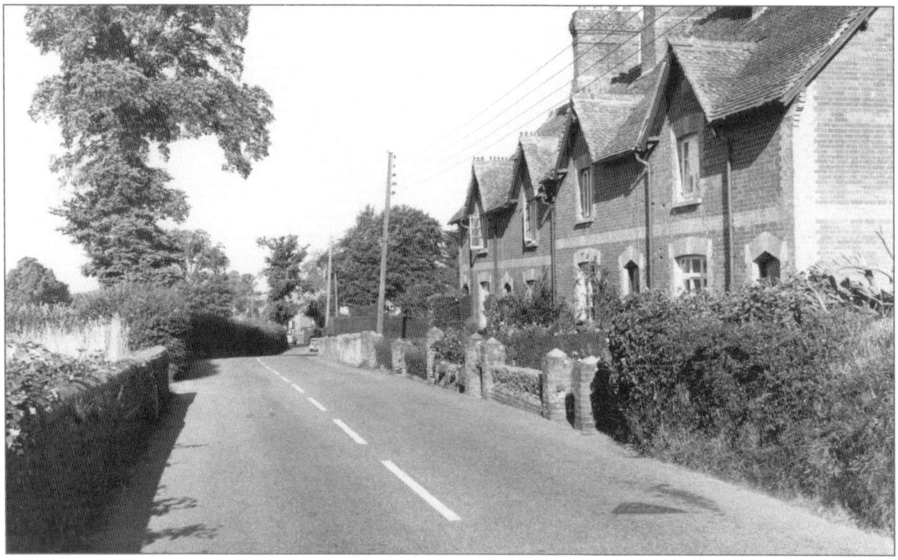

WOODBURY
The Village c1960
W129018

Travellers heading along the broad highway from the East Devon coast to Exeter often miss the heart of Woodbury. This is a pity, as it is a settlement of much charm, and it is best explored on foot.

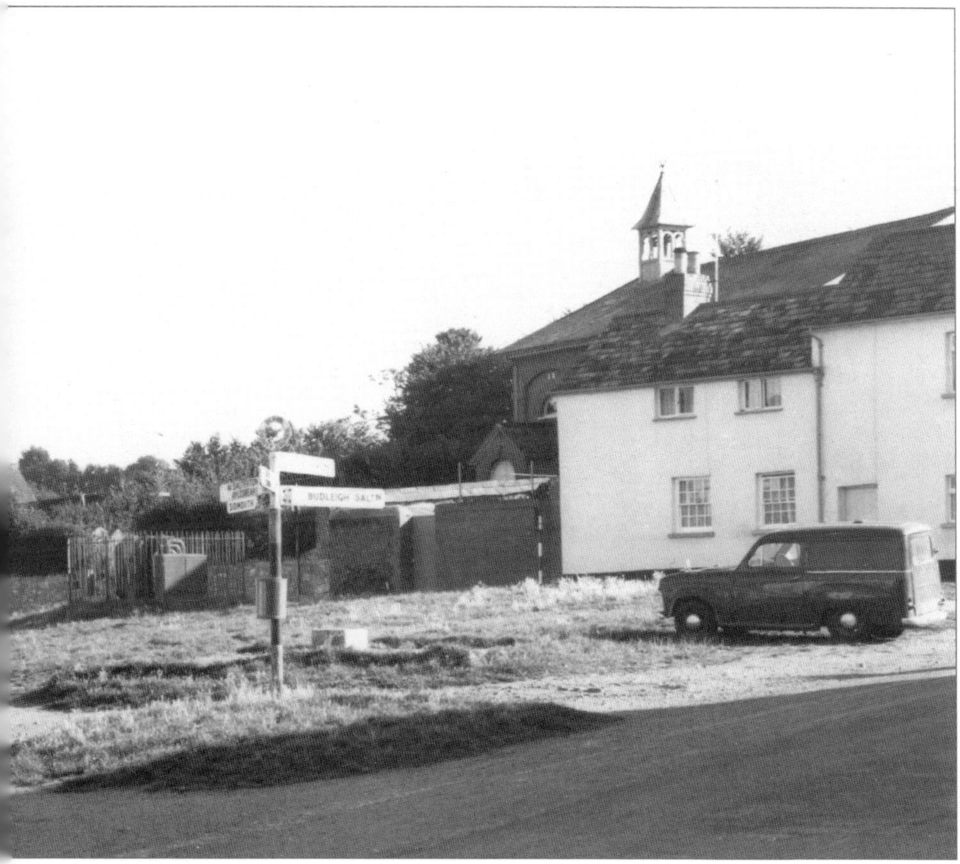

WOODBURY
The Village c1960
W129021

Woodbury's village green is rarely as empty of parked cars as it was in this day in the 1960s. On the left are the Church Rooms, and just beyond is the then village shop, an adjunct to a residential cottage.

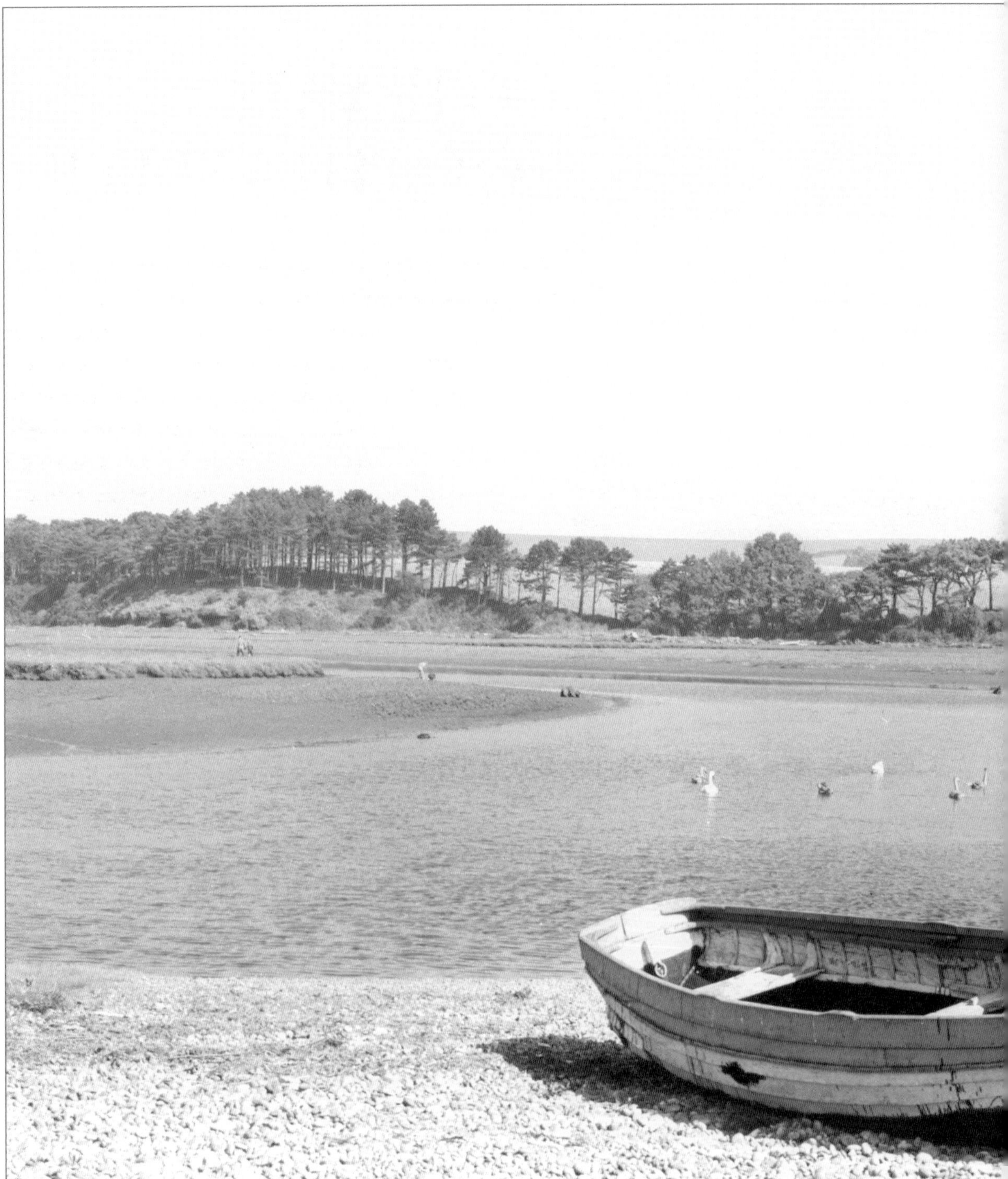

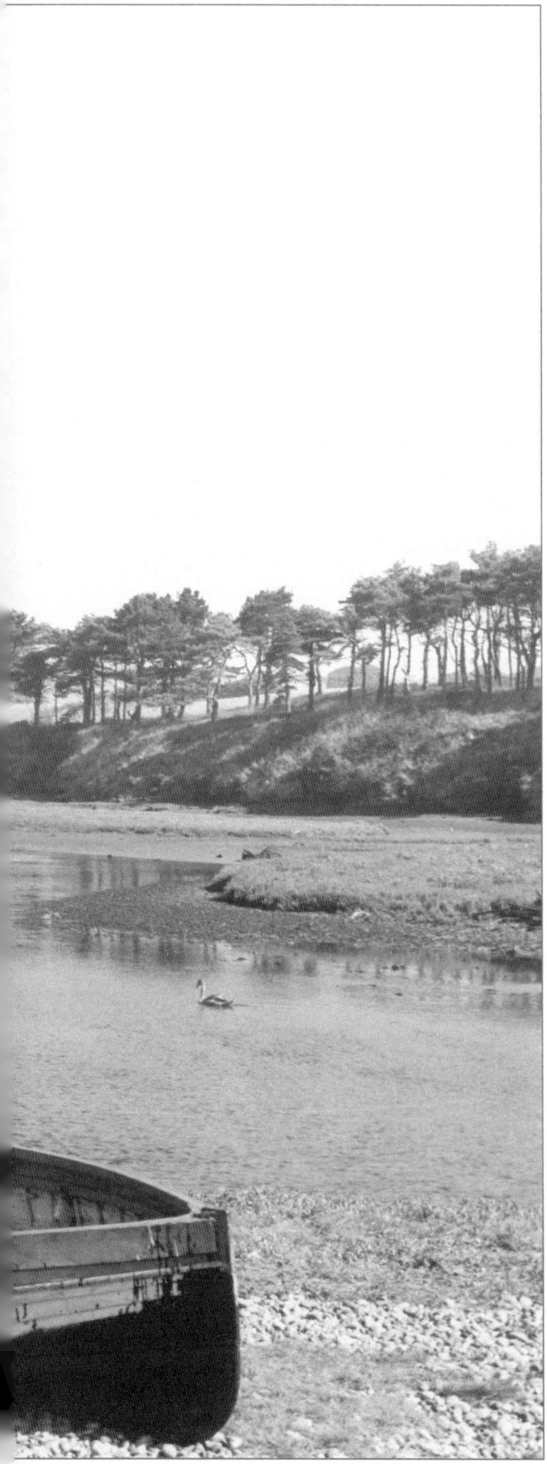

THE VALE OF THE OTTER

ALTHOUGH tiny in comparison with the great estuary of the River Exe, the Otter is very much the river that defines East Devon. It meanders across much of the East Devon landscape to a source across the border in Somerset. It can be and should be walked for much of its length. The Otter earned the admiration of one of England's greatest poets, Samuel Taylor Coleridge, who called it his 'dear native brook, wild streamlet of the west'. Coleridge was born in Ottery St Mary, and spent a childhood and youth walking the river's banks.

Sir Walter Raleigh, explorer, statesman and man of letters, wrote no poem about the Otter, but he loved the river. His earliest explorations would have been in the Vale of the Otter, perhaps down to Budley Haven, the port that once existed below East Budleigh in the days before the estuary silted up. The villages along this length of the river, Otterton, Colaton Raleigh and Newton Poppleford, would have been known to Raleigh. Exiled in London, he yearned for these boyhood scenes, but never relived those early and carefree adventures. Honiton is the largest settlement on the Otter, with its long history of lace manufacture and its busy ancient market - a good centre for seeking out the upper reaches of the 'wild streamlet of the west'.

BUDLEIGH SALTERTON
The Mouth of the Otter c1960 B243025

The River Otter meets the sea just to the east of Budleigh Salterton after a 30-mile journey across Somerset and East Devon. The river's estuary has been silted up for centuries, but in medieval times a prosperous port once lined the Otter's banks. The mouth of the Otter is now an important nature reserve, famed for is wild birds.

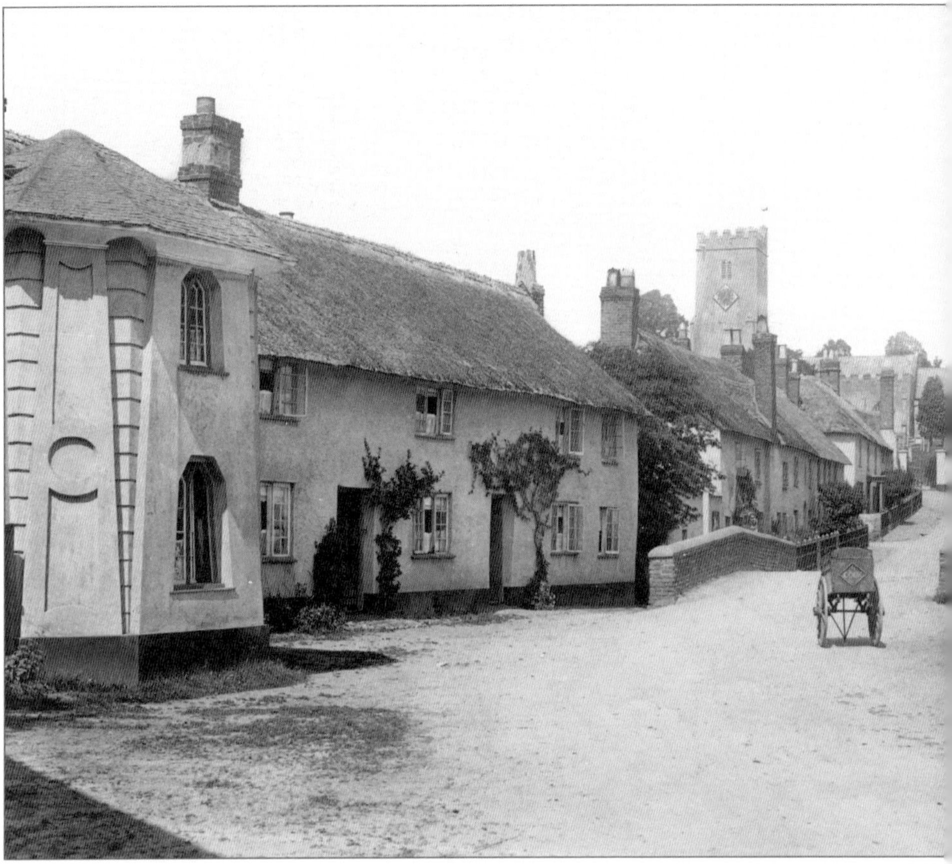

EAST BUDLEIGH
The Main Street 1914 56662

East Budleigh's main street has changed little since this photograph was taken at the outbreak of the Great War. The village was an important market town when neighbouring Budleigh Salterton consisted of a few scattered fishermen's cottages. The unusual house on the left was demolished soon after this photograph was taken.

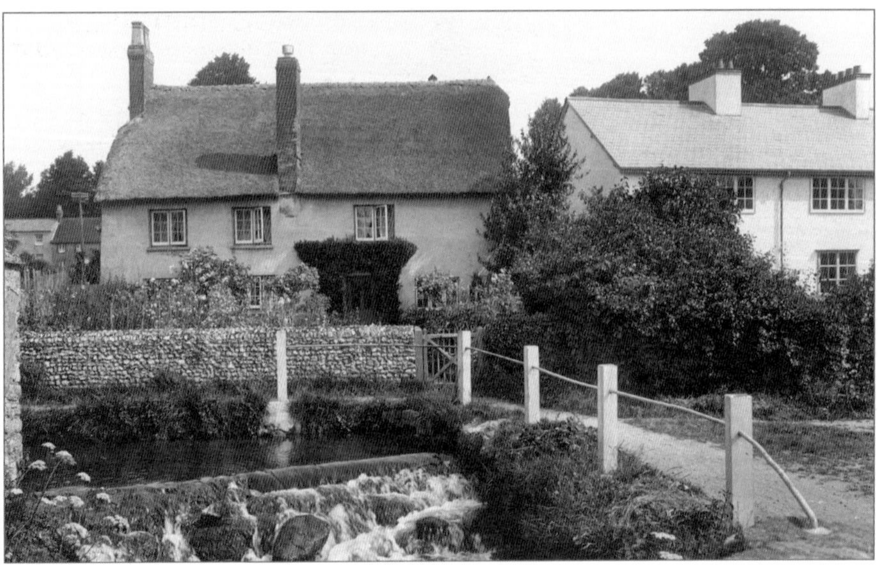

EAST BUDLEIGH
The Waterfall 1928
81070

A feature of several East Devon villages is a brook running alongside a main street. East Budleigh's waterway adds to the delight of this picturesque village, filling the air with the sound of tumbling water.

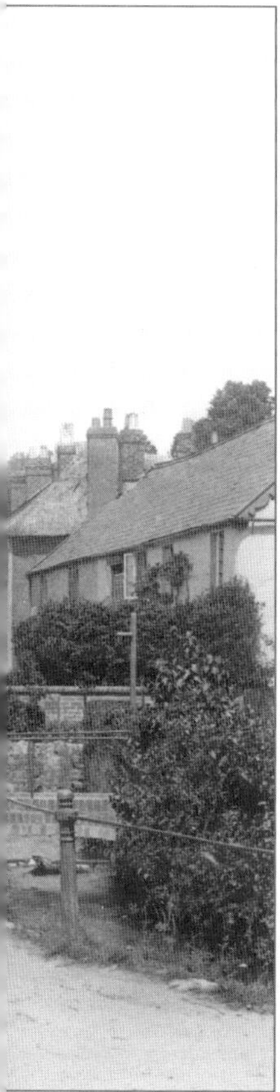

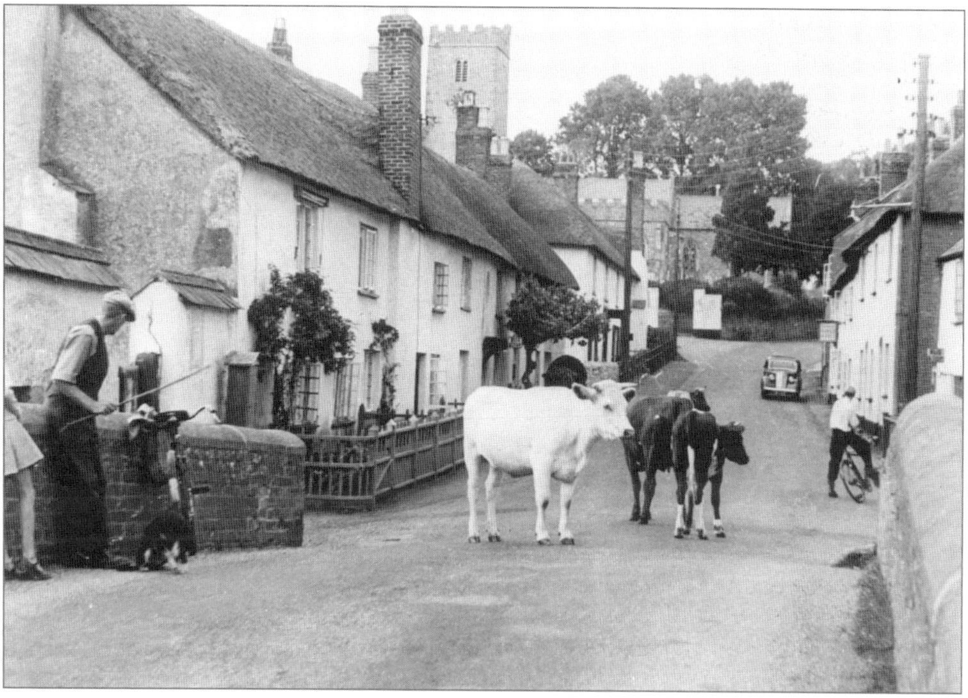

▲ **EAST BUDLEIGH,** *The Village c1955* E6010

It is still not unusual to see a scene such as this in East Budleigh, for the farms in the vicinity are very active. On the right-hand side of the street by the parked car is the village inn, the Sir Walter Raleigh, named in honour of East Budleigh's most famous son. In the distance is the parish church of All Saints, built of the local red sandstone. The Raleigh family pew survives, marked by Sir Walter's coat of arms.

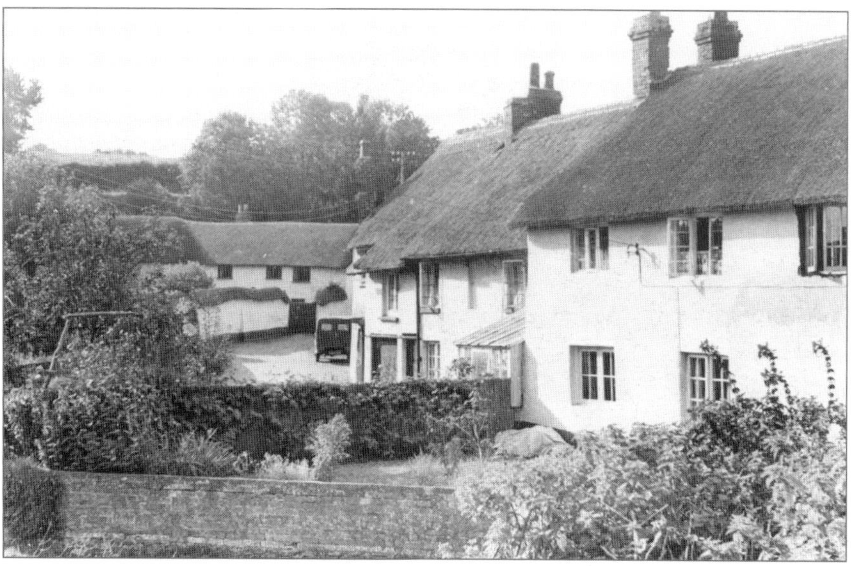

◄ **EAST BUDLEIGH**
The Old Vicarage c1955
E6025

In the distance is East Budleigh's charming old thatched vicarage with its delightful walled garden. Known today as Vicar's Mead, this is where Sir Walter Raleigh went to school. In later years it was the headquarters of Ambrose Stapleton, vicar and leader of the local smuggling gang. It is reputed to have secret rooms and passageways where contraband was stored.

HAYES BARTON
The Birthplace Of Sir Walter Raleigh 1928
81362A

A country lane leads from East Budleigh to Raleigh's birthplace at Hayes Barton. The explorer, poet and statesman was born here in 1552, and spent his boyhood exploring the local countryside. Raleigh never forgot his first home, and made several attempts to purchase it in later life. In a letter of 1584 he wrote: 'I had rather seat my sealf ther than any where else'. Unfortunately, all his attempts to regain the family home came to naught.

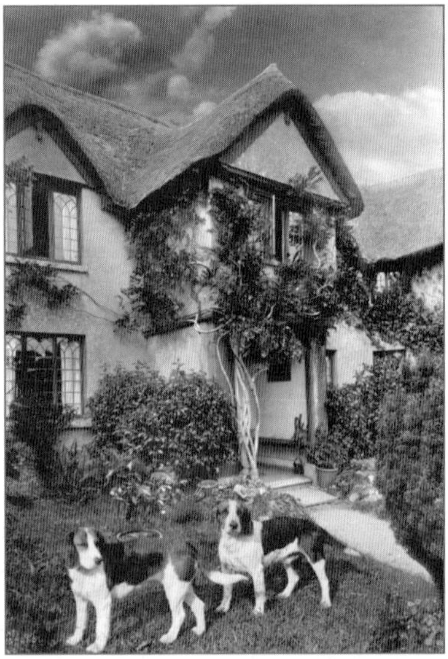

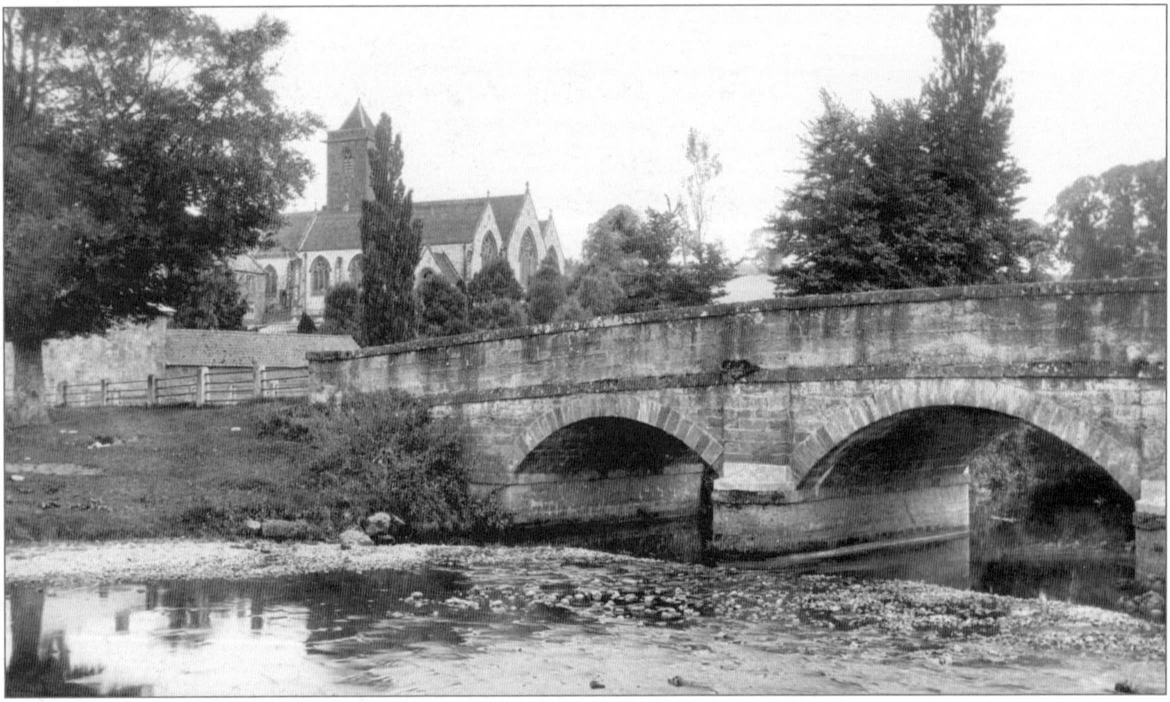

OTTERTON, *The Church and the Bridge 1890* 26238

A little further upstream we come to the village of Otterton, built around one long main street. A bridge has spanned the Otter here since medieval times, though the structure we see here dates from 1827. Dominating the village is the church of St Michael, restored in 1869 by the local benefactress Lady Rolle. A priory was located here until the Reformation, when the village was purchased by Richard Duke, who converted some of the monastic buildings into a home.

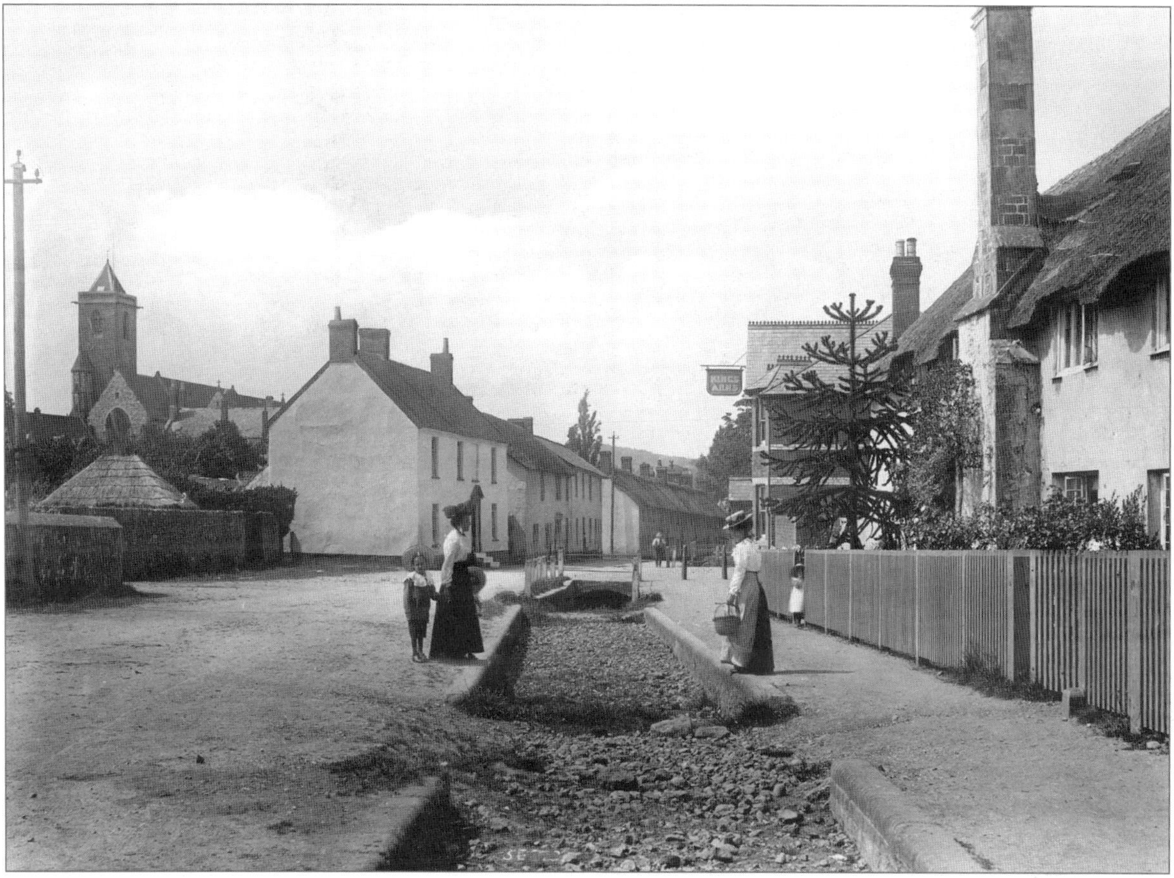

OTTERTON, *The Village 1906* 56673

Otterton's brook seems to be dry in this photograph, as it sometimes is during long dry summers. Just beyond the two Edwardian ladies is the King's Arms inn, named in honour of George III and rebuilt in 1889. One Victorian landlord, Edwin Snow, rests in the nearby churchyard with his baby daughter - both died within a few months of each other. The King's Arms now serves as the post office and village store as well as a public house.

▼ **OTTERTON,** *The Village Green 1914* 66531

Otterton's village green was the setting for medieval village fairs, and it is still a venue for local events. To mark George III's jubilee in 1809, a couple danced a hornpipe there - their joint ages totalled 180 years! The cottages beyond were demolished in 1939 and replaced by homes for workers on the Rolle estate.

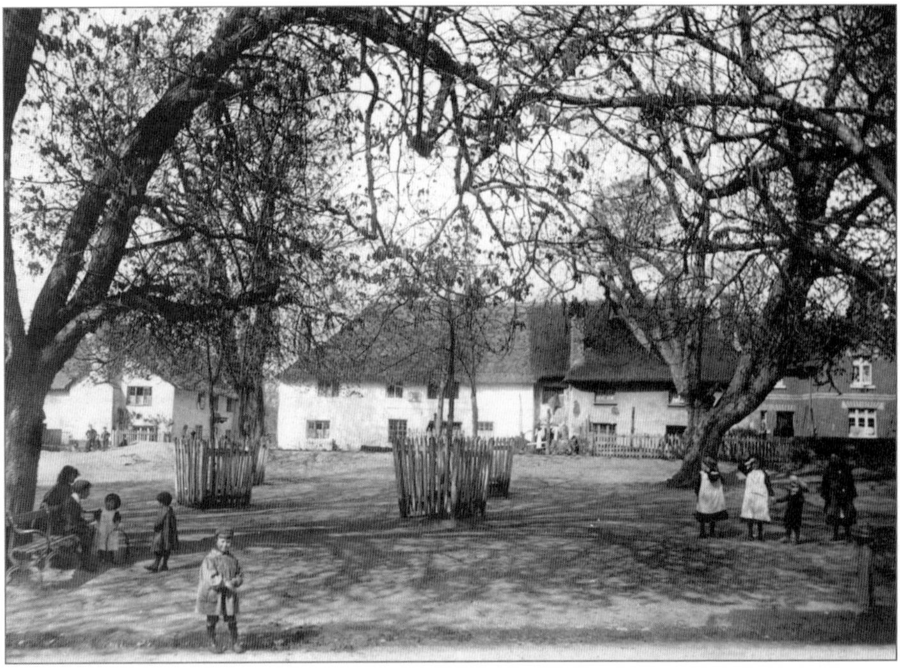

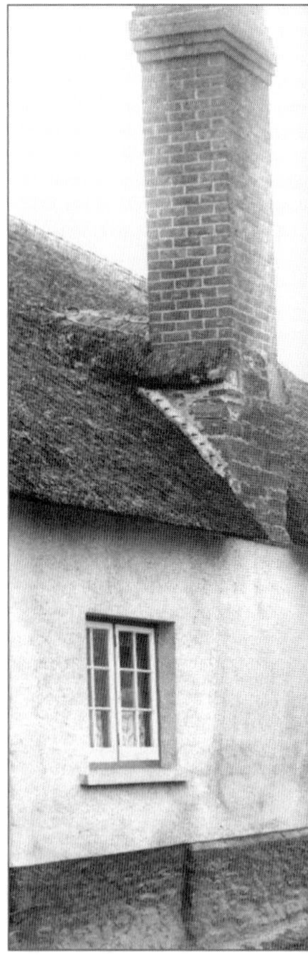

► **OTTERTON**
The Village c1955
O27047

Otterton has some of the best examples of cob and thatch cottages in Devon. Many of the homes we see in this photograph date from between the 15th and 18th centuries. In the spring, when the little gardens and window boxes are filled with flowers, Otterton is one of the delights of the county.

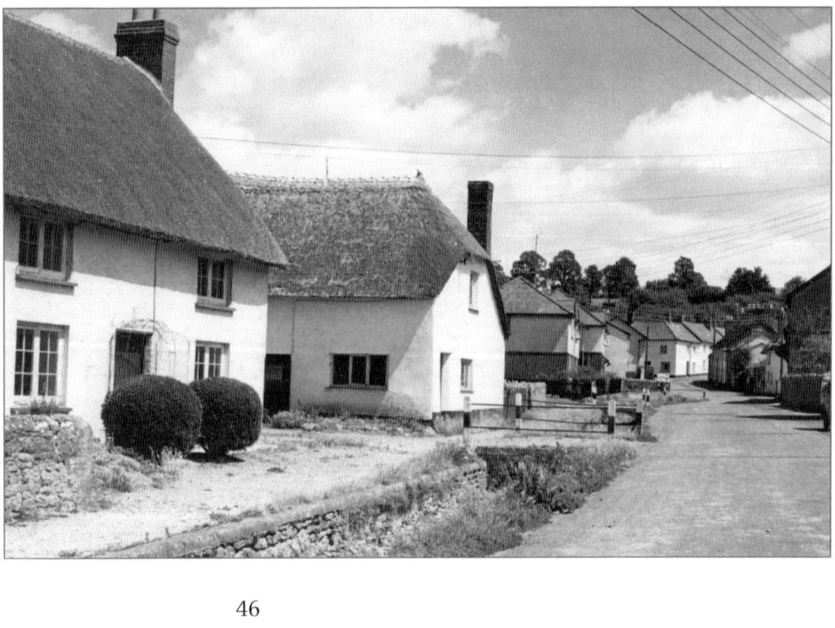

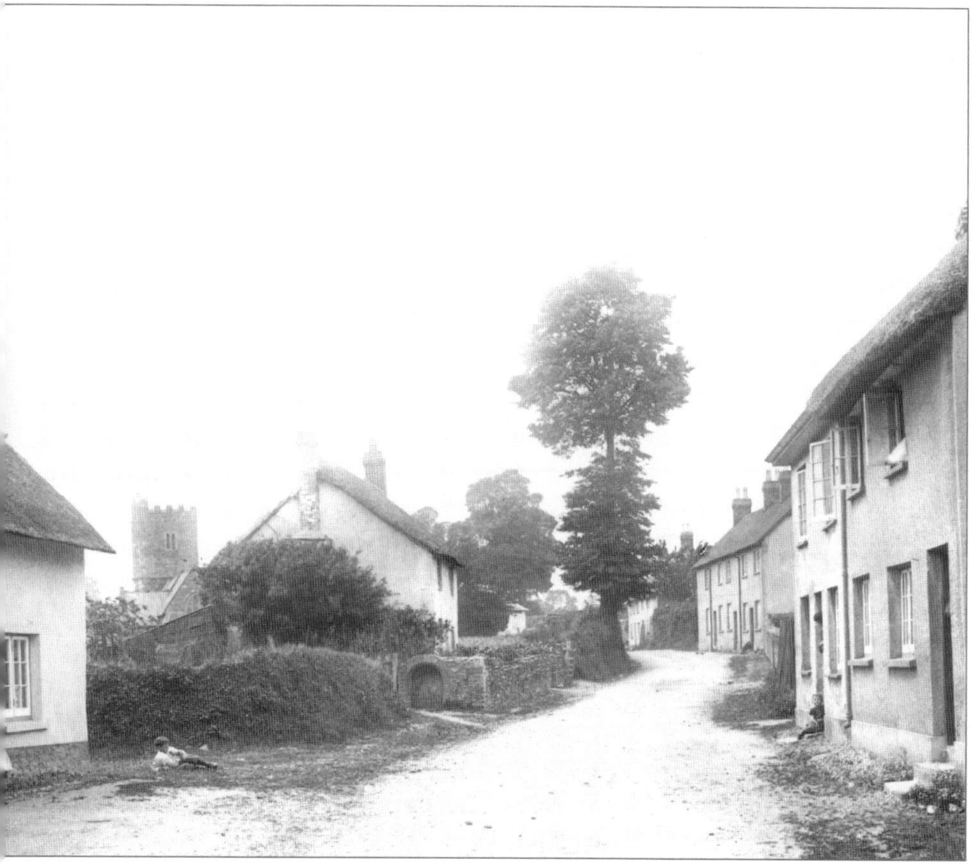

◀ **COLATON RALEIGH**
The Village 1906
53828

Colaton dates from at least Saxon times, and it was a royal manor at the time of the *Domesday Book*. The first links with the Raleigh family, from which the village now takes the second part of its name, came in 1346 when Peter de Raleghe owned certain manorial rights. Contrary to popular belief, Sir Walter Raleigh was not baptized in the parish church, but in the tiny chapel at nearby Place Court house.

▶ **NEWTON POPPLEFORD**
Ye Olde Toll House c1965 N82029

Newton Poppleford takes its name from the round stones, or popples (like the pobbles of Budleigh Salterton), that abound in the area; it was a fording place over the Otter for centuries before its stone bridge was built. Its delightful thatched toll house was built in 1758, and has been recently renovated and slightly extended.

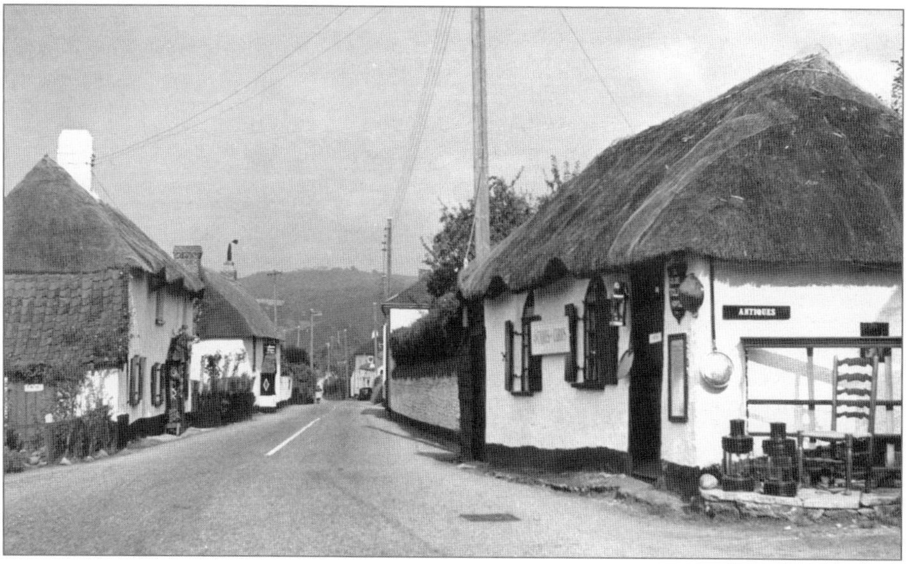

NEWTON POPPLEFORD
The Main Street c1965 N82067

Newton Poppleford clusters for a mile along the highway from Exeter to Lyme Regis. In the middle distance is the Exeter Inn, and to the left is P J White's grocer's shop and mini-market - supermarkets were a relatively new concept in the 1960s.

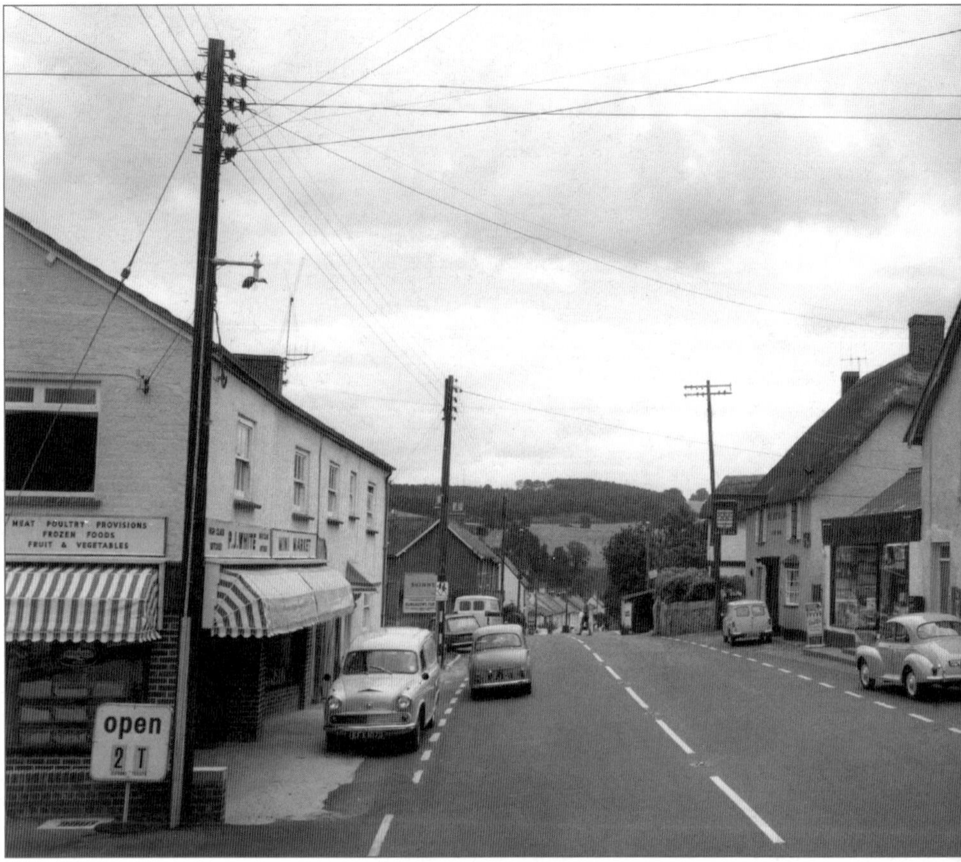

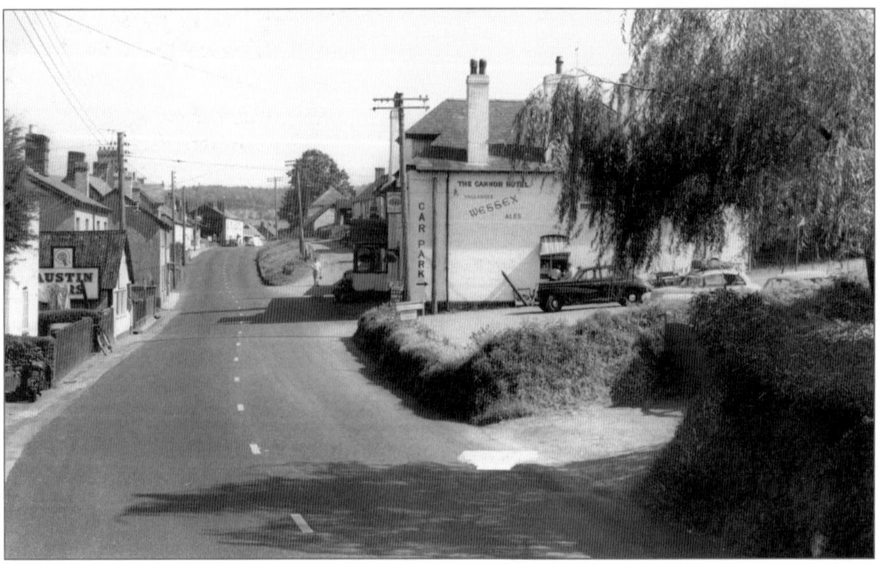

NEWTON POPPLEFORD
The Cannon Hotel c1965 N82046

Newton Poppleford is a good base for exploring the Vale of the Otter, with footpath, bridleways and ancient green lanes heading out to all points of the compass.

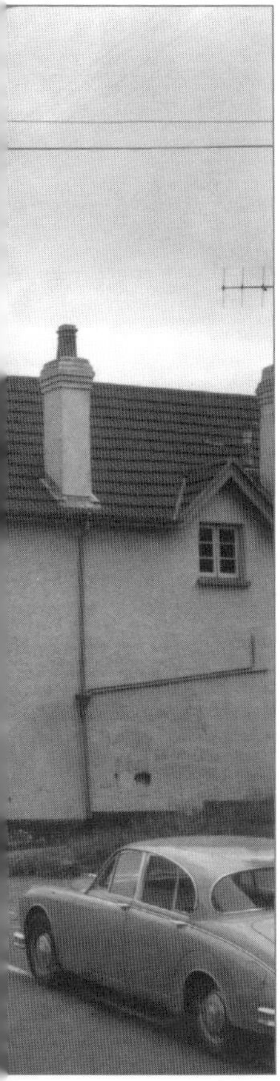

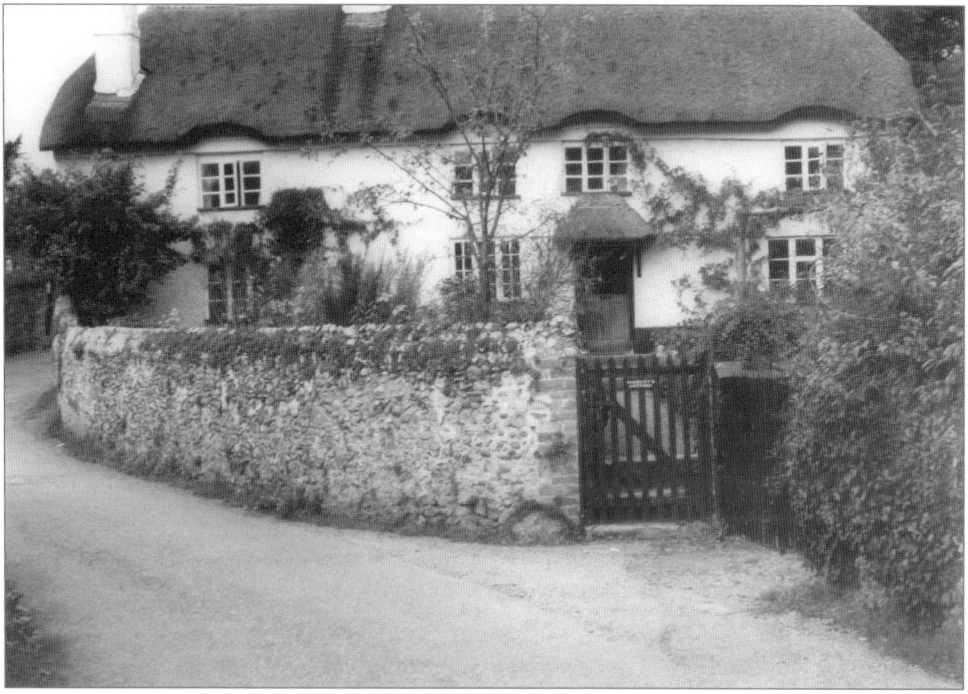

▲ **HARPFORD,** *Podbury's Cottage c1960* H389080

Harpford clings to a hillside between the sparkling waters of the River Otter and the green dells of Harpford Woods. It has been suggested that the village's name means 'ford of the musical river'. In the churchyard is a memorial to Augustus Toplady, vicar for two years from the year 1766, the author of the hymn *Rock of Ages*.

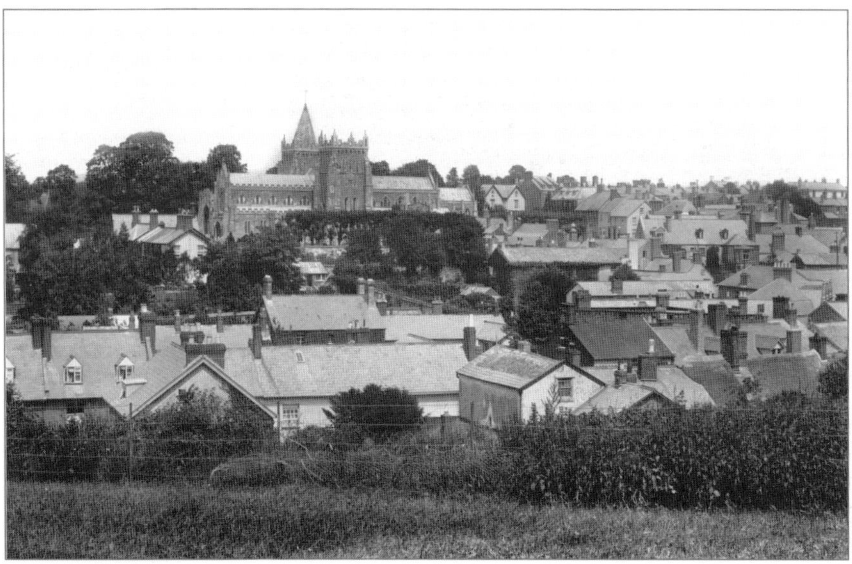

◄ **OTTERY ST MARY**
General View 1907
58180

Ottery St Mary, with its cathedral-like parish church, was the birthplace of Samuel Taylor Coleridge, poet and critic. His love of the River Otter never left him, and his earliest walks were along its banks. The poet is buried in Highgate, London, but there is a memorial in Ottery bearing words from *The Rime of the Ancient Mariner*: 'He prayeth best who loveth best all things both great and small.'

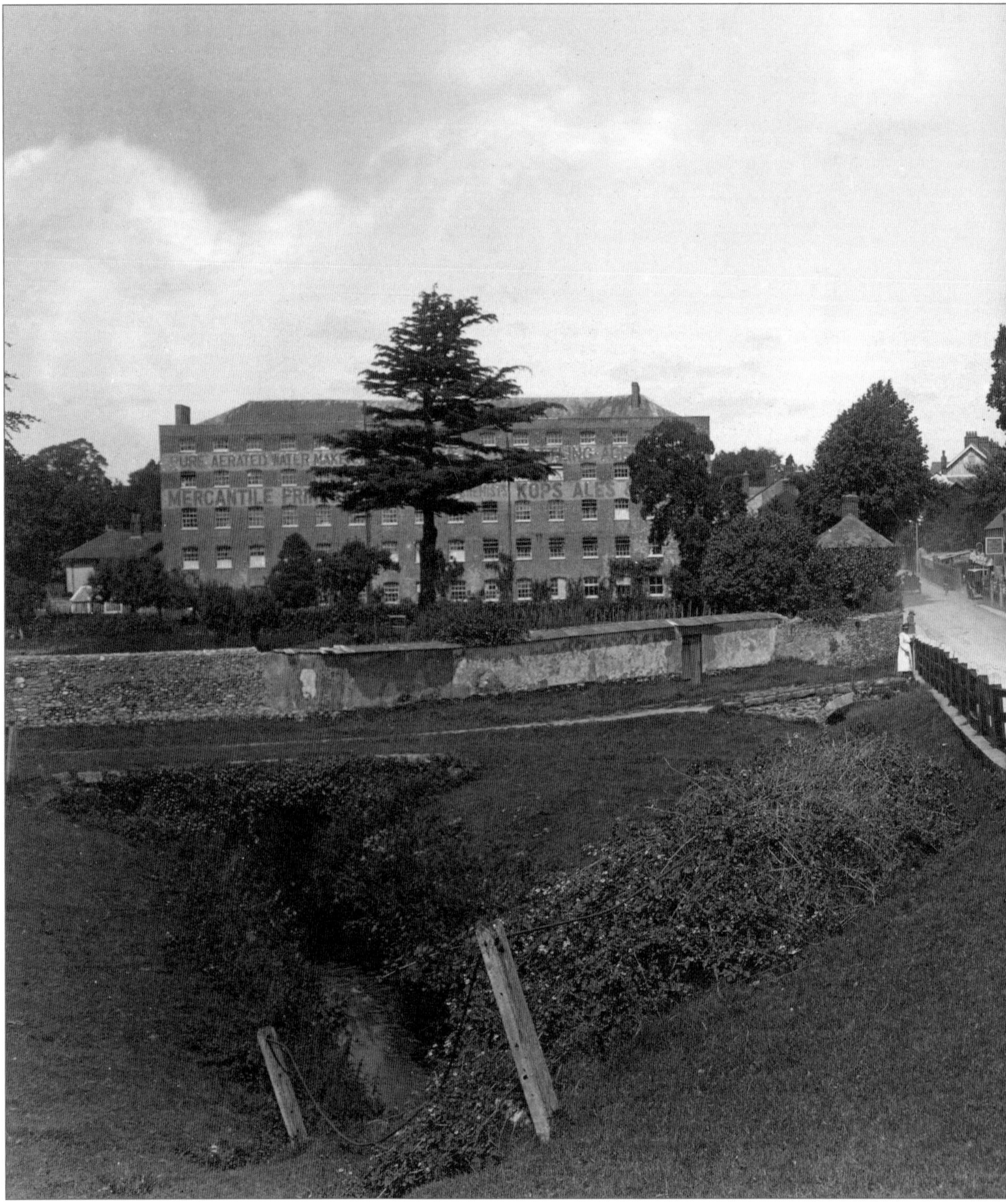
AERATED WATER
MERCANTILE
KOPS ALES

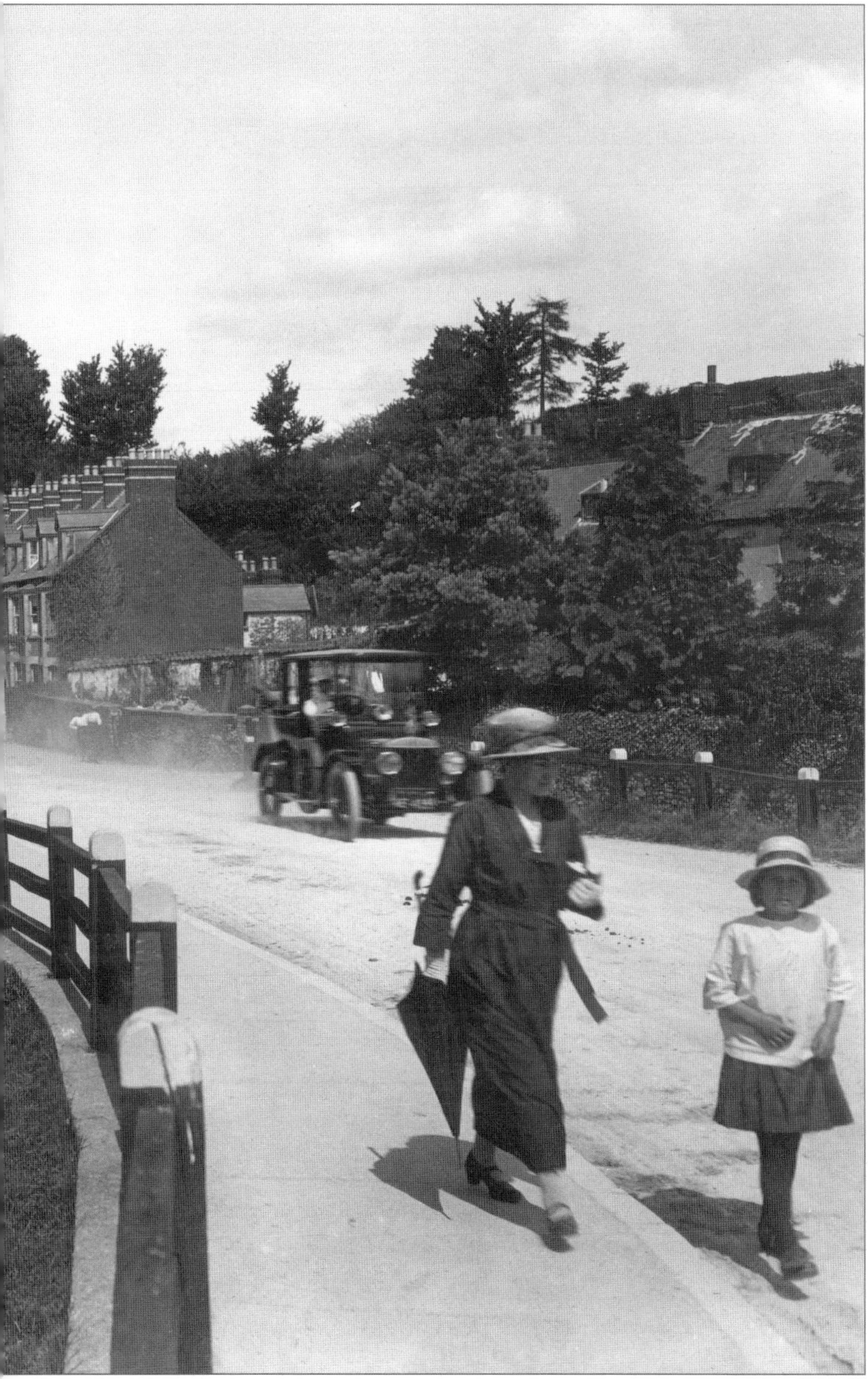

OTTERY ST MARY
The Factory 1922 72970

These industrial buildings, now an engineering works, are a reminder of Ottery's industrial heritage, for the town was famous for the production of serge and lace in previous times. To the rear of these buildings is an unusual circular weir, built in 1790 to provide power for the serge factories.

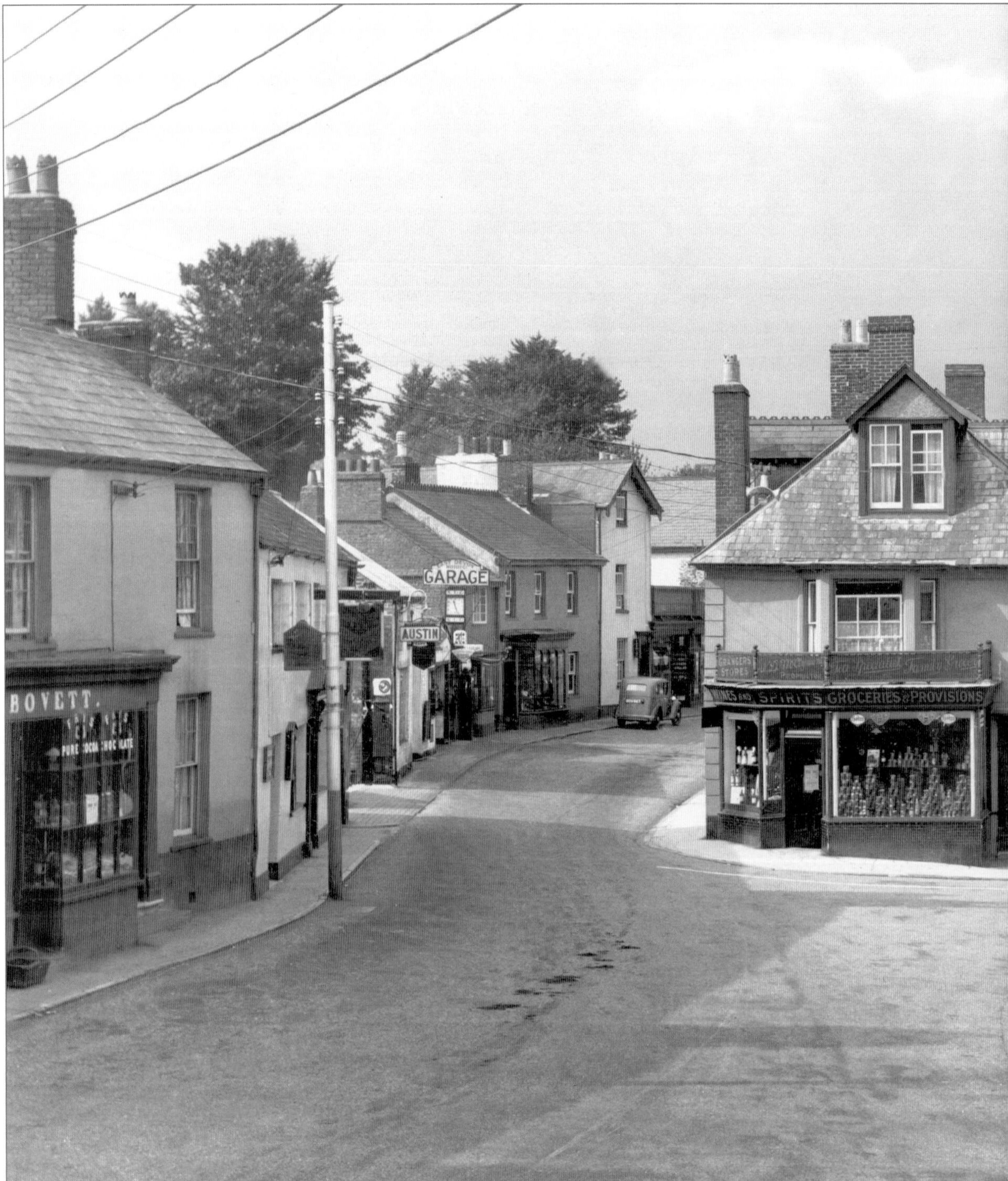
BOVETT.
GARAGE
AUSTIN
WINES AND SPIRITS GROCERIES & PROVISIONS

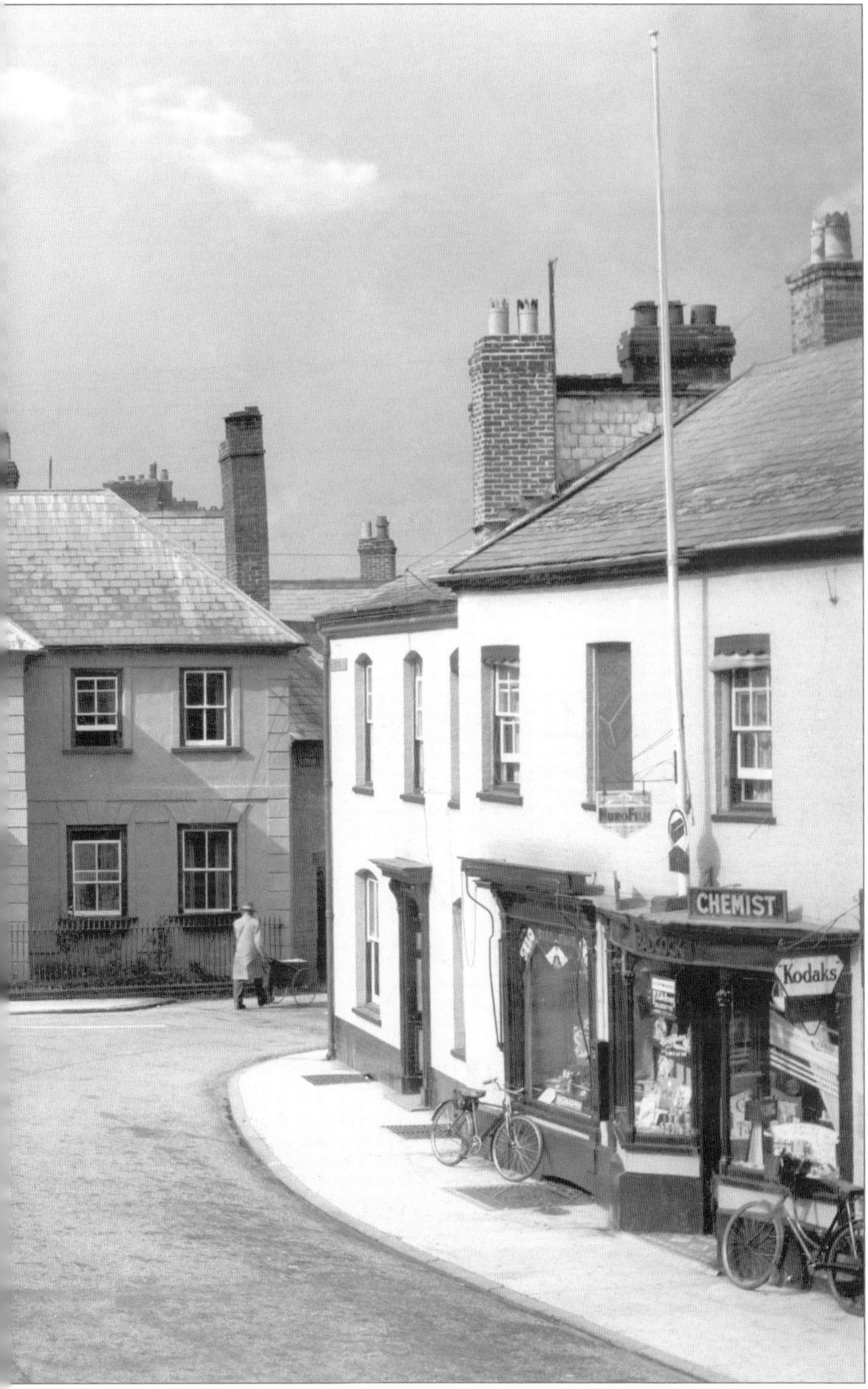

OTTERY ST MARY

Broad Street 1938 88624

Broad Street hints at Ottery's original Saxon street layout. To the left is the confectionary shop of H Bovett; then comes the Volunteer Inn, and in the distance the premises of the East Devon Motor Company - unchanged in use today, for it is still a garage. In the centre of Broad Street is Granger's Stores. In 1938 the proprietor was W D McClymont.

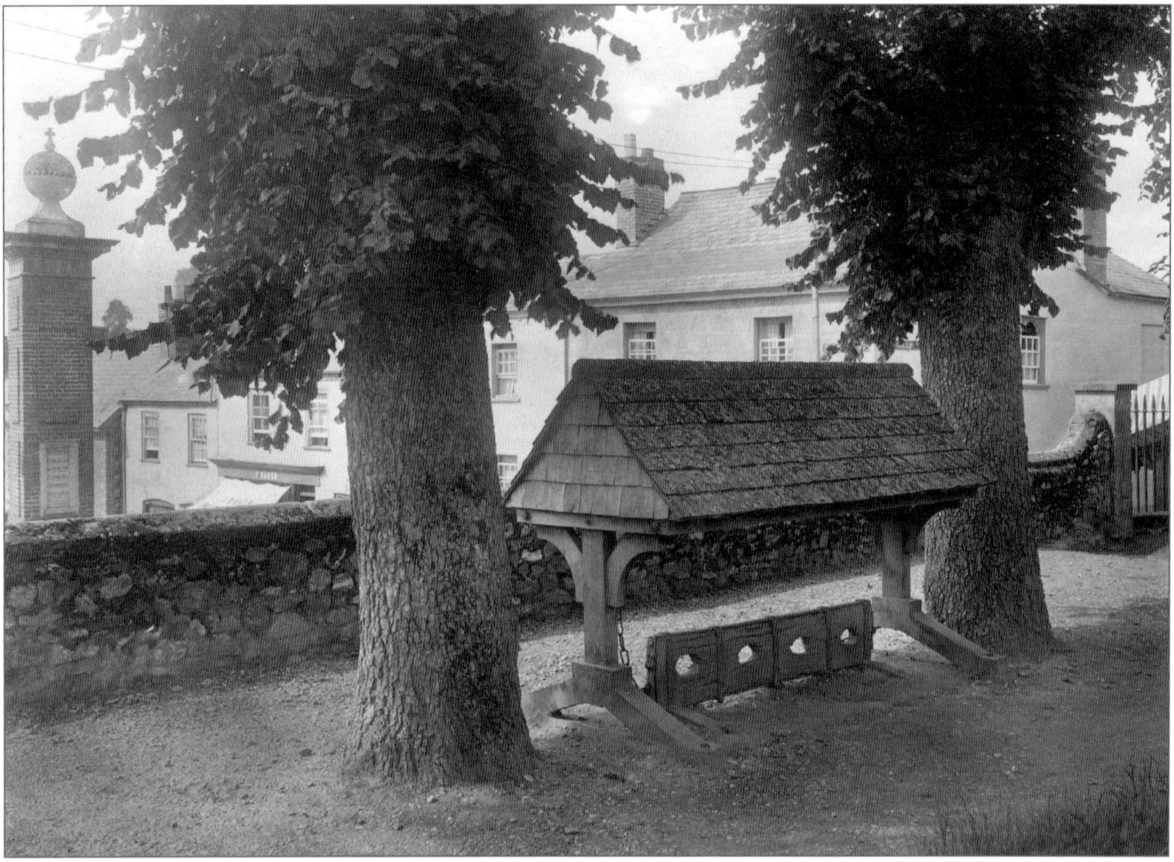

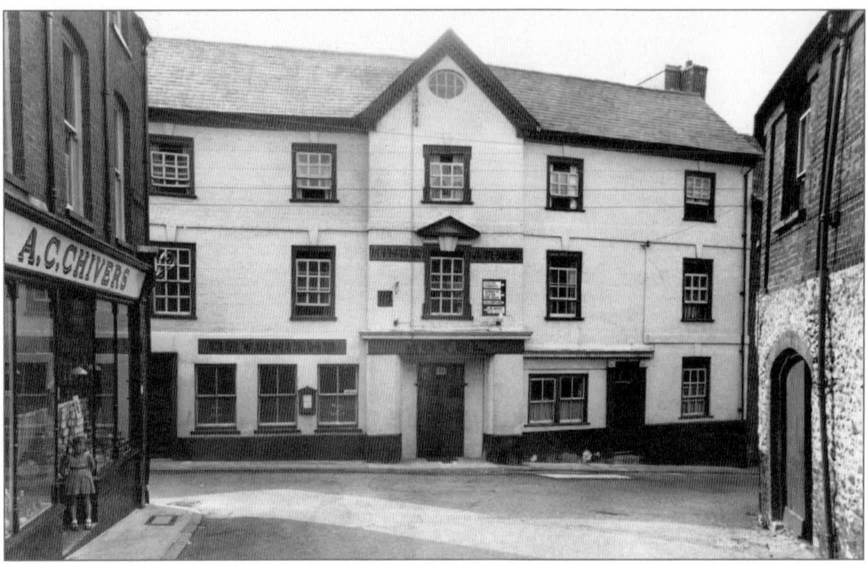

◄ **OTTERY ST MARY**
The King's Arms c1960 O28049

This old coaching inn was built in 1756 and named in honour of King George II. It survived the great fires of 1767 and 1866 which devastated other parts of Ottery St Mary.

◄ **OTTERY ST MARY**
The Stocks in the Churchyard 1922 72971

Ottery's stocks have been moved to the far side of the church path since this photograph was taken over eighty years ago. The original wooden stocks are now very fragile, and are protected by the later housing we see here. To the left is the stone monument commemorating Queen Victoria's Jubilee.

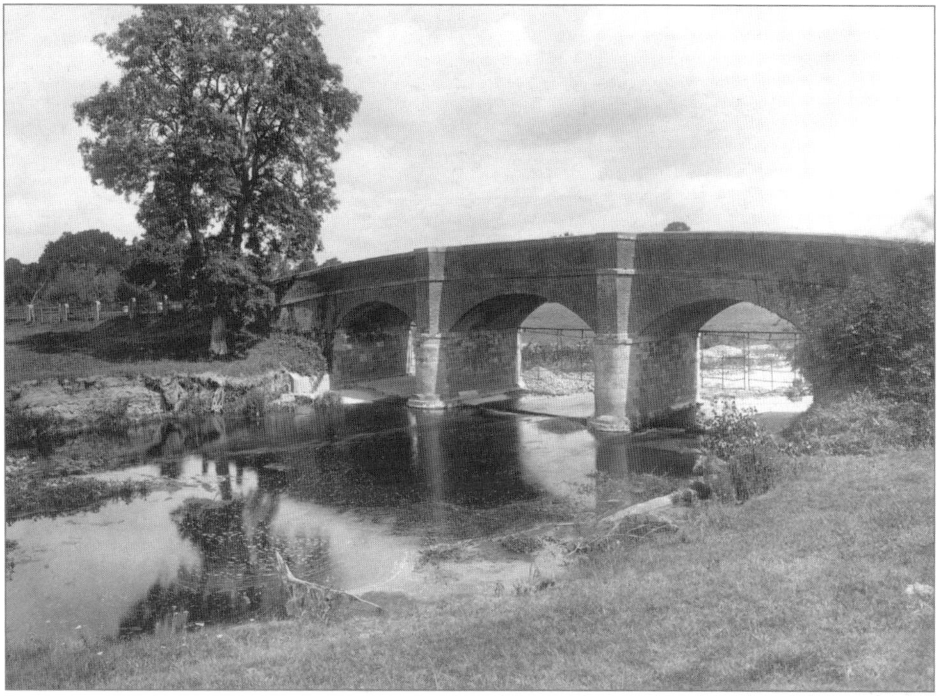

▲ **OTTERY ST MARY,** *Cadhay Bridge 1922* 72975

In earlier times, before the construction of its many bridges, the Otter presented a formidable barrier to travellers, particularly when the river was in flood and its ford impassable. Cadhay Bridge dates back to the time of Queen Elizabeth I.

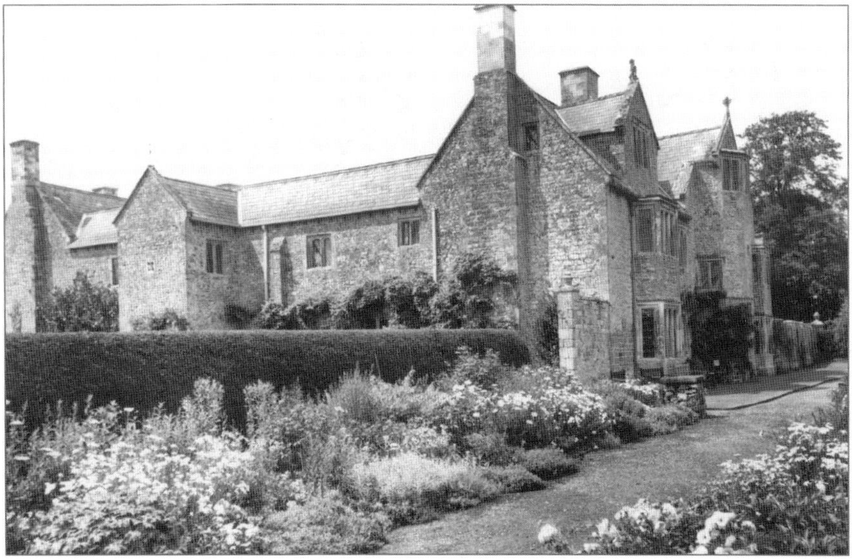

◄ **OTTERY ST MARY**
Cadhay House c1955
O28066

Cadhay House was built by the Elizabethan lawyer John Haydon, who now rests in Ottery's parish church. As well as this beautiful Tudor mansion, built partly from stones salvaged from the pre-Reformation monastic college in Ottery, Haydon also built the first of the parish's bridges across the River Otter.

GITTISHAM
The Post Office c1955 G136001

Gittisham, pronounced 'Gitsam', was the birthplace of the mystic Joanna Southcott. She worked as a domestic servant in the village for some years before claiming the gift of prophecy. At the age of 64 she announced that she was to be the mother of a second Messiah, but she died of dropsy soon afterwards.

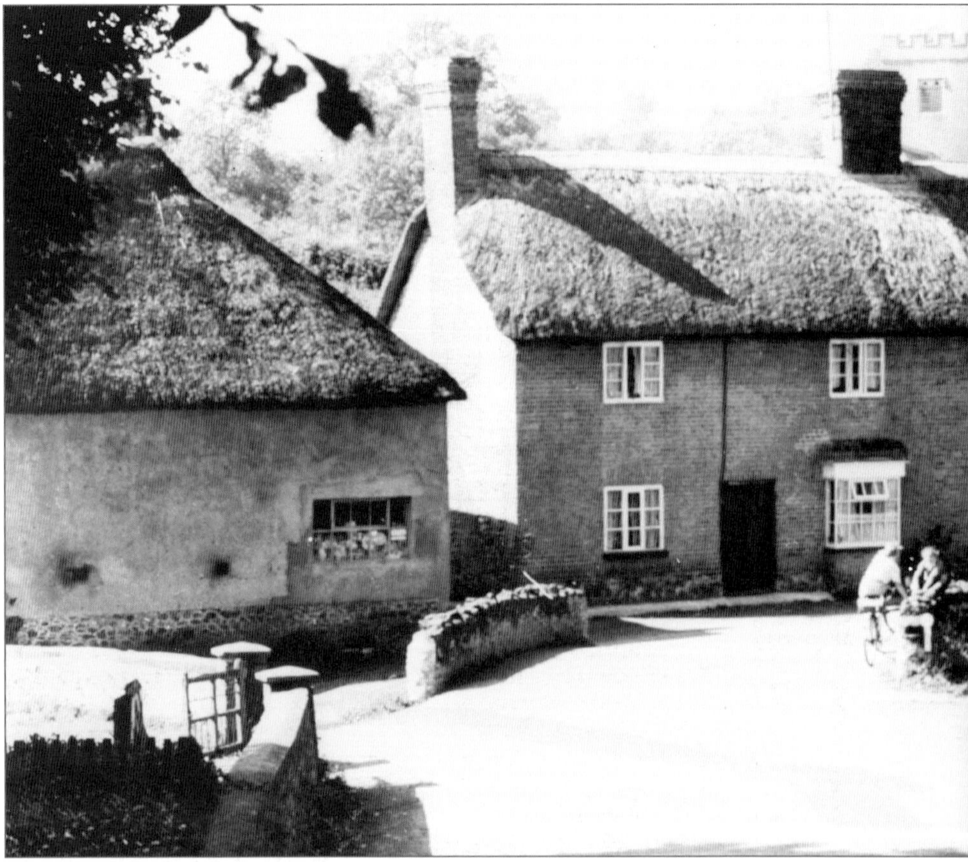

FENITON
The Village 1906 56681

Villagers pose for the Frith photographer in this charming study taken in Feniton nearly a century ago. The meadows below the village, on the banks of the Otter, were the scene of terrible slaughter in a battle during the Prayer Book Rebellion of 1549.

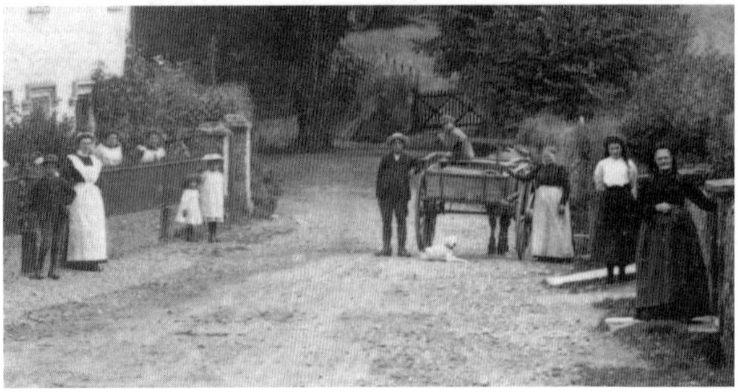

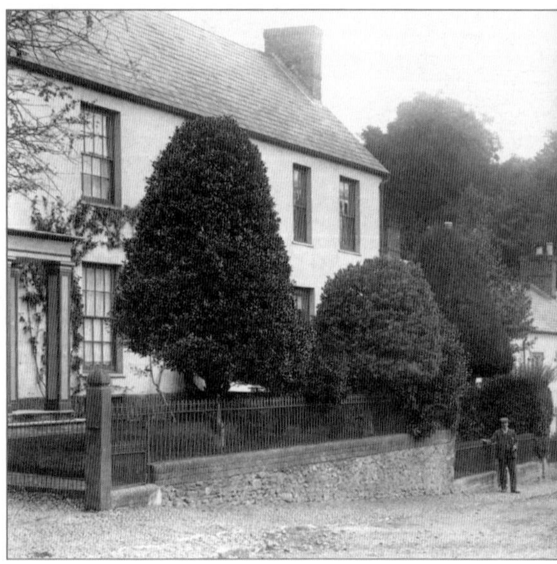

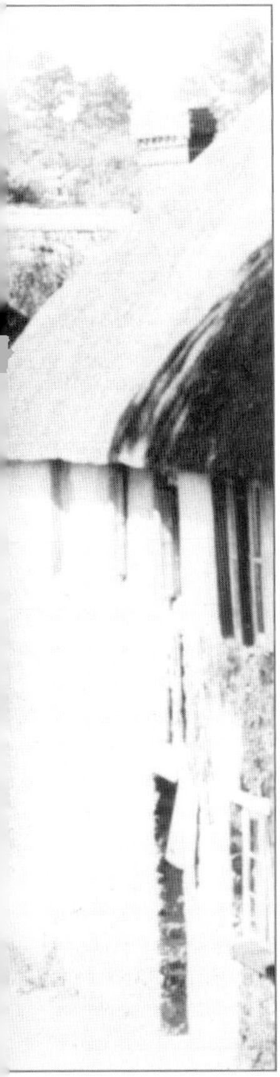

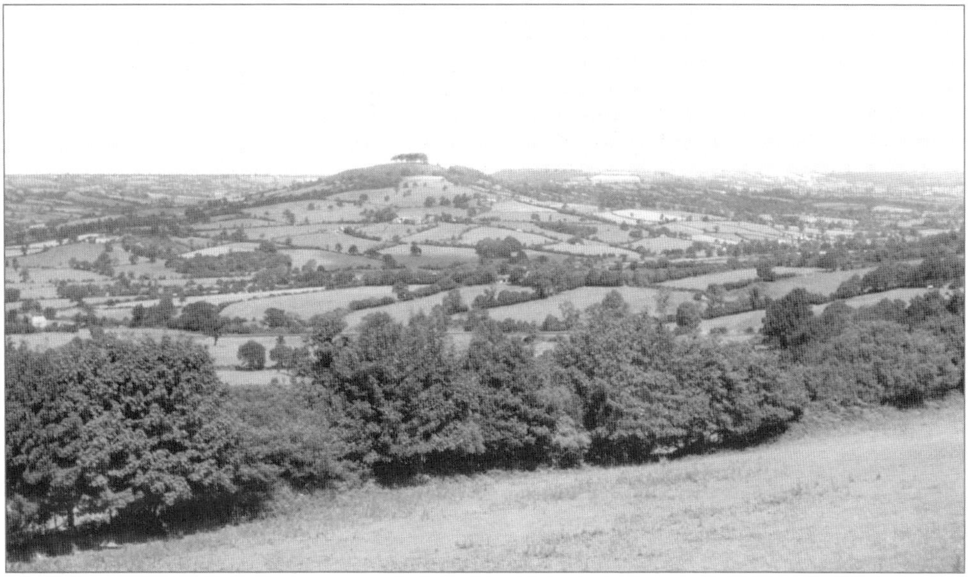

▲ **HONITON,** *The View from Honiton Hill c1955* H111020

The high ridges surrounding the upper reaches of the River Otter offer wonderful views across the East Devon countryside. This rural splendour remains relatively unchanged since this photograph was taken half a century ago.

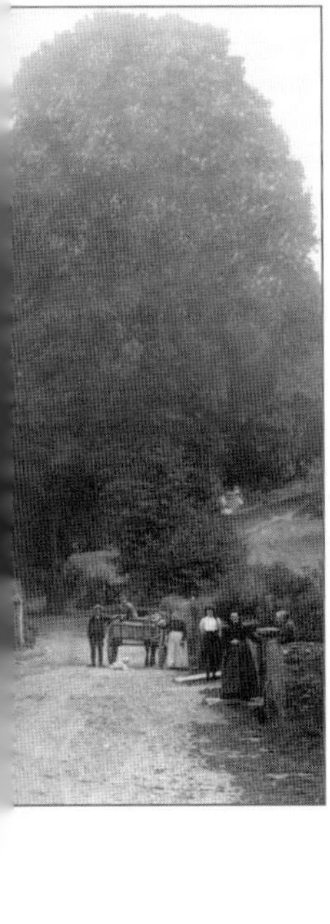

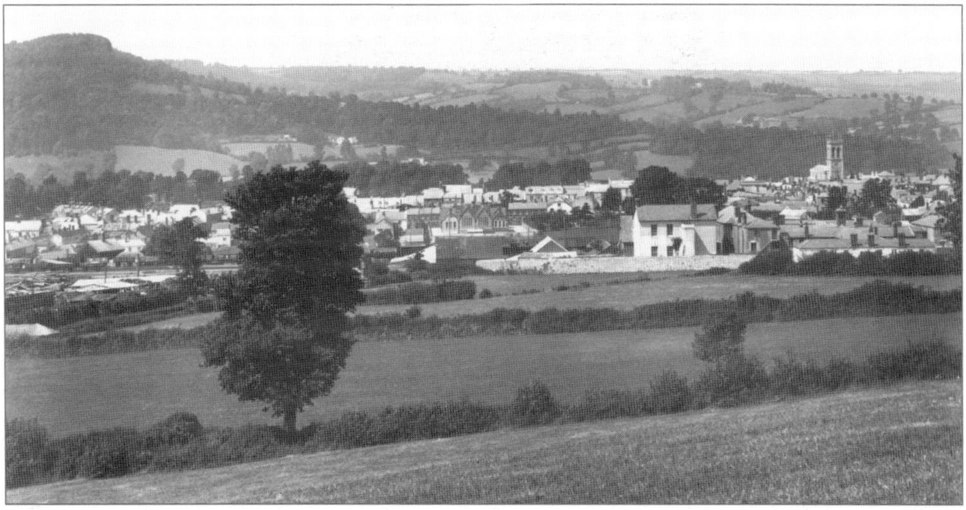

▲ **HONITON**
General View 1904 52106

Honiton is the largest settlement on the River Otter; this ancient market town stretches along a mile of Roman road. In recent centuries, Honiton was a staging post on the coaching route between London and Exeter, and some of its inns catered for the stagecoaches and their passengers. The town is now bypassed.

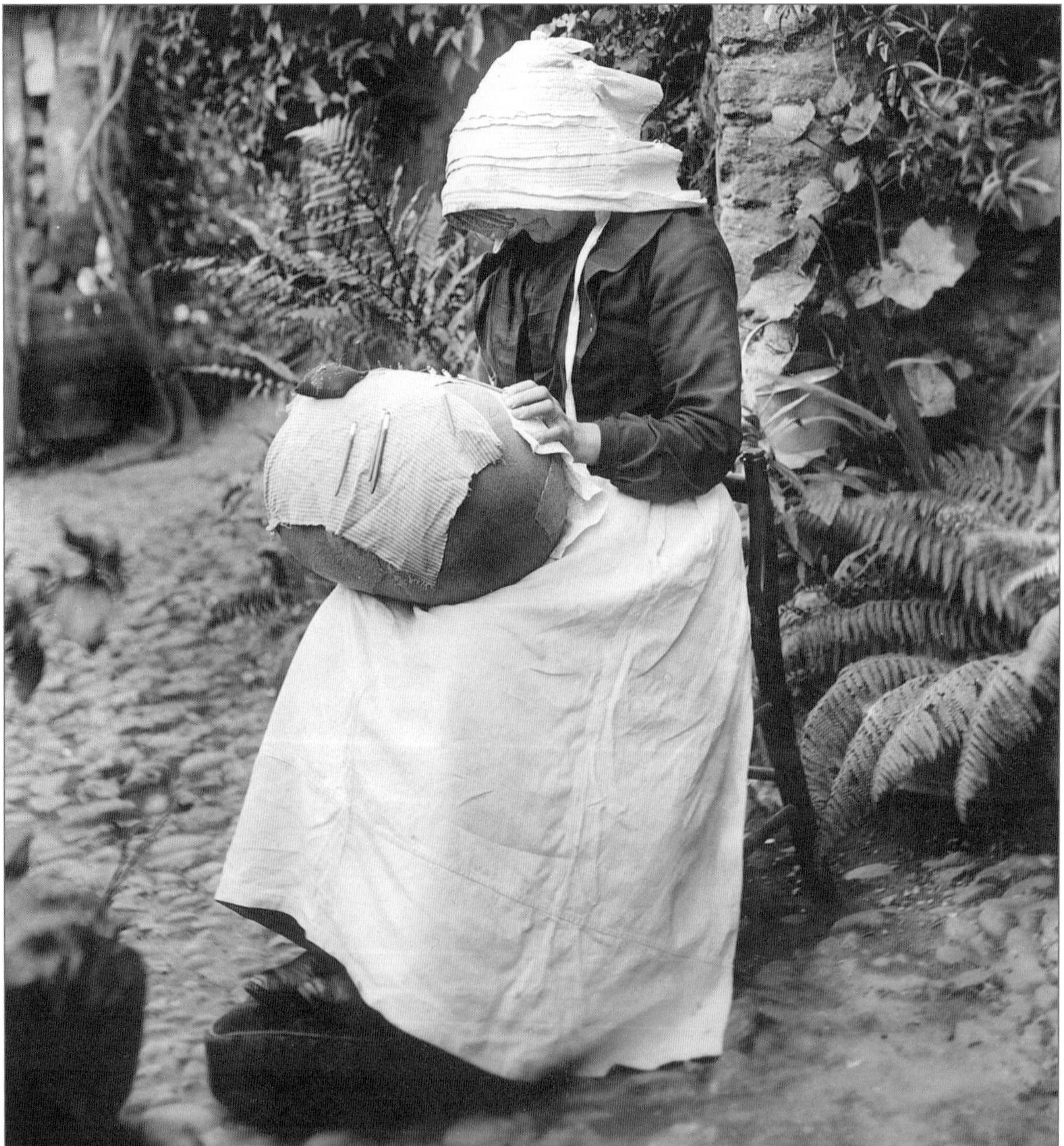

HONITON, *A Lace Maker (Mrs Freeman) 1907* 58189

Honiton's lace production was at its peak during and in the years after the reign of Elizabeth I. It seems to have declined after a series of devastating town fires in the 18th century. Even in Mrs Freeman's heyday, a century ago, there were only a few lace makers left in Honiton - now there are even fewer. Examples of Honiton lace can be purchased in the town, and the town museum has an excellent exhibition of Honiton lace.

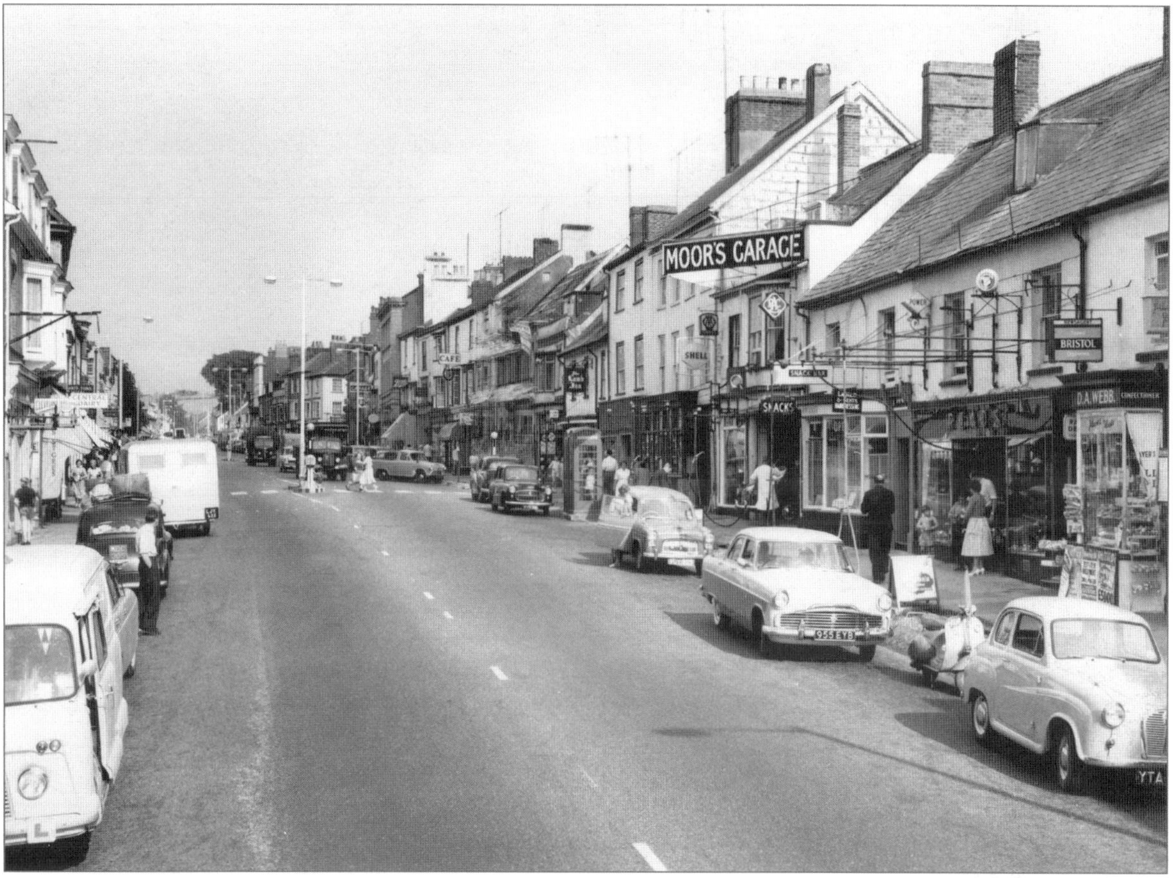

HONITON, *High Street c1960* H111040

Before the days of motorways and bypasses, Honiton was the gateway to Devon for travellers coming from the south and east of England, who passed along this long straight road. Just beyond Moors Garage (right) is the old Lamb Inn, closed by its parent brewery in the 1970s and now a café. Moors Garage has gone too, and is now a photographic shop.

HONITON
High Street c1965
H111049

A Dimond had already traded on the High Street for some 80 years when this photograph was taken, and Dimond's (left) are happily still in business, though the shop front has changed slightly. The family has had a recent tradition of naming all of their children with names beginning with the letter A so that the shop sign need never be changed. The Black Lion Hotel, the lower white building in the centre of the photograph, was demolished soon afterwards to allow New Street to enter the High Street.

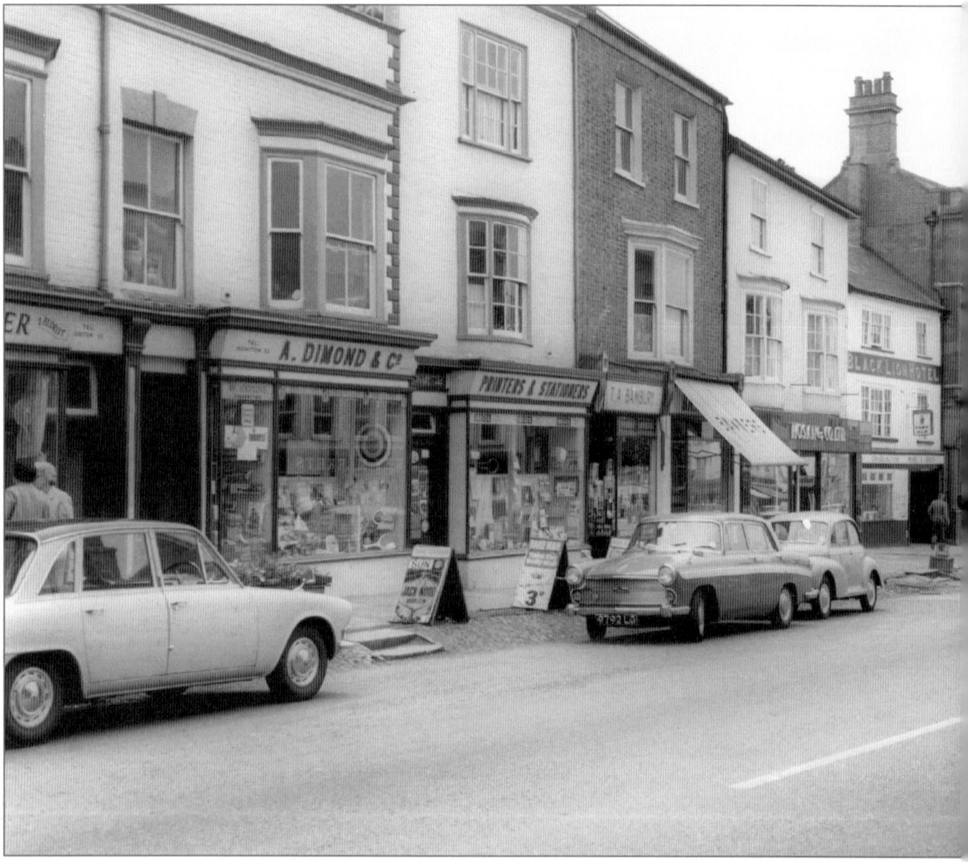

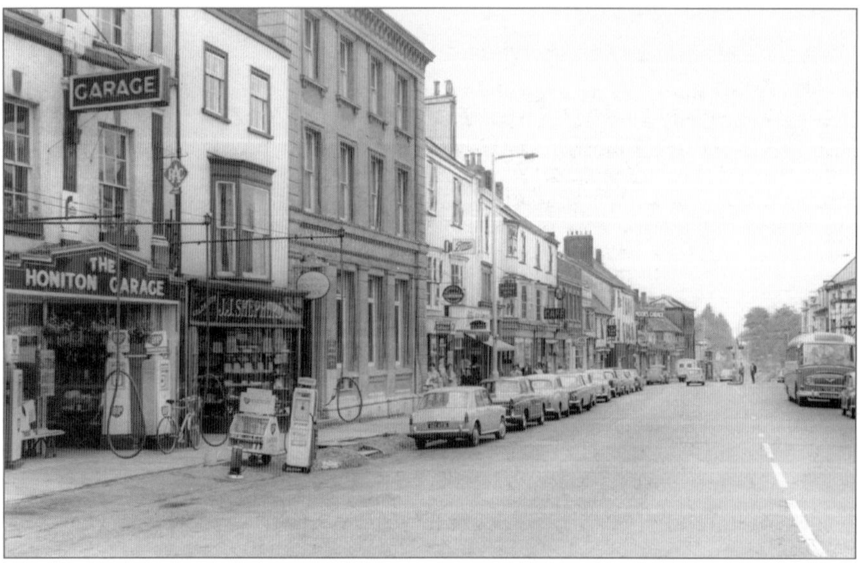

HONITON
High Street c1965
H111051

Each week, on market day, colourful stalls line the pavements of the High Street, and shoppers come from all over East Devon as they have for centuries. The Honiton Garage (left), a reminder of carefree motoring days, has been replaced by a supermarket. The solid brick building two doors down, then the National Provincial Bank, is now Natwest. Further down is Boots the Chemist, the Midland Bank, the Lamb Inn and Moors Garage.

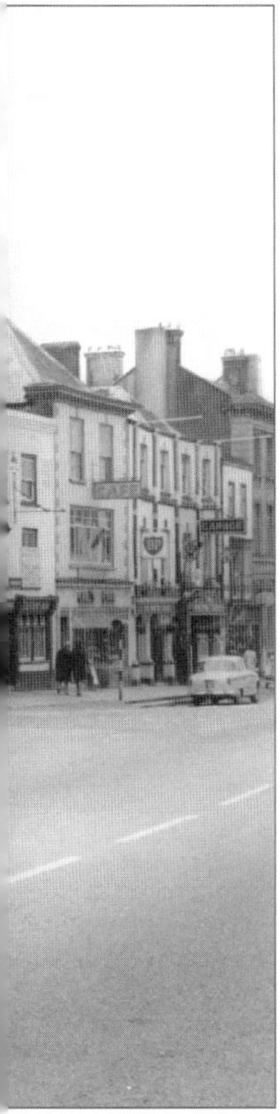

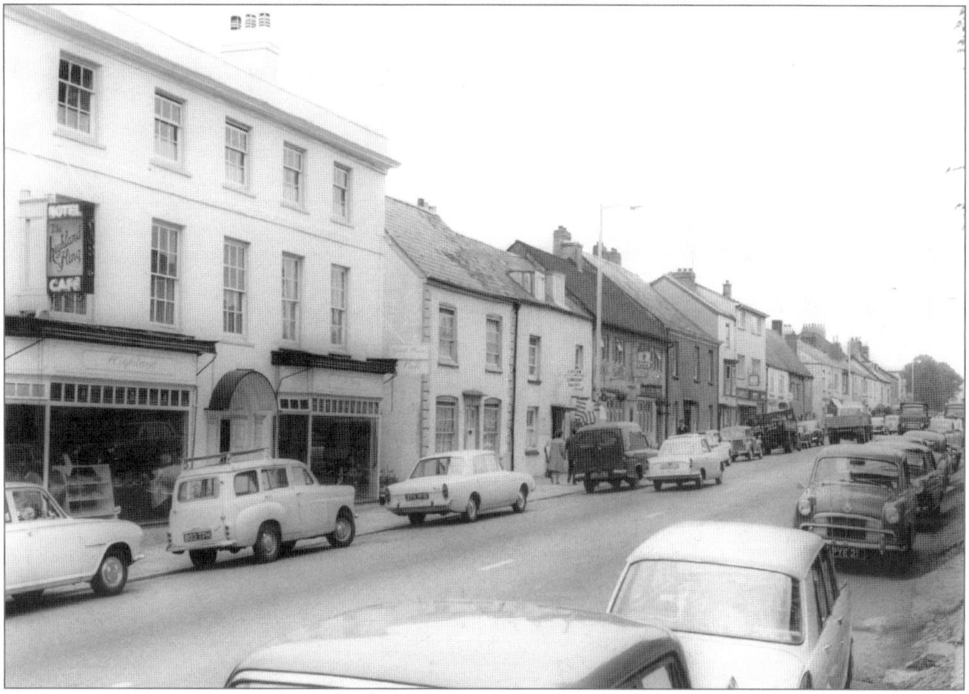

▲ **HONITON,** *High Street c1965* H111060

Here we see the eastern end of the High Street, with the wall of the Congregational Church on the right. The Highland Fling hotel and café (left) spent some years as an extremely large antiquarian bookshop and antiques centre before reverting back to being a café. The inn in the middle distance is the Red Cow, which had a wild reputation in Victorian times.

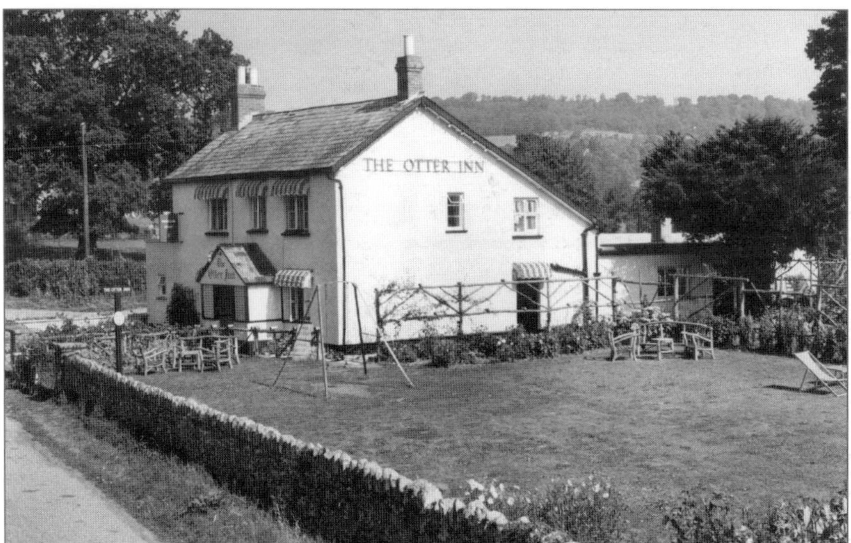

◄ **HONITON**
The Otter Inn c1960
H111042

The Otter Inn, just outside Honiton in the hamlet of Weston, has changed very slightly since this photograph was taken. The garden we see here is now the car park, and the inn building is now somewhat larger. It is much frequented by walkers exploring the Vale of the Otter.

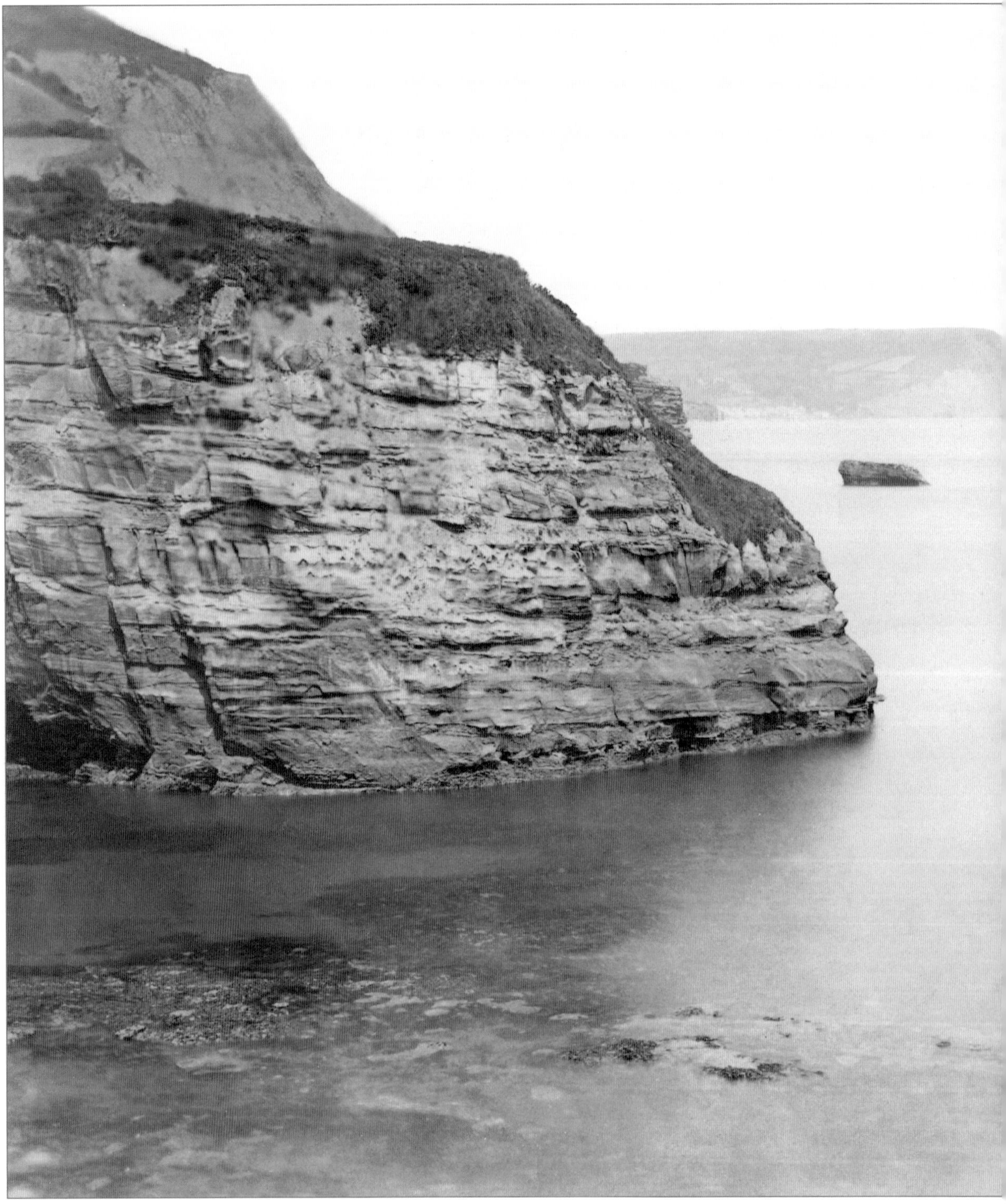

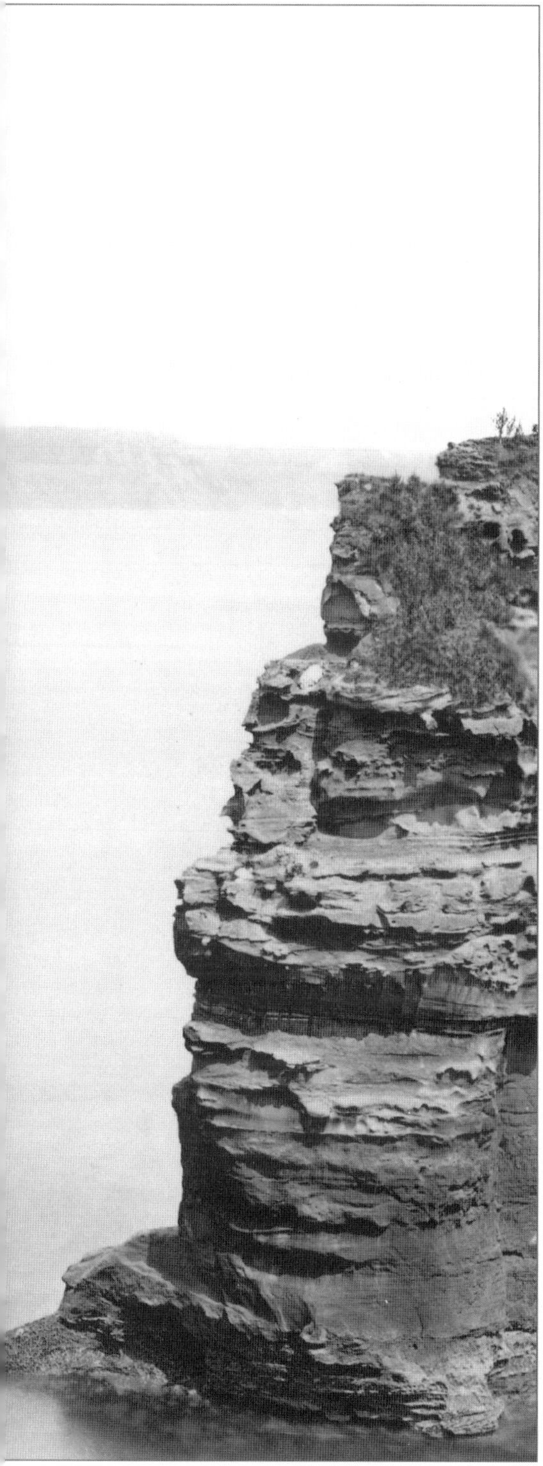

THE LONELY COAST

EAST DEVON has one of the quietest, least spoiled stretches of coastline in England. Much of it can only be explored on foot, and is all the better for that. The cliff paths are by turn steep, as they descend almost to sea level into the numerous combes that tumble towards hidden, secret coves, then level as they breast the high cliffs with views far out across Lyme Bay.

This coast was made for smuggling. Tales are told of Jack Rattenbury of Beer, who landed many a cargo on these beaches on dark nights two centuries ago. The Mutters, who lived in and around Sidmouth, treated smuggling as very much the family business, carrying contraband far inland hidden under the turf and wood of their farm cart.

The resorts of the lonely coast still have the feel of those watering places of earlier times, particularly genteel Sidmouth. Beer is at heart a fishing village. Seaton has a great deal of modern building, and comes the closest to a commercial holiday town with its tourist shops and takeaways. But even here there is a sense of people seeking a quieter holiday break.

This is the coast where the red sandstone cliffs of South Devon run into the white chalk of southern England. It is a lonely coast, a place to walk, to linger and to remember what peace and quiet are really all about.

LADRAM BAY, *King William Rock c1874* 7234

Ladram Bay, with its spectacular rock stacks, is halfway between Budleigh Salterton and Sidmouth. Smugglers used the area so much that a coastguard cottage was built here in 1834 to deter the landing of contraband. Jack Rattenbury of Beer landed many a cargo, all taken inland on a turf cart by his accomplice Abraham Mutter.

LADRAM BAY
c1965 L3091

Towards the end of Queen Victoria's reign, Ladram Bay had become a popular destination for trippers, who would arrive by boat from neighbouring resorts. The bay is now the site of a vast caravan park, established by Mr Tovell in the 1930s.

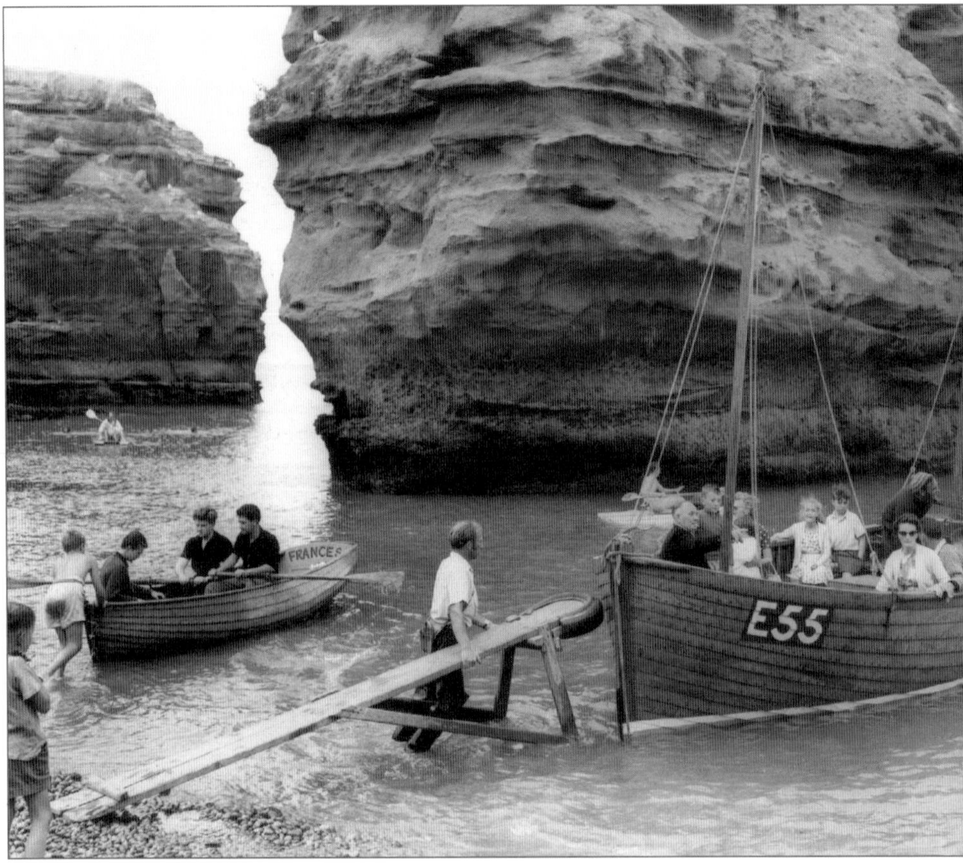

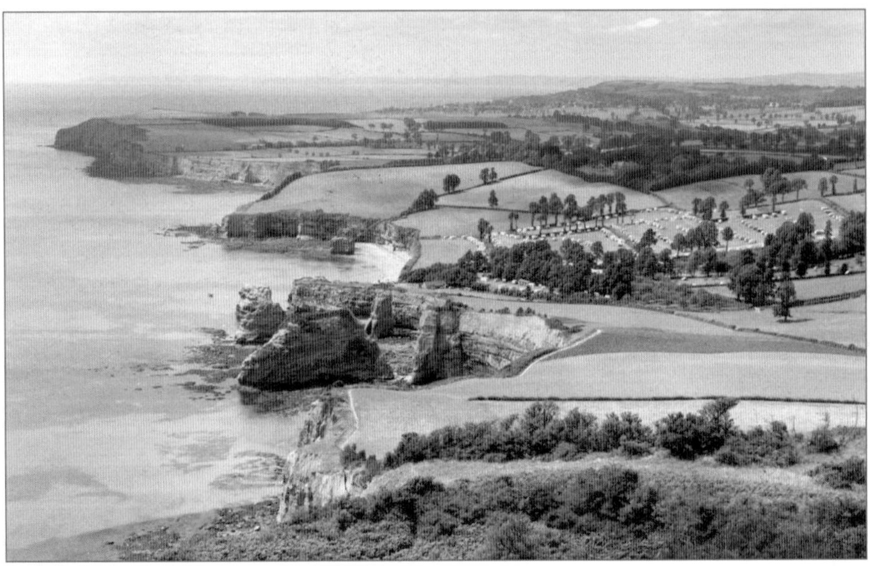

LADRAM BAY
From High Peak
c1965 L3069

This wonderful view shows the East Devon coast from the great cliff of High Peak to distant Exmouth, circling part of the great sweep of Lyme Bay. All of this coastline can be walked by following the South West Coast Path, ancient routes originally taken by the coastguards who patrolled the lonely coast.

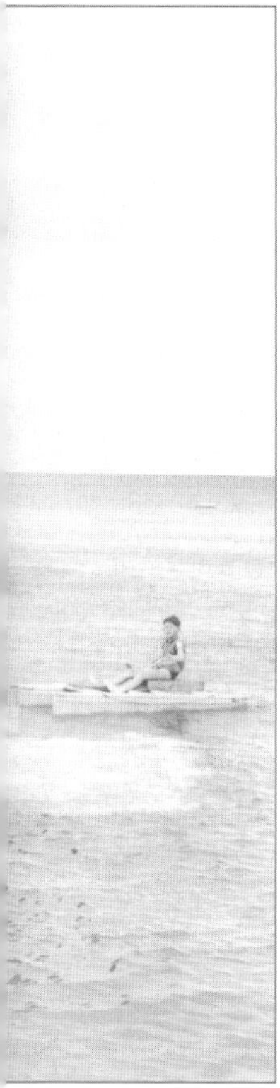

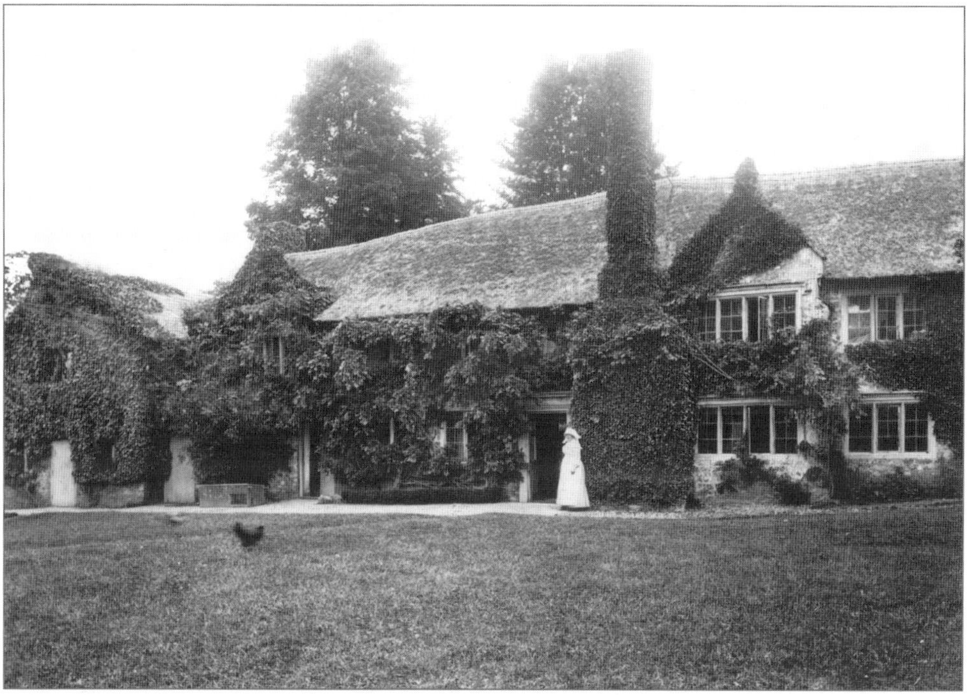

▲ **SIDMOUTH,** *Sid Vale Dairy 1906* 53827

Sidmouth nestles in a broad valley where the pastoral countryside of East Devon sweeps down to the sea. It was a centre for fishing and farming long before it became popular with tourists.

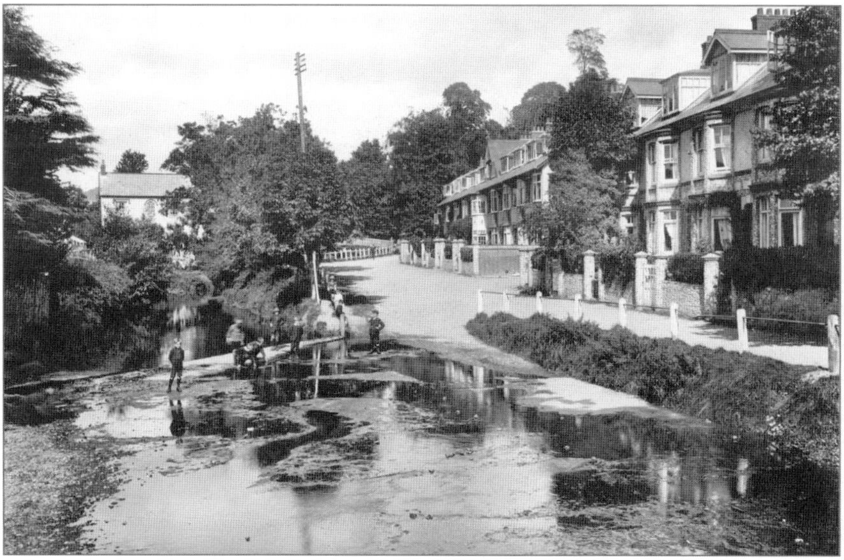

◄ **SIDMOUTH**
Milford Road 1918
68750

The River Sid starts its short journey to the sea amidst the high land at Broad Down and Farway; here the Bronze Age inhabitants of East Devon buried their dead. These ancient peoples journeyed the length of the river to collect salt at the seashore. Despite its modest size, the River Sid is one of Devon's most charming rivers.

SIDMOUTH
Fore Street 1918 68745

Sidmouth remained a fishing village until the tourists began to arrive in the late 18th century; it became extremely popular during the long Napoleonic Wars, when the continent was closed to visitors. The town's mild climate persuaded many people to settle here, and the architecture reflects these Georgian and Victorian influences. Trump's Café, on the left, is now the Dove public house.

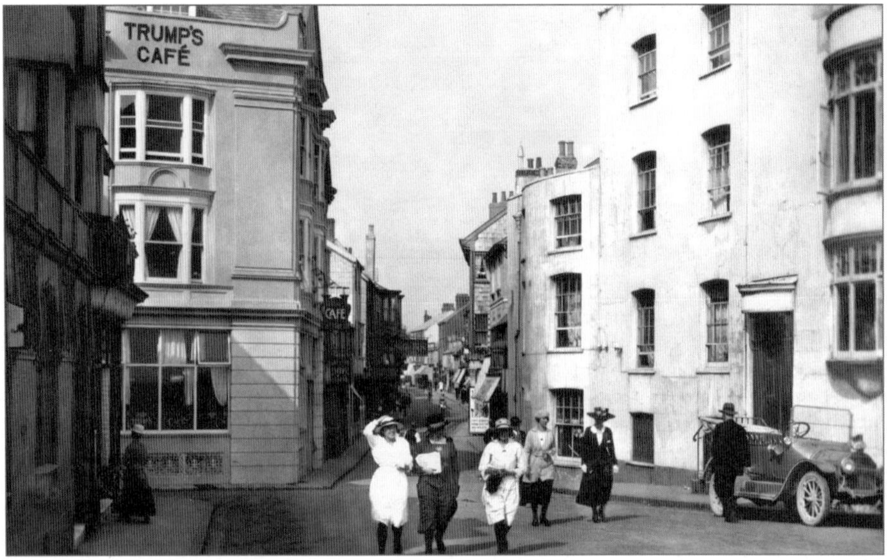

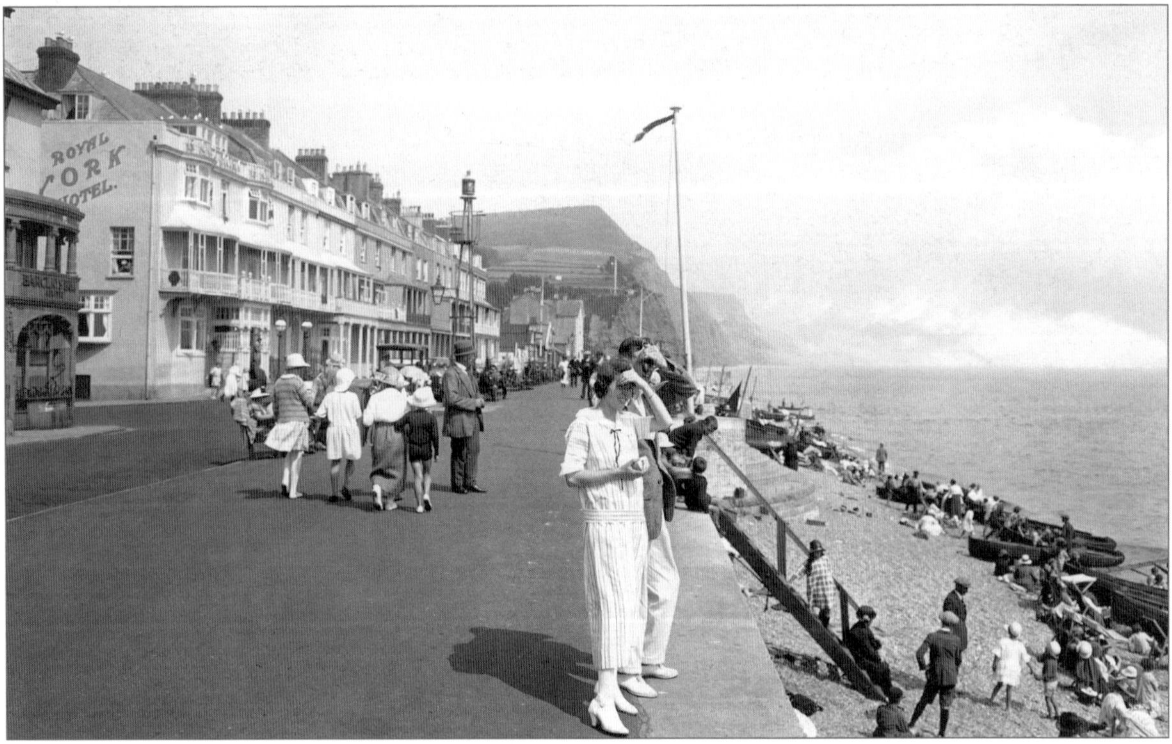

SIDMOUTH, *York Terrace 1924* 76352

In the 1920s, Sidmouth had a reputation as an up-market resort, as renowned for its climate and setting as for its sea bathing. The town's first library was situated in one of the houses in York Terrace.

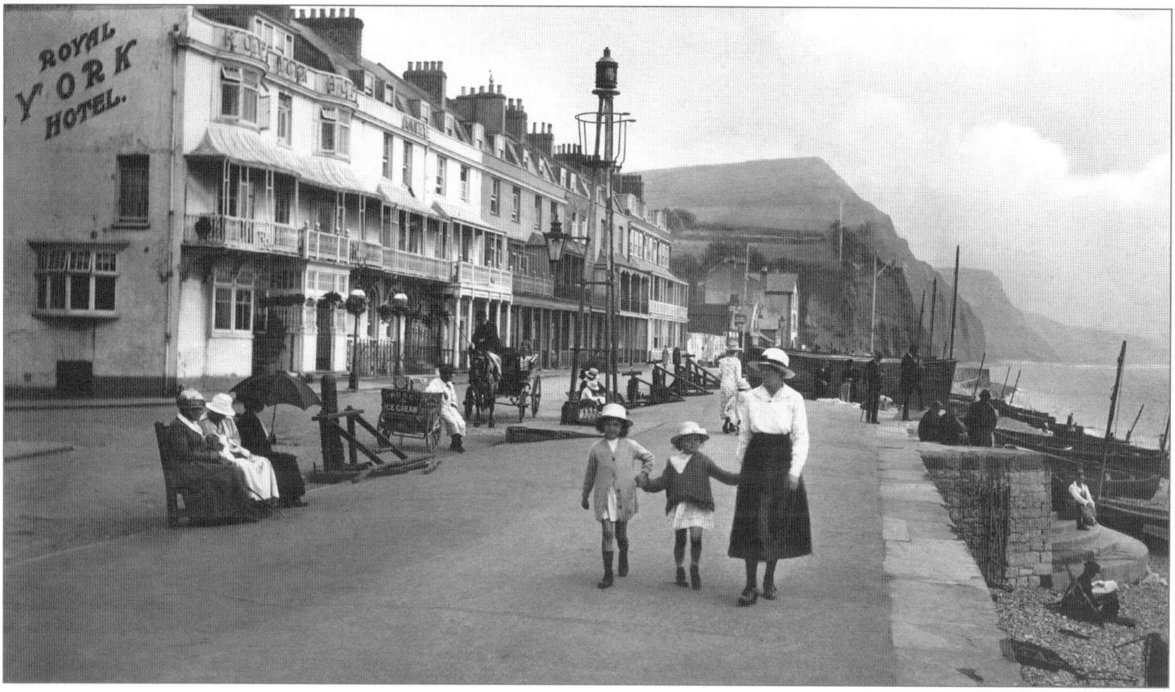

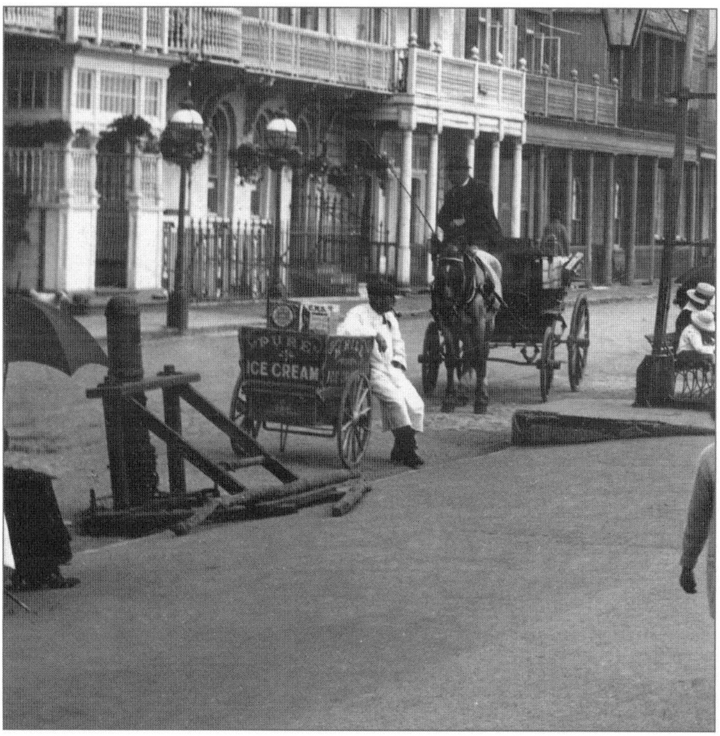

▲ **SIDMOUTH**
The Esplanade 1919 68738

The Royal York (left) opened in 1810 as Sidmouth's first purpose-built hotel. The Duke of Kent, father of Queen Victoria, was an early visitor. His grandson, the Prince of Wales, later Edward VII, stayed here on a boyhood walking tour with his tutor. The building survives as the Royal York and Faulkner Hotel. The children here have obviously resisted the temptations of the ice cream on sale at the edge of the promenade.

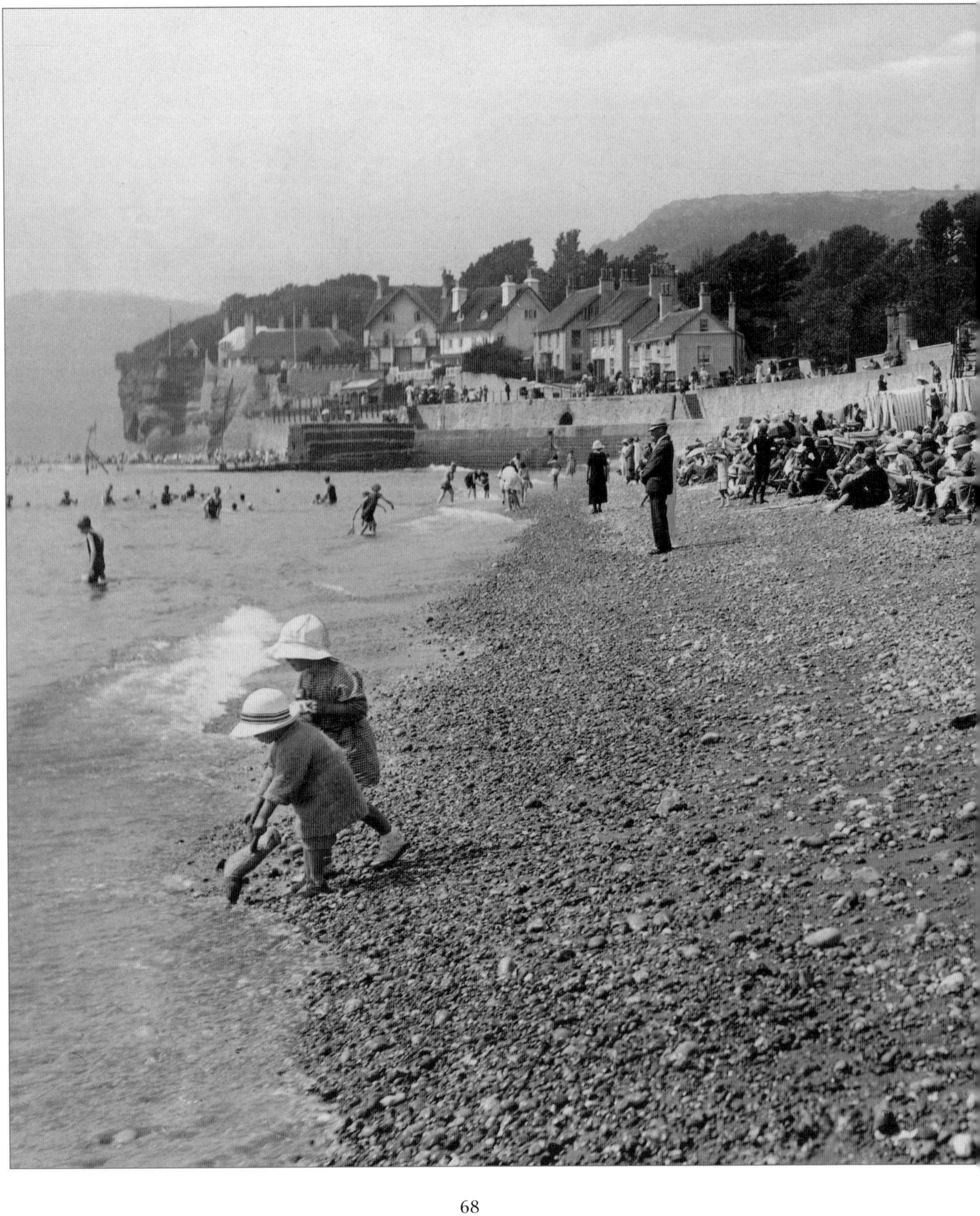

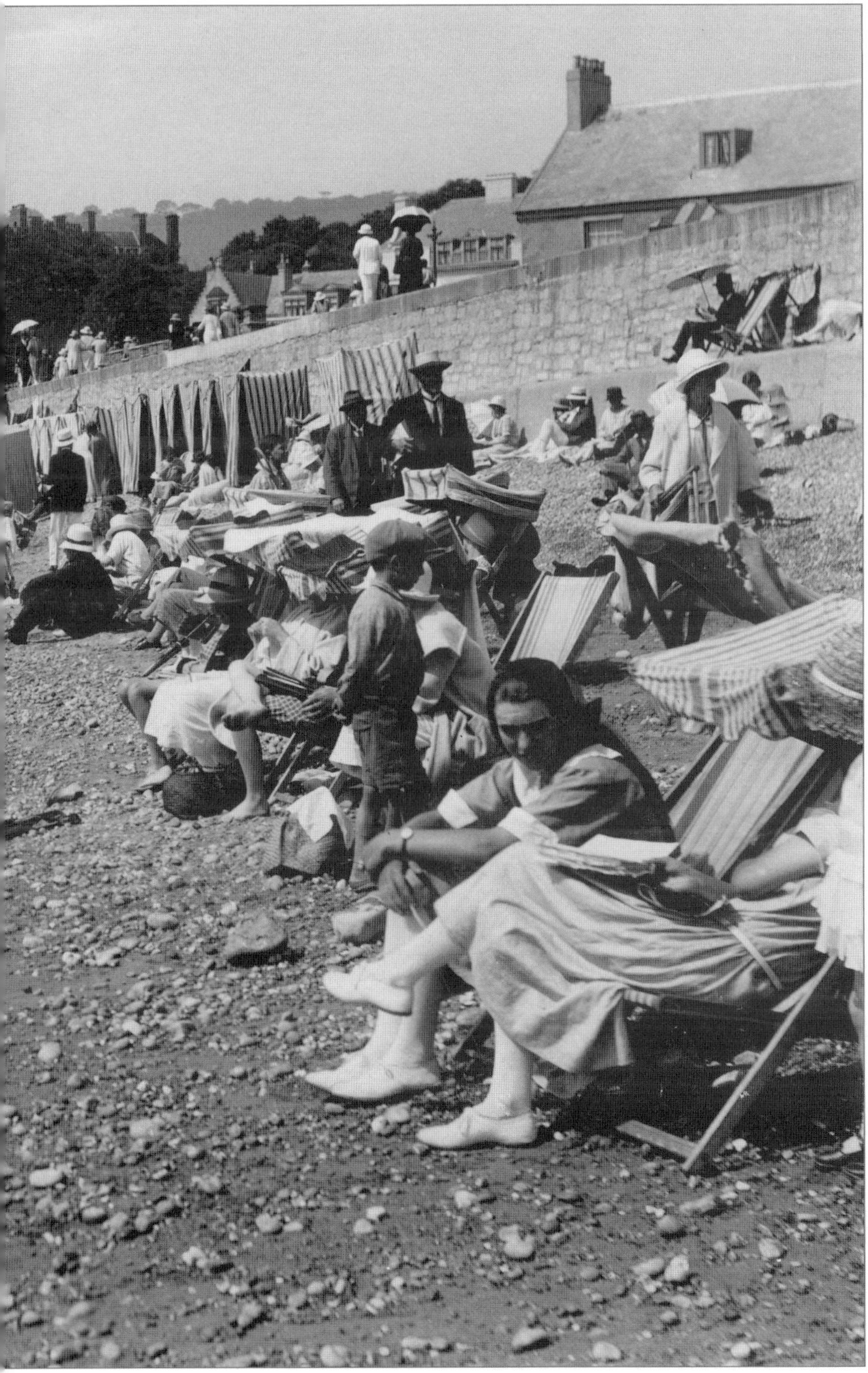

SIDMOUTH
The Beach 1924 76365

Sidmouth's pebbly beach has never deterred sea bathers and paddlers, though building sandcastles was a harder task. There is more sand on the resort's beaches today, and it is a favourite sun trap on long summer days. On the skyline is the long stretch of Mutter's Moor and the huge cliff of High Peak.

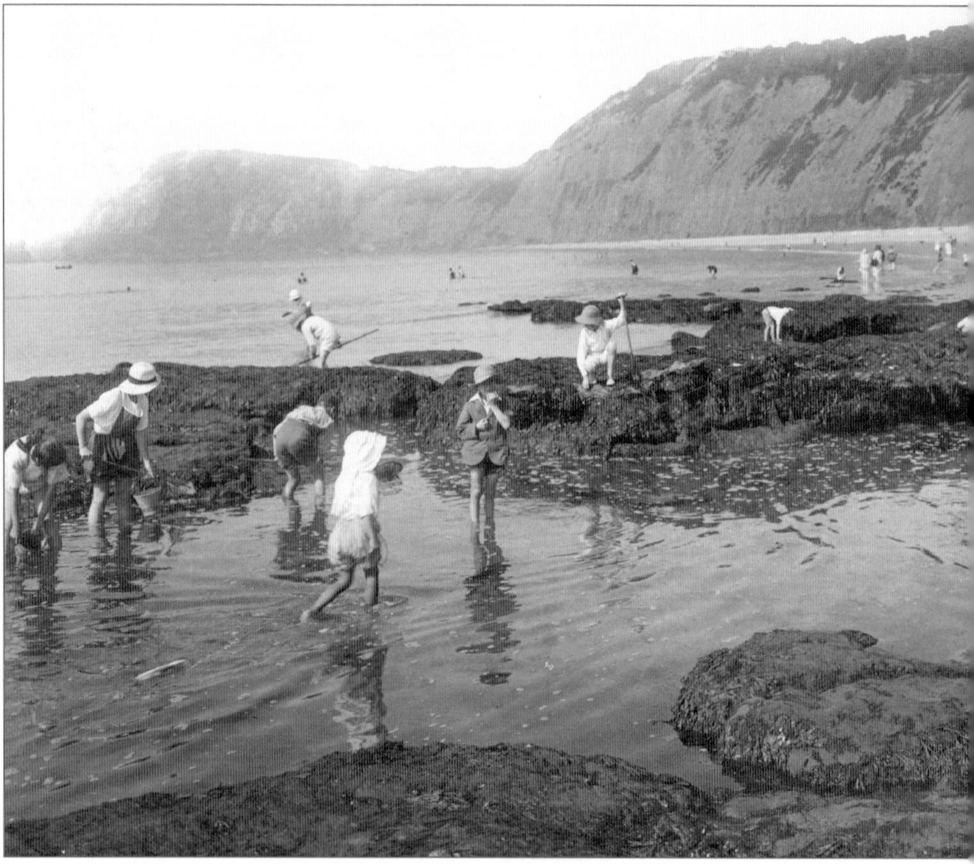

► **SIDMOUTH**
The Western Bay
1924 76367

Rock-pooling has always been one of the joys of a seaside holiday, and these children are obviously enjoying themselves. In the distance is High Peak and the distant rock stacks of Ladram Bay.

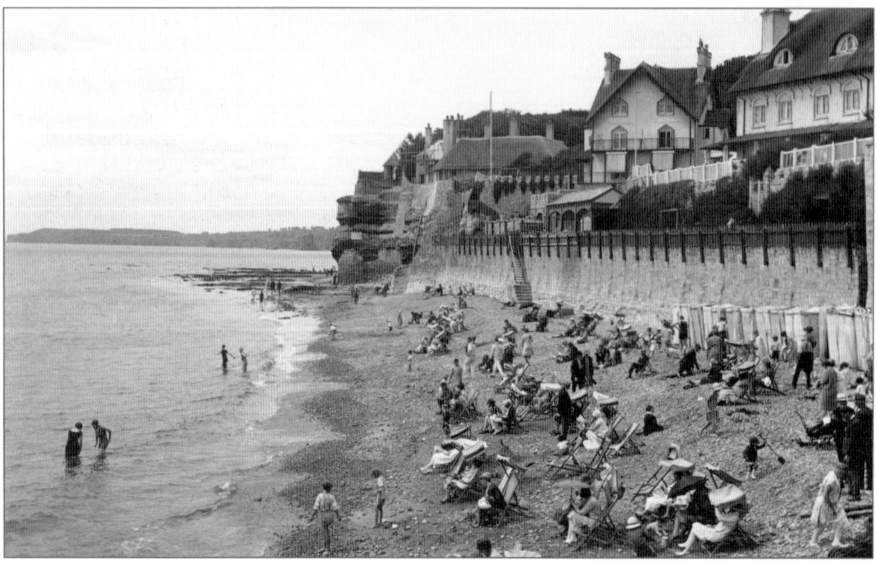

◄ **SIDMOUTH**
The Bathing Beach
1925 78585

It was to this western corner of Sidmouth that the Duke of Kent brought his baby daughter Alexandrina Victoria in 1819. The impoverished duke died here in 1820, though not before he had taken the child in his arms to see the sea, telling locals 'one day she will be your queen'. Years later, Queen Victoria placed a window in the parish church as a memorial to her wayward but adored father.

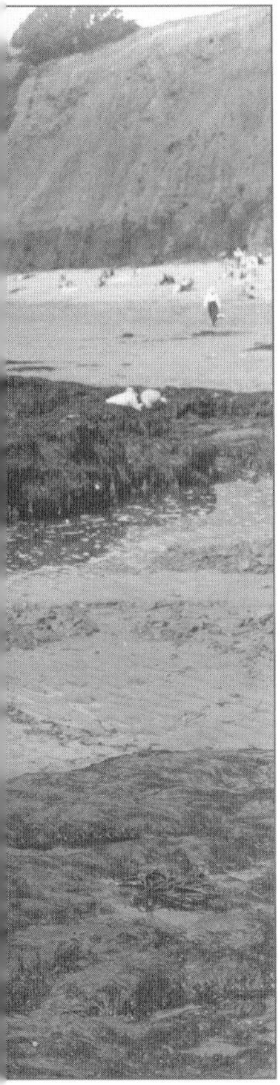

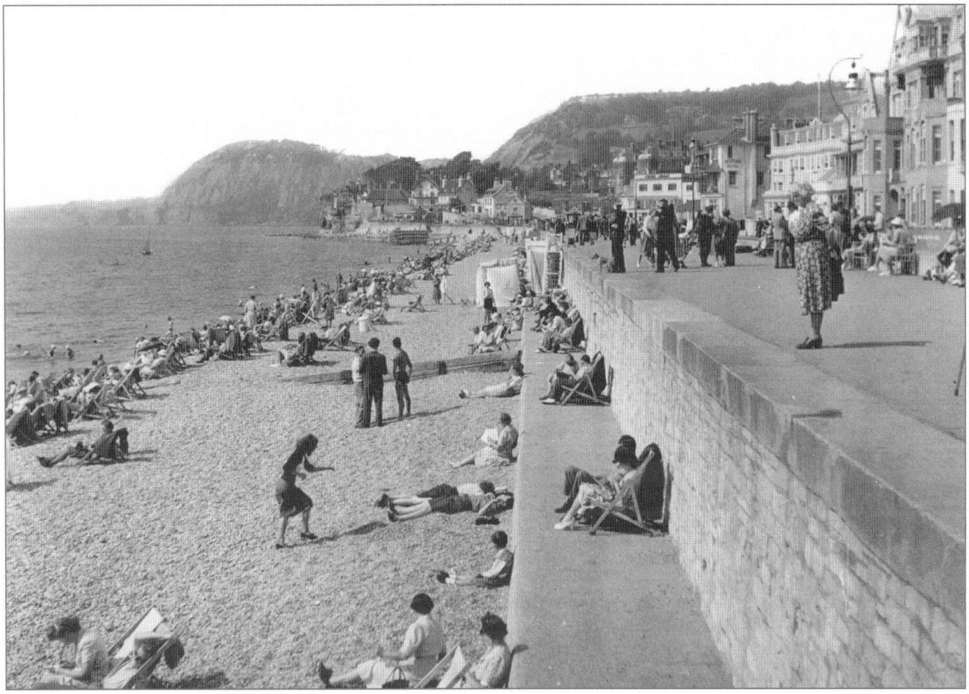

▲ **SIDMOUTH,** *The Beach and the Esplanade Looking West c1955* S129039

Wider car ownership and a busy railway station helped Sidmouth develop as a holiday resort in the 20th century. It remains a popular holiday destination in this new century for tourists enjoying short break holidays and day trips, and it has become a fashionable shopping centre.

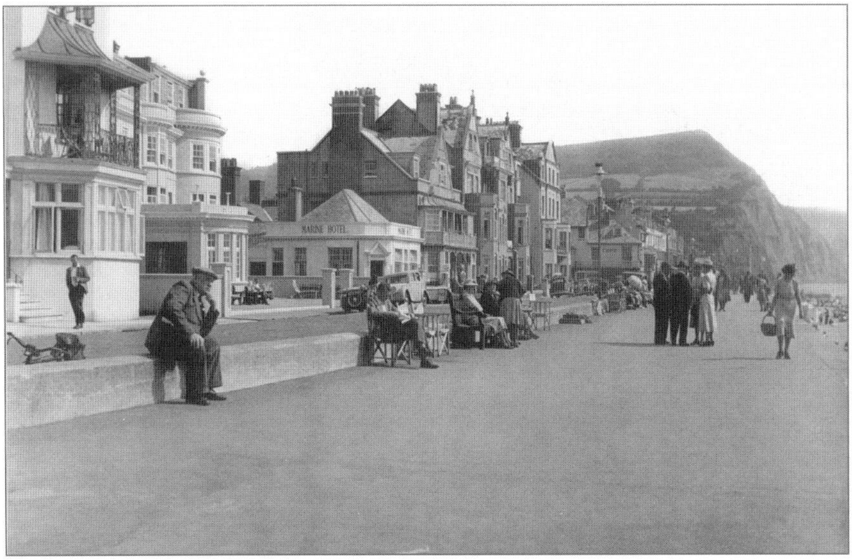

◀ **SIDMOUTH** *The Esplanade Looking East c1955* S129037

An elderly visitor contemplates a busy Sidmouth sea front on a summer's day in the 1950s. Just beyond the Marine Hotel is the site of the Sidmouth Brine Baths, where visitors to the town could have massage and 'electrical treatment' - probably a low current passed through the water - as well as the opportunity to bathe in salt and fresh water.

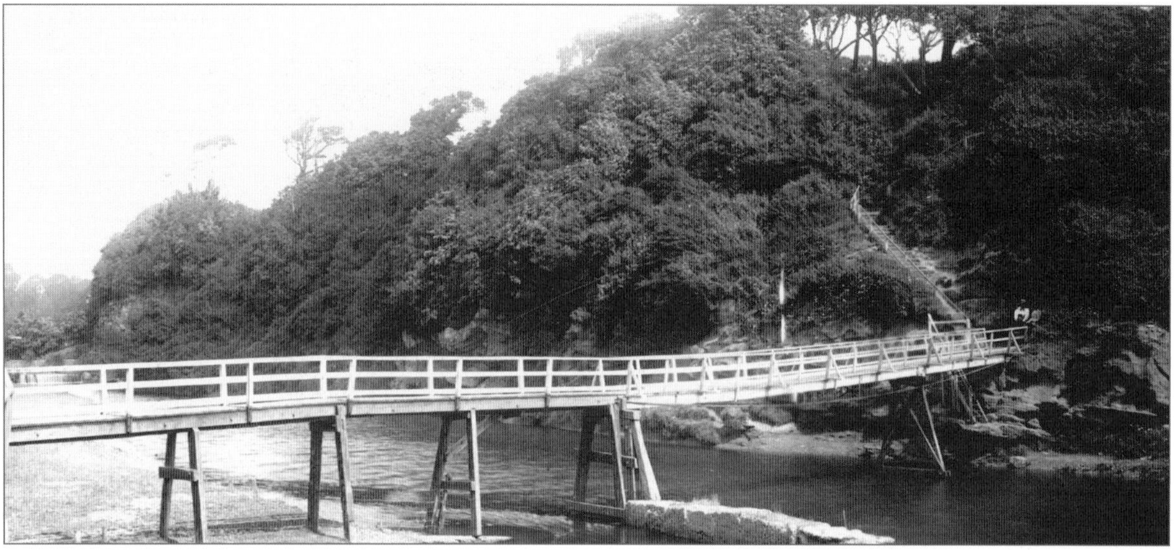

SIDMOUTH, *Alma Bridge 1895* 36076

Alma Bridge spans the Sid at the point just before the river tumbles across a pebbled ridge into the sea. The first bridge here dated from 1855, when local worthy Mrs Cornish allowed its construction at a cost of £26 10s using timbers taken from the sailing vessel *Laurel*, which had been wrecked on Sidmouth Beach. A heavy storm in 1877 battered the bridge, and we see it in its repaired state in photograph 36076 (above). In 1900 the architect R W Sampson was commissioned to design the present bridge, which we see here in photograph 84087 (below).

SIDMOUTH, *Alma Bridge 1931* 84087

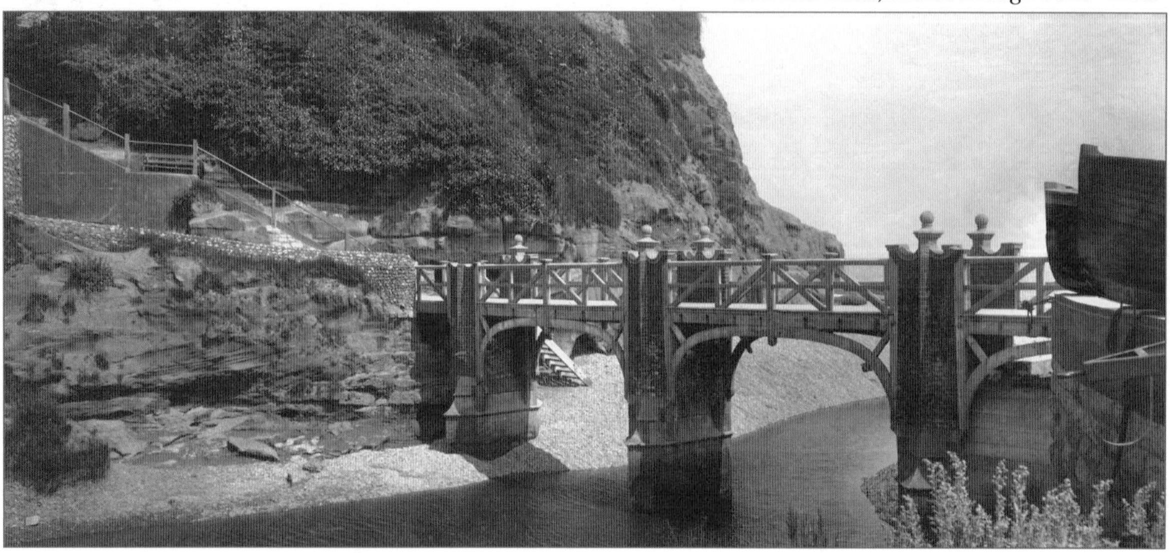

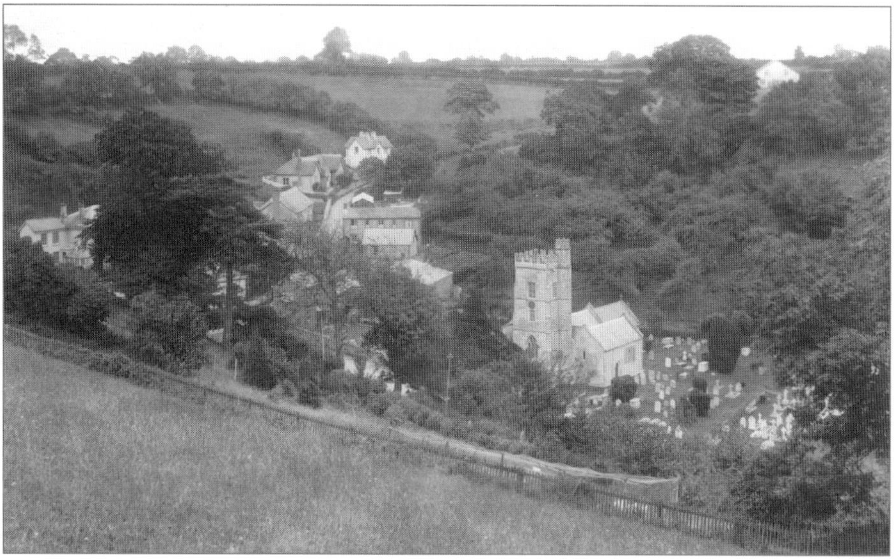

SALCOMBE REGIS *The Village and the Church 1928* 81056

Salcombe Regis shelters at the head of a secluded combe high above the sea to the east of Sidmouth; it has been a farming settlement since Saxon times. In the churchyard lies Sir Norman Lockyer, the great astronomer, his gravestone bearing the words: 'The heavens declare the glory of God; and the firmament sheweth his handywork.' Lockyer's observatory is nearby on Salcombe Hill.

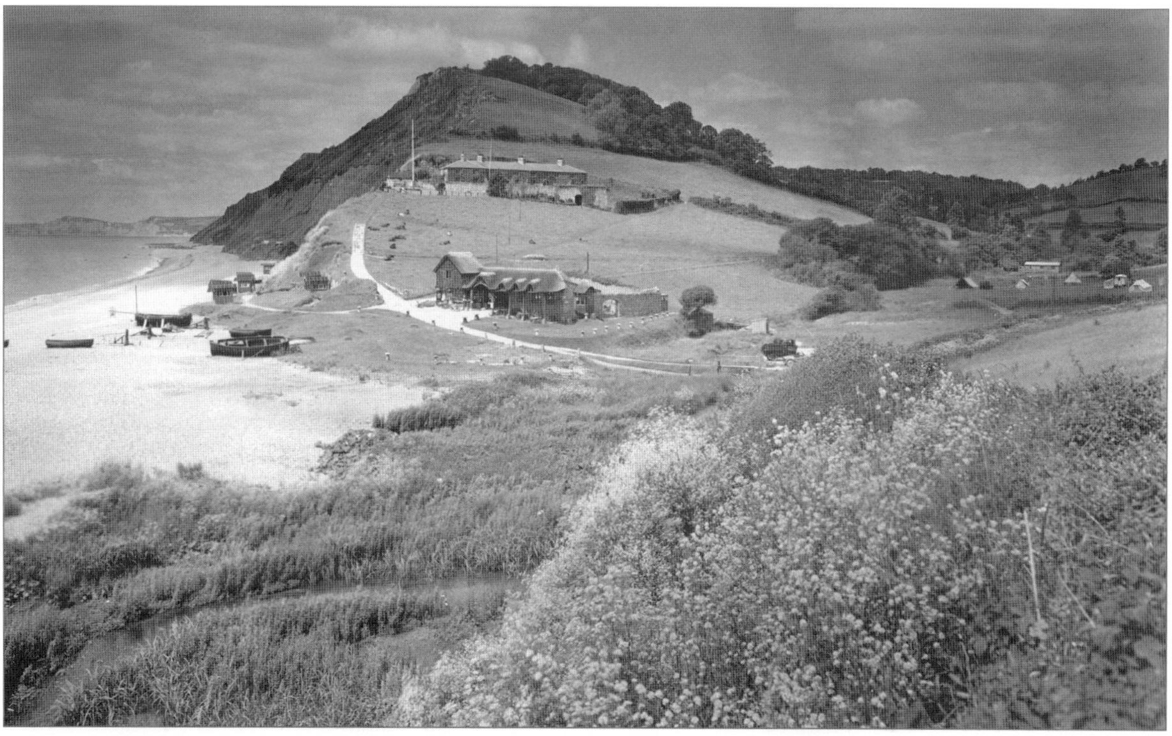

BRANSCOMBE, *The Beach and the Tea Shanty 1931* 84110

A deep valley, miles long, meets the sea at Branscombe Mouth, a steep-sided gap in a long line of high and rugged cliffs. This scene has changed little since the photograph was taken.

BRANSCOMBE
General View 1931
84106

Branscombe lies amid what a previous vicar described as 'a perfect jumble of hills'. The village is certainly one of Devon's prettiest, not least for its setting, strung in a series of hamlets around the junction of several pastoral and wooded combes. The parish church of St Winifred is thought to date from the Dark Ages.

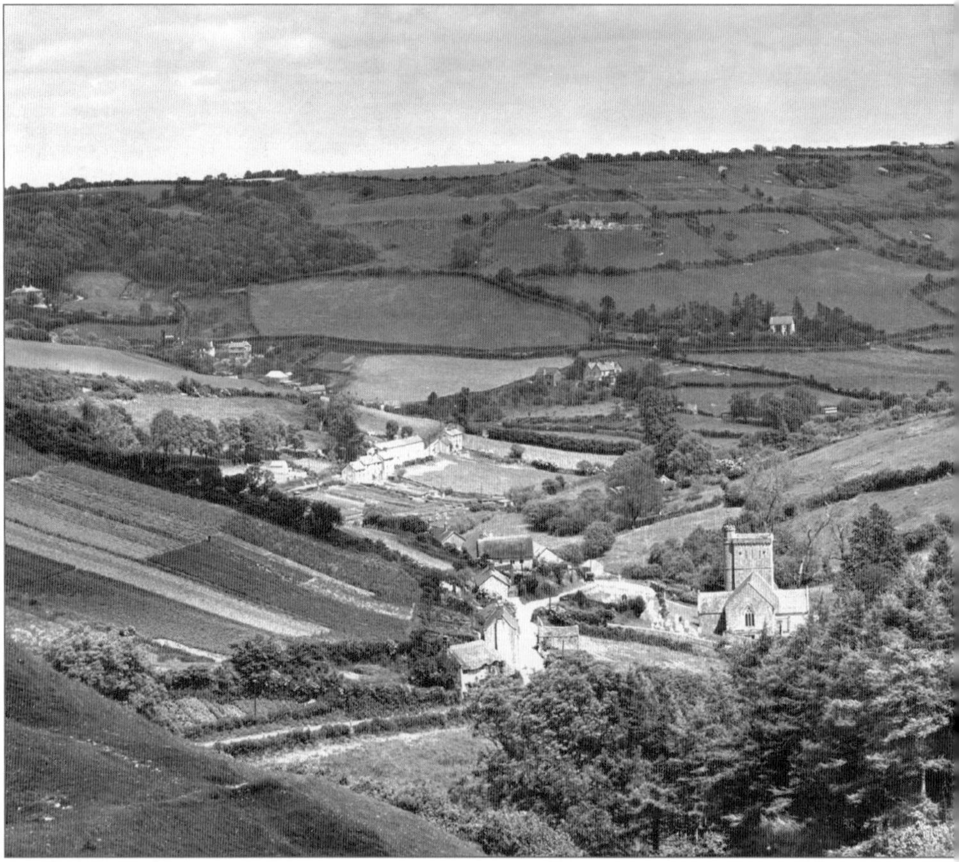

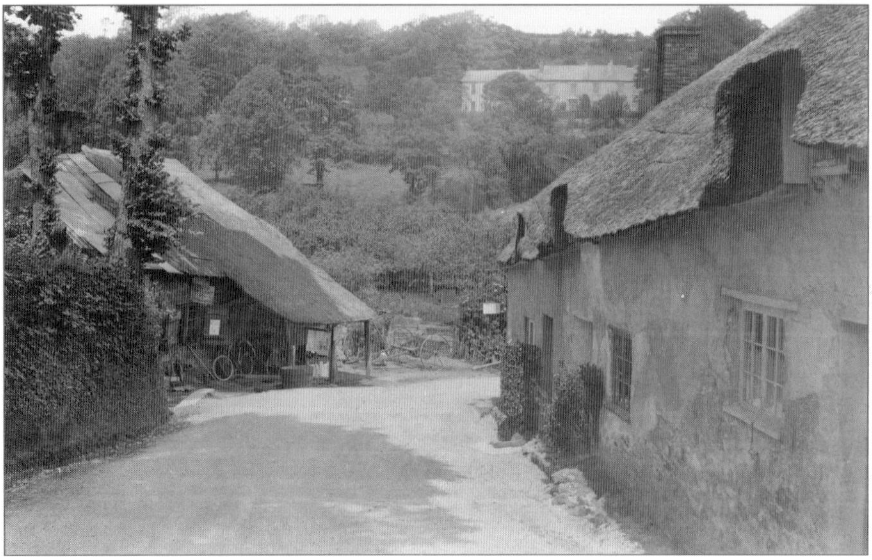

BRANSCOMBE
The Old Forge 1931
84116

Branscombe is fortunate indeed that its forge has survived as a working building – it is now owned by the National Trust. Visitors can see the smith at work in a scene that can have changed little over the centuries. The tiny sign at the far end of the row of cottages reads 'Teas - Weekdays Only'.

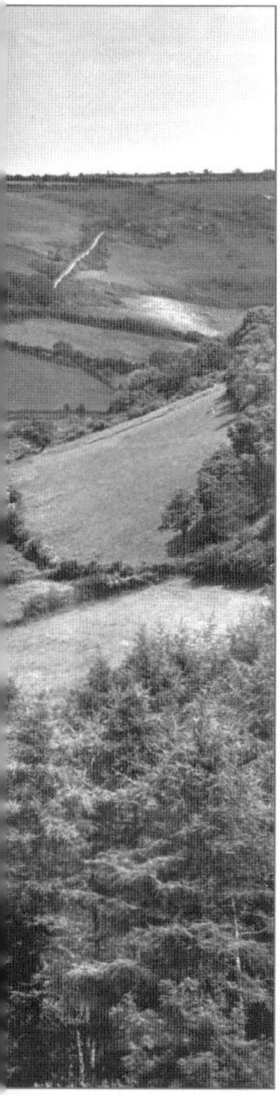

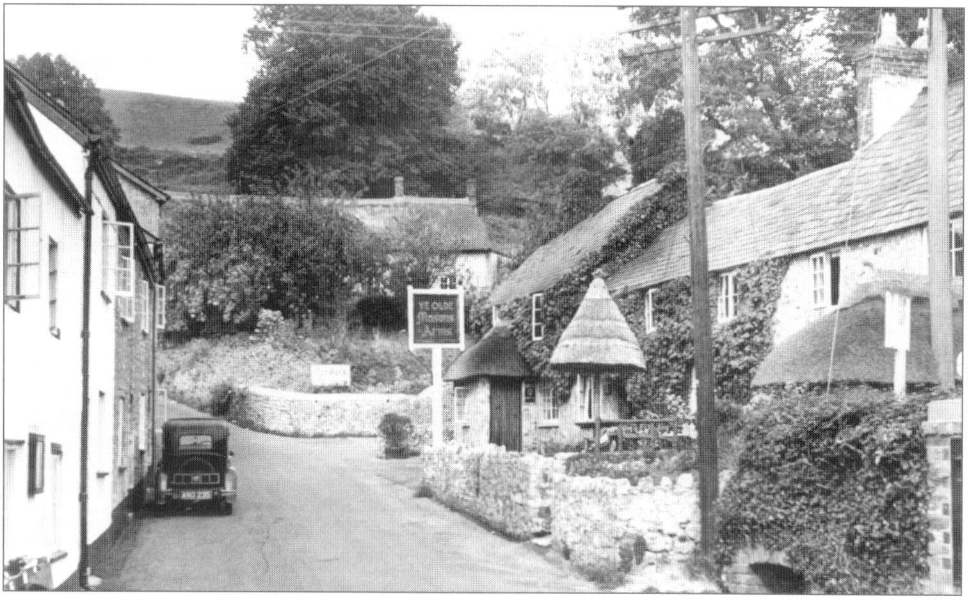

▲ **BRANSCOMBE,** *The Village c1955* B188011

The Mason's Arms serves as the inn for the seaward end of Branscombe, and it has links to both the smuggling and quarrying industries. It is a popular haunt with the many ramblers who walk the steep paths of the parish.

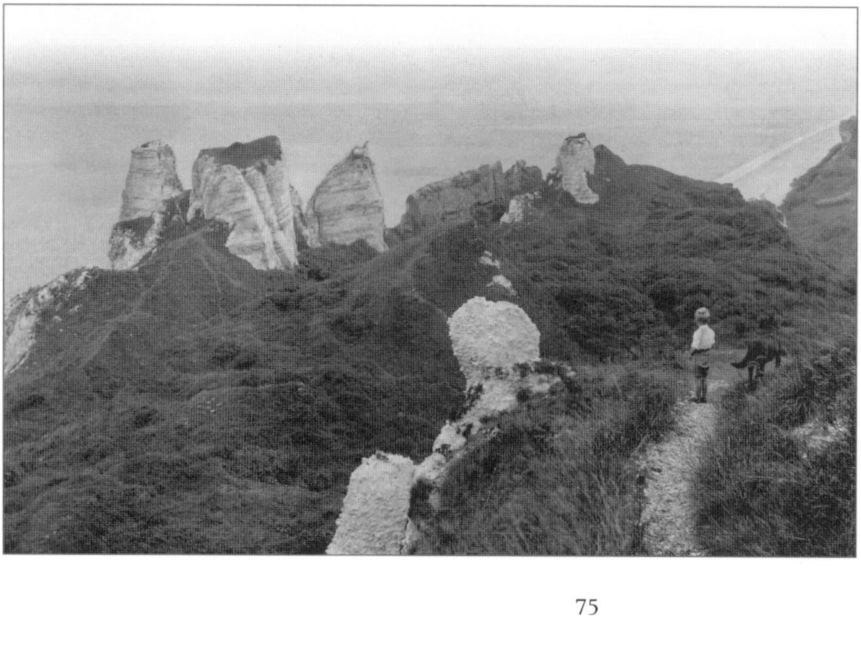

◄ **BEER**
Under Hooken Landslip 1927 79812

This wild cliffscape midway between Branscombe and Beer was formed on a day in March 1790 when 10 acres of land tumbled towards the sea. Trees and bushes have grown on the fallen chalk, creating a perfect haunt for wildlife and a great adventure for hardier ramblers.

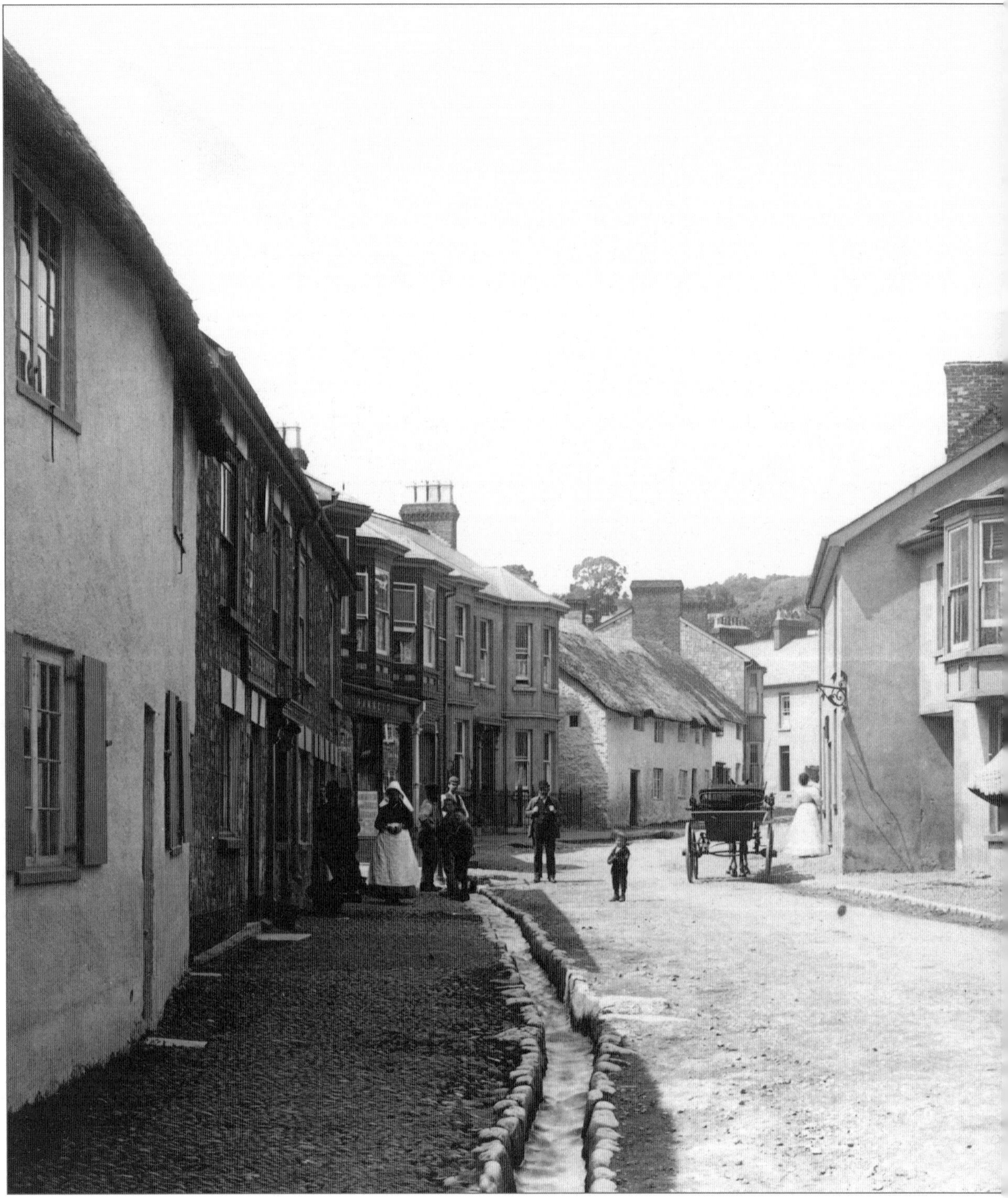

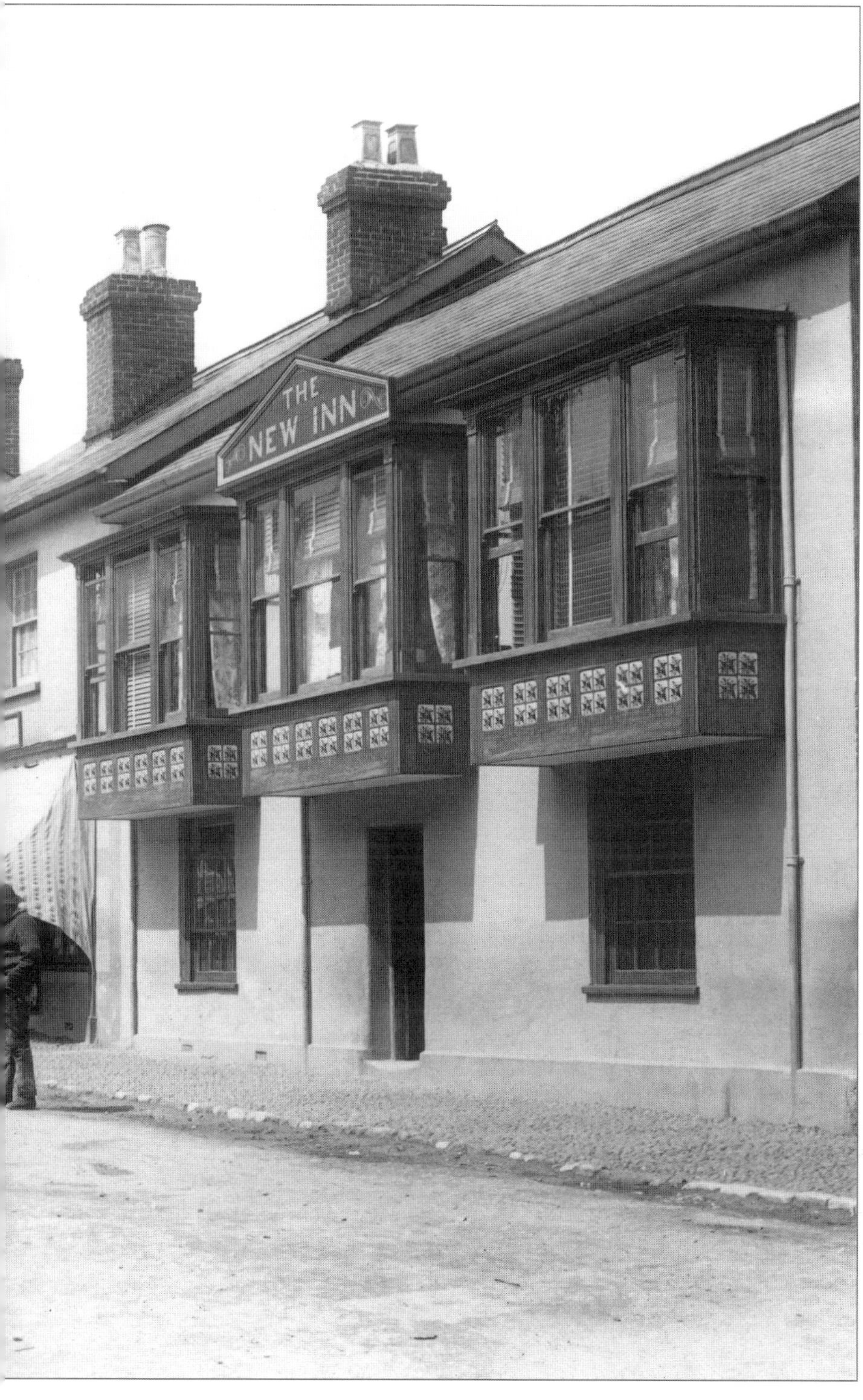

BEER

The Village 1895 36092

Once a modest fishing village, Beer became a small resort during Victoria's reign. This led to some changes: one 1920s guidebook writer complained that 'the newer, stoutly built houses have almost replaced the cottages that were the joy of artist and photographer'.

BEER
The Beach and the Boats 1898
42435

Jack Rattenbury, the 'Rob Roy of the West', was born at Beer in 1778 and experienced a series of adventures at sea before settling down to a life of smuggling along this wild and lonely coast. Rattenbury wrote of his experiences in his book *Memoirs of a Smuggler*; he spent his latter years living on a small pension provided by the local landowner, Lord Rolle.

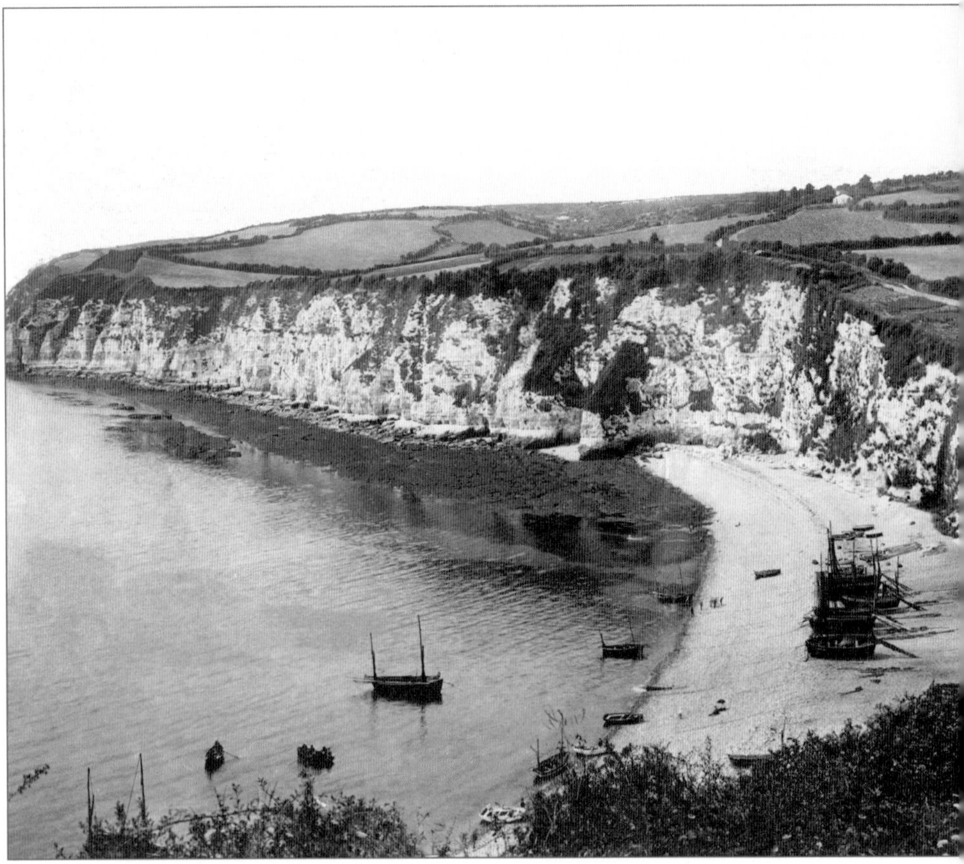

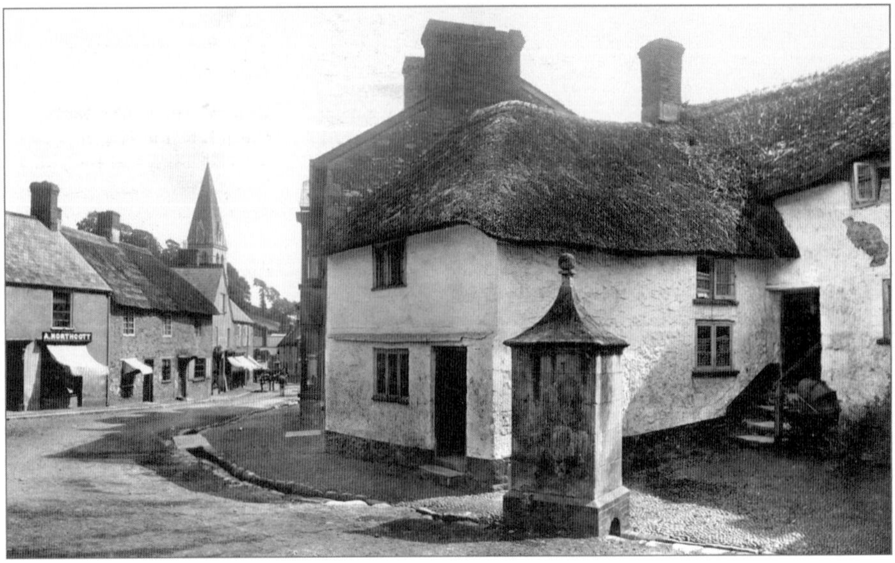

BEER
The Village 1898
42430

As with so many East Devon villages, a tiny stream - the Beer Brook - runs down the main street, first on one side of the road and then on the other. In the foreground is a water pump, made of the local Beer stone. Little has changed in more than a century, though the cottages just past Northcott's shop (left) are no longer thatched.

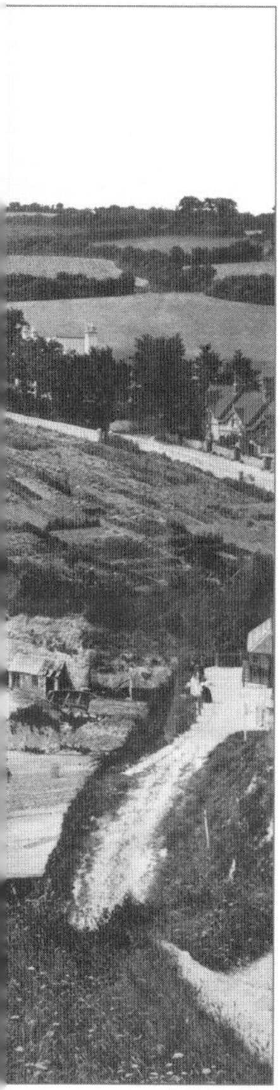

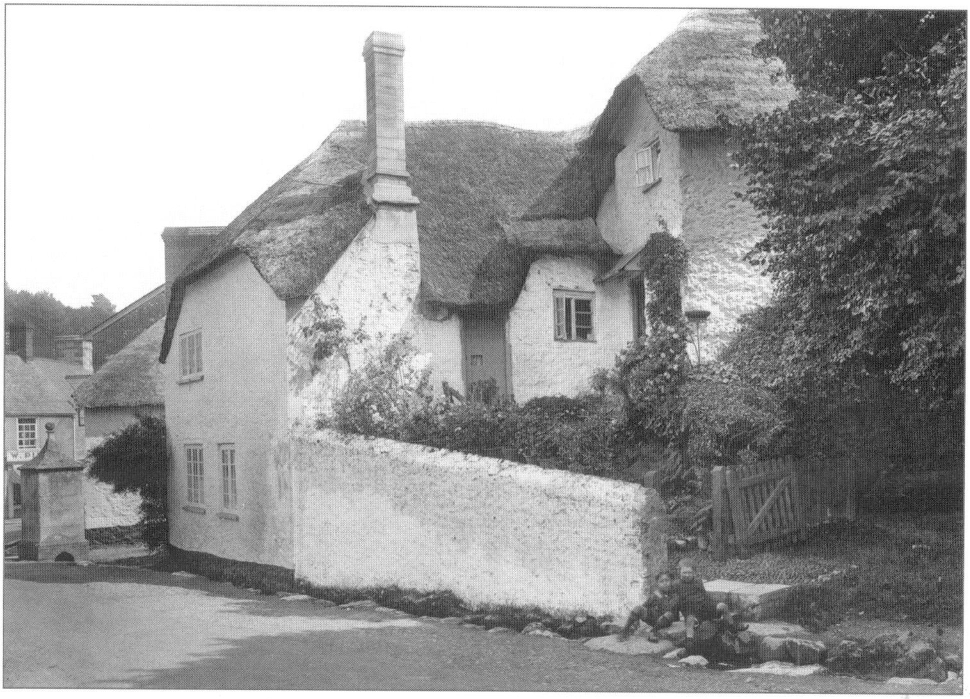

▲ **BEER,** *Shepherd's Cottage 1922* 72948

Children sit astride the Beer Brook outside the vast, sprawling Shepherd's Cottage. This marvellous house has survived almost unchanged into our new century, and is one of Beer's oldest buildings.

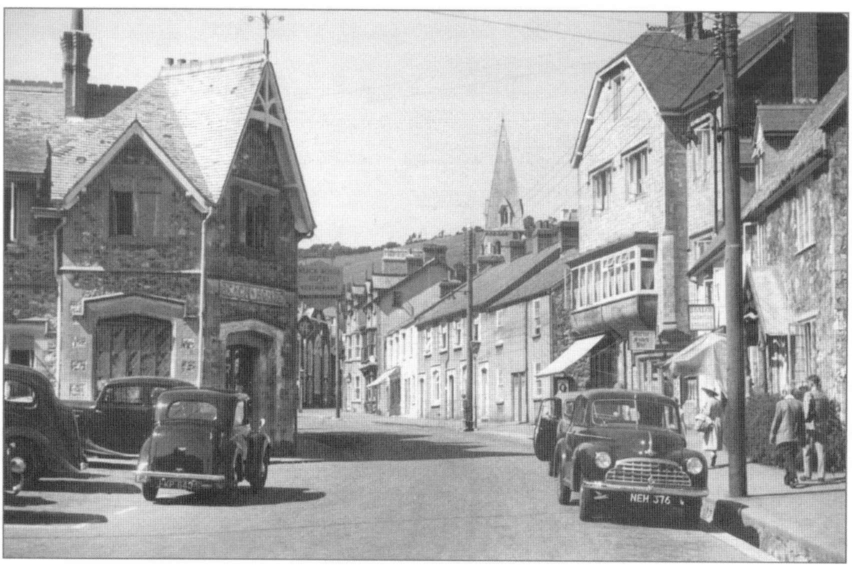

◄ **BEER**

The Village c1955

B55047

Here we see St Michael's Church topped by its original spire (centre right). The spire was removed in 1962 after being weakened first by an exploding mine out at sea, and then by a lightning strike, leaving only the square-topped tower that we can see today. In the foreground is the Beach House Hotel, now Beach Court (left), with the Marine Snack Bar on the opposite side of the road.

▼ **BEER,** *Fore Street c1955* B55077

We are looking down Fore Street, with the Victorian St Michael's Church in the distance. To the right is Mutter's fish shop and the Central Steam Bakery, now the Steam Gallery. On the opposite side of the road are the chemist's Hinton Lake and the post office.

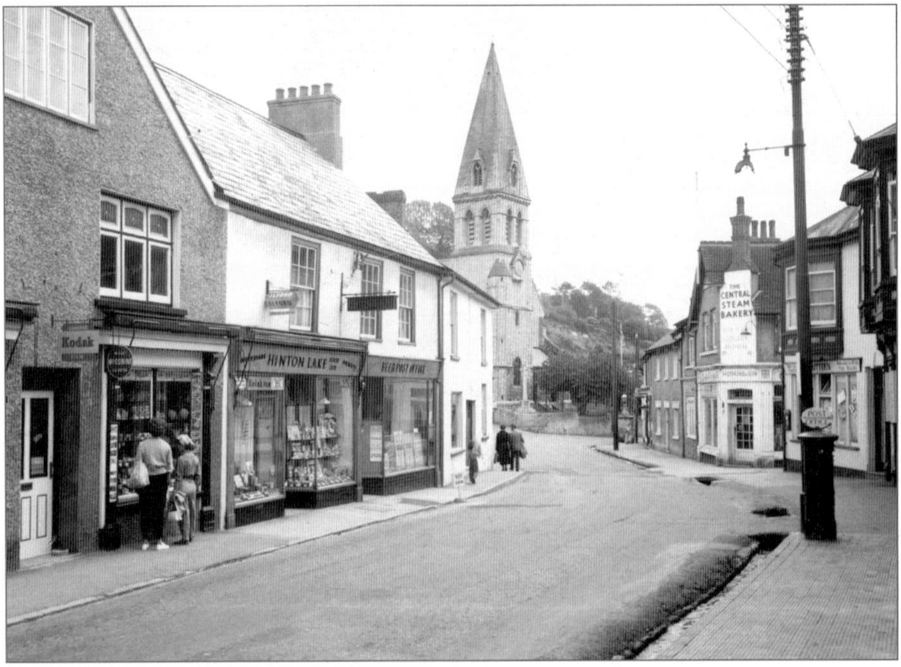

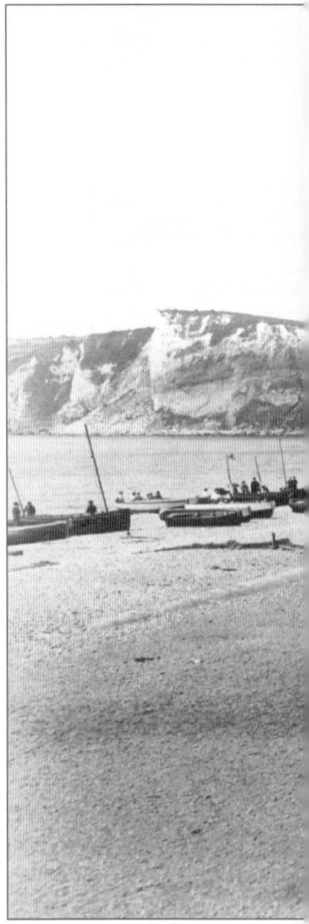

► **BEER**
Sea Hill c1965 B55060

Beer remains a fishing village, if not quite on the scale of yesteryear, and there are still a number of family-owned boats. There is no harbour at Beer, so the boats are drawn up on the beach at the end of each fishing trip. The BP garage (right) no longer exists.

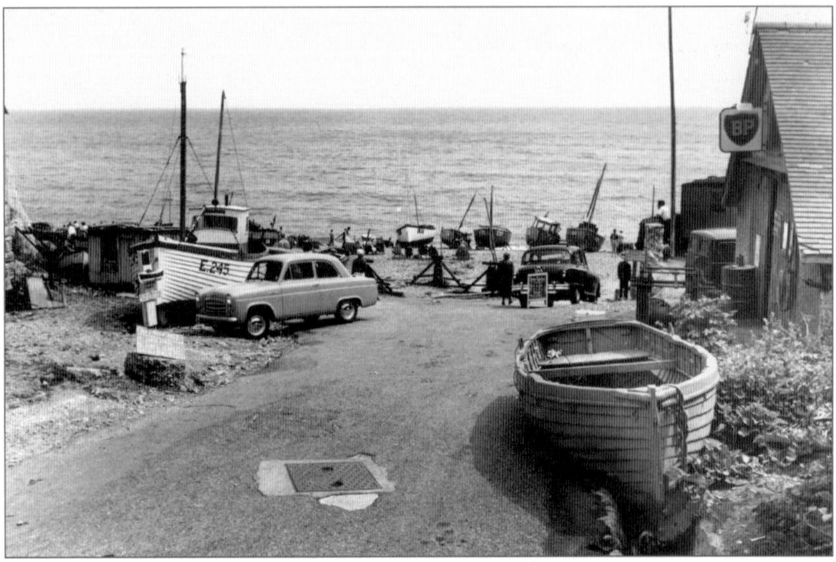

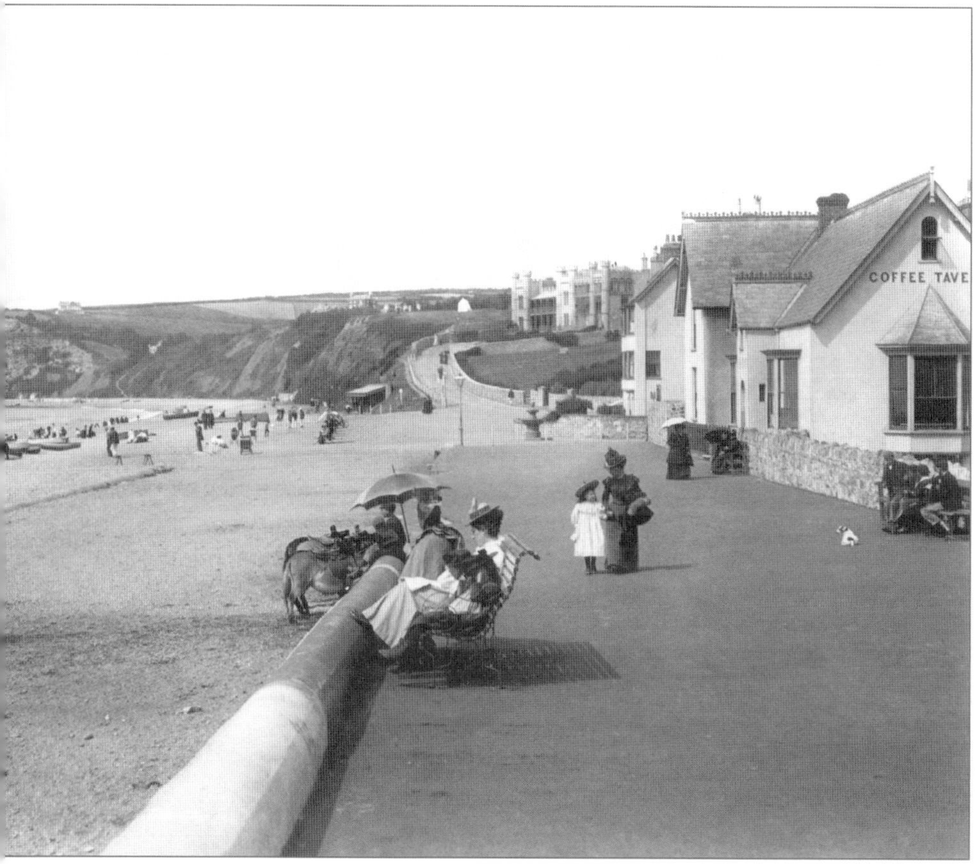

◄ **SEATON**
The Beach and the Promenade 1898
42420

Seaton is Devon's easternmost resort, with only a few miles of rugged cliffs and landslips separating the town from neighbouring Dorset. Seaton's fishing industry declined soon after this photograph was taken; notice the fishing boats drawn up on the beach. It is now a much larger town, and a popular resort. The Coffee Tavern (right) has survived as part of the Hook and Parrot public house.

► **SEATON**
The Beach and the Castle 1898 42419

Seaton developed as a resort in the 1850s, and in the years that followed a number of hotels were built to cater for the town's popularity with visitors. In the distance is the distinctive Castle Hotel. The building to the right, Cliff House, gained another storey soon after this photograph was taken; in the 1920s, it offered 'furnished apartments - an ideal spot for summer or winter residence'. The stout sea wall of today had not been built at the time of this photograph, hence the wide appearance of the beach.

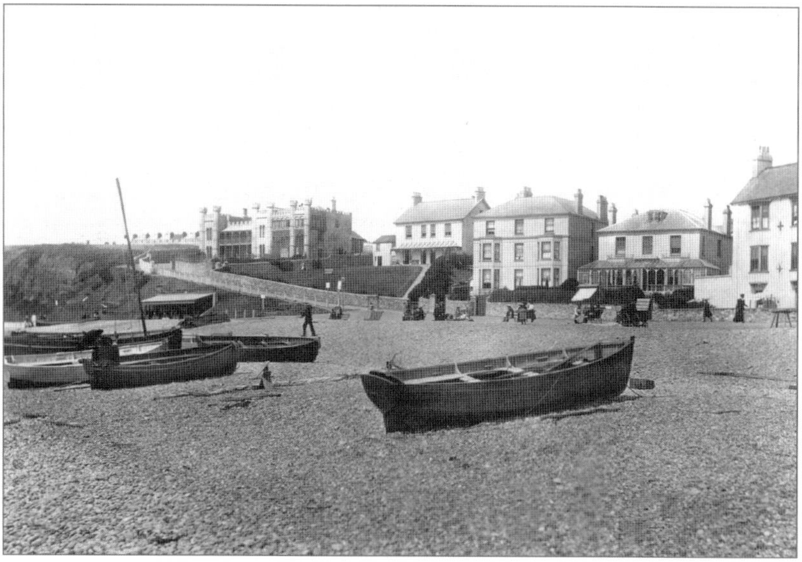

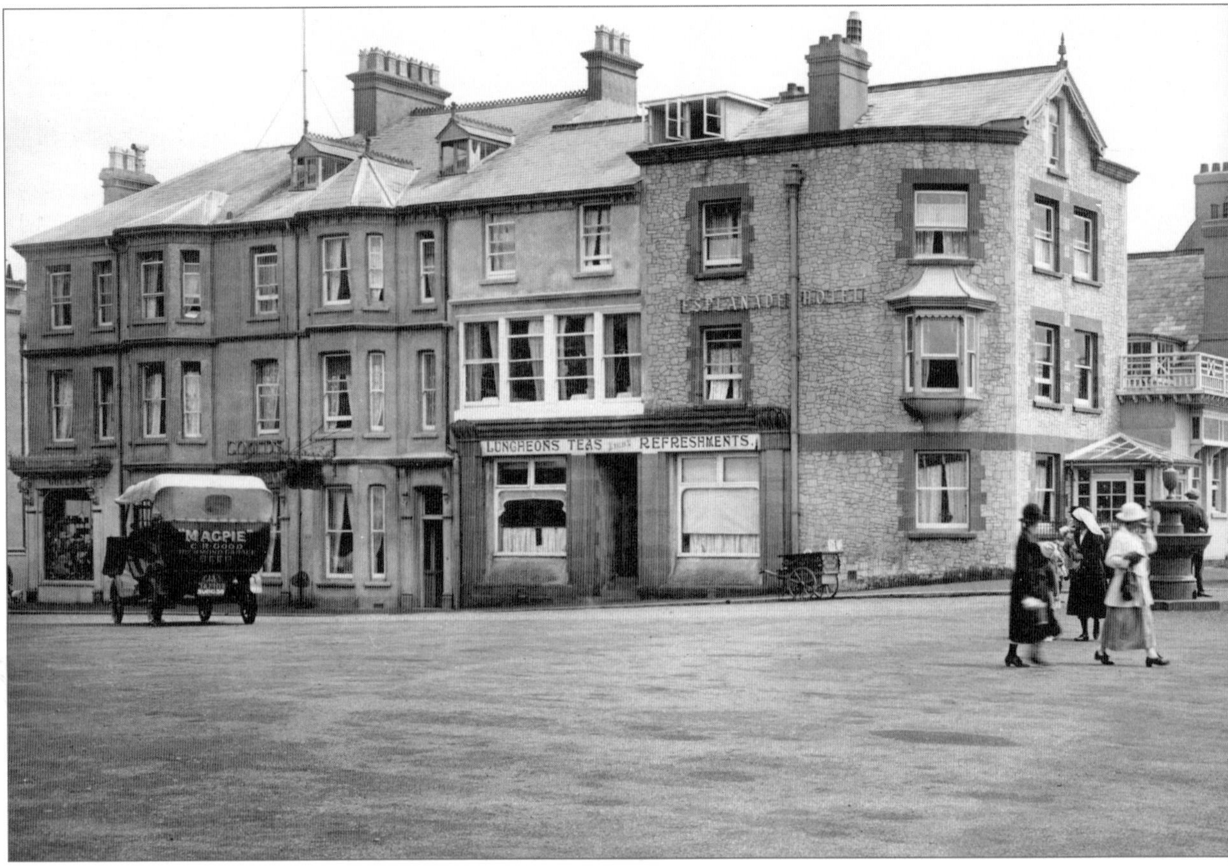

► **SEATON**
The Sea Front 1922
72915

Looking beyond Castle Hill, we see the cliffs around Beer in the distance. This open plain of sea front has since been divided by the sea wall and a modern motor road. These buildings were extremely vulnerable to the ferocious gales that would hurl pebbles in their direction. A group of local lads, one with a delivery bicycle, congregate for a chat by the parked van.

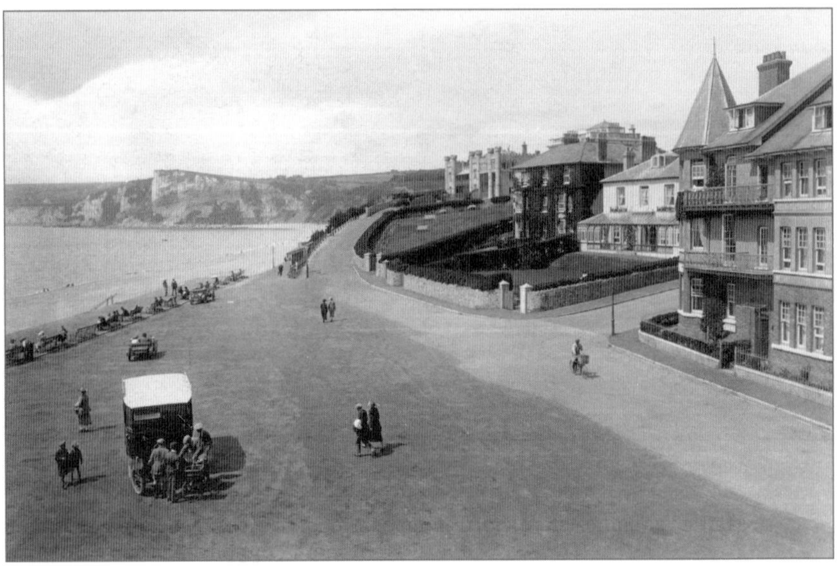

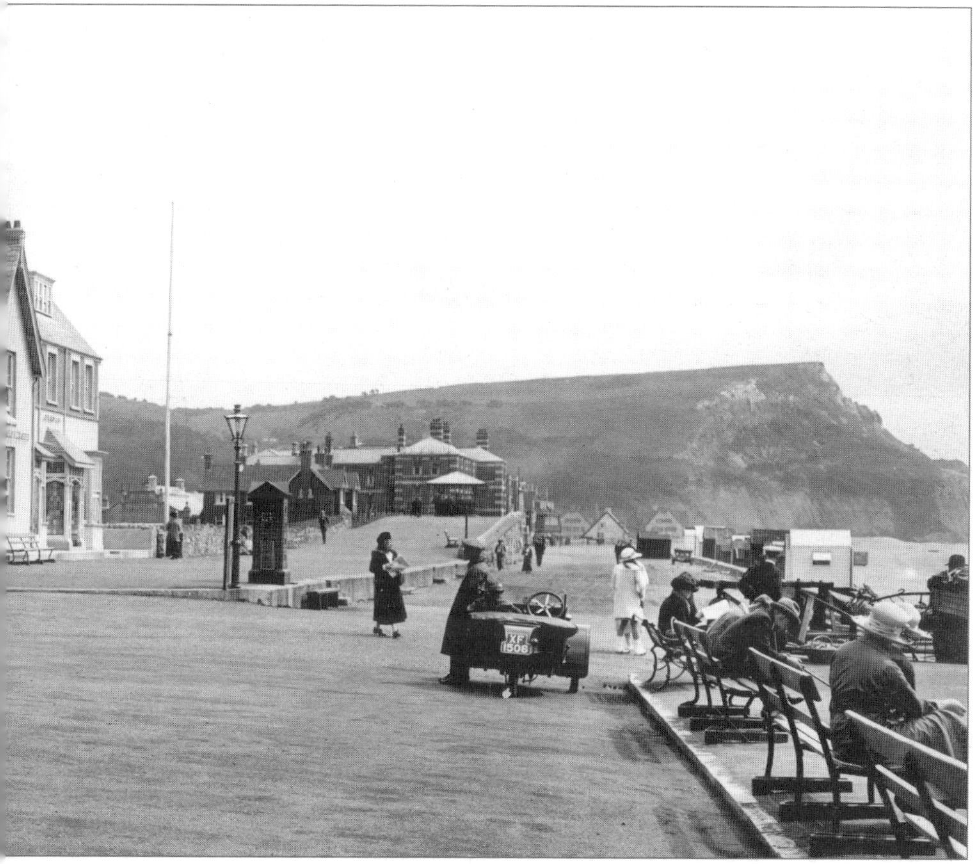

SEATON
The Promenade 1922 72907

This view shows the sea front before the construction of the modern sea wall that holds back the sea on stormy days. The Esplanade Hotel, on the right-hand end of the terrace, had incorporated the neighbouring Gould's Hotel by the 1920s, when a guide book described it as 'a well-appointed and comfortable establishment'. In the street is the tourist car Magpie (left), owned by C R Good of the Richmond Garage.

SEATON
Looking East 1927
79821

From Castle Hill we look down on the Esplanade, with the Beach Hotel in the middle distance. A guidebook of this time told prospective visitors that 'the water supply and sanitation is perfect. Seaton is highly recommended by the medical profession for invalids and convalescent cases'.

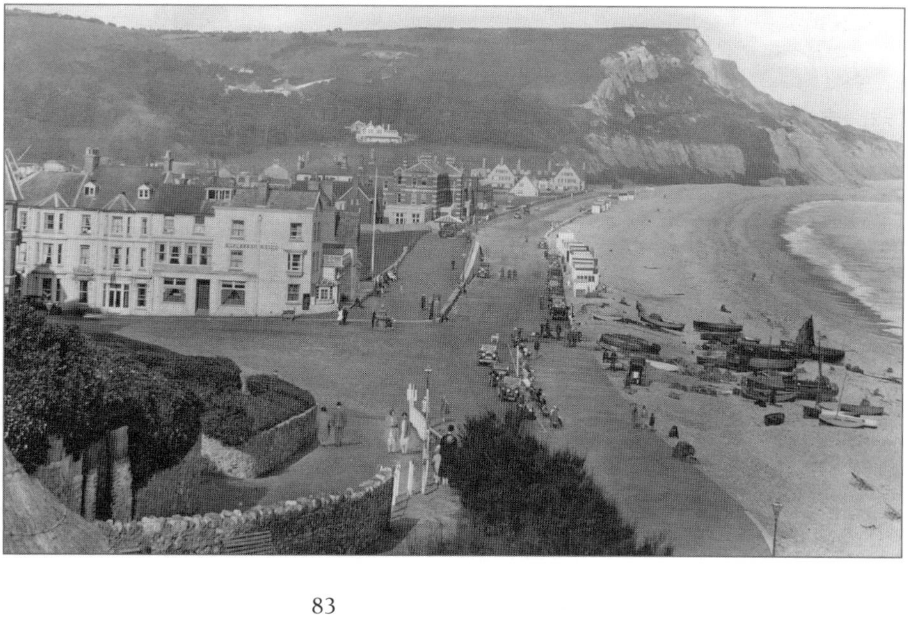

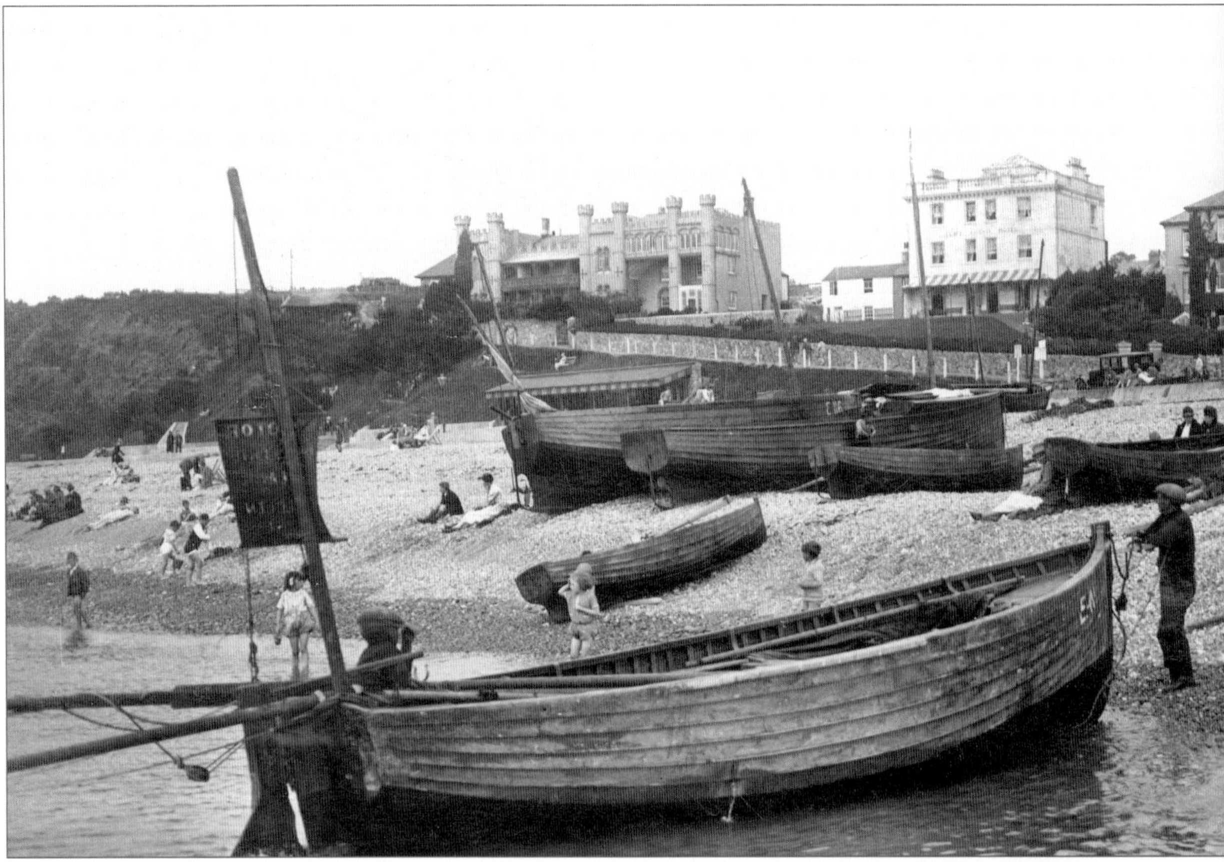

► **SEATON**
The Town from the Car Park c1950 S84050

Harbour Road has changed considerably since this photograph was taken. The car park has disappeared with the building of flats and shops. But the shop on the right has survived, albeit with the loss of its decorative railings. At this time it belonged to E H Rodger, and traded as a stationer's, confectioner's and lending library. It is now a newsagent.

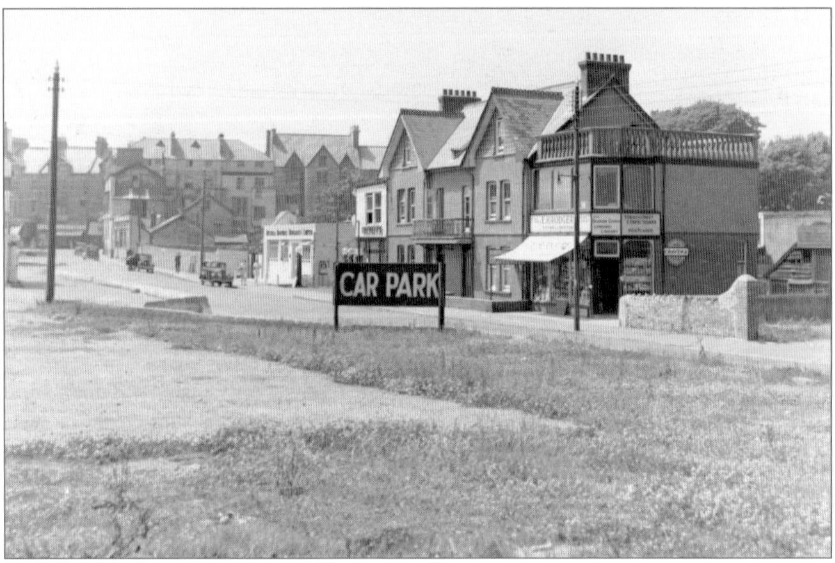

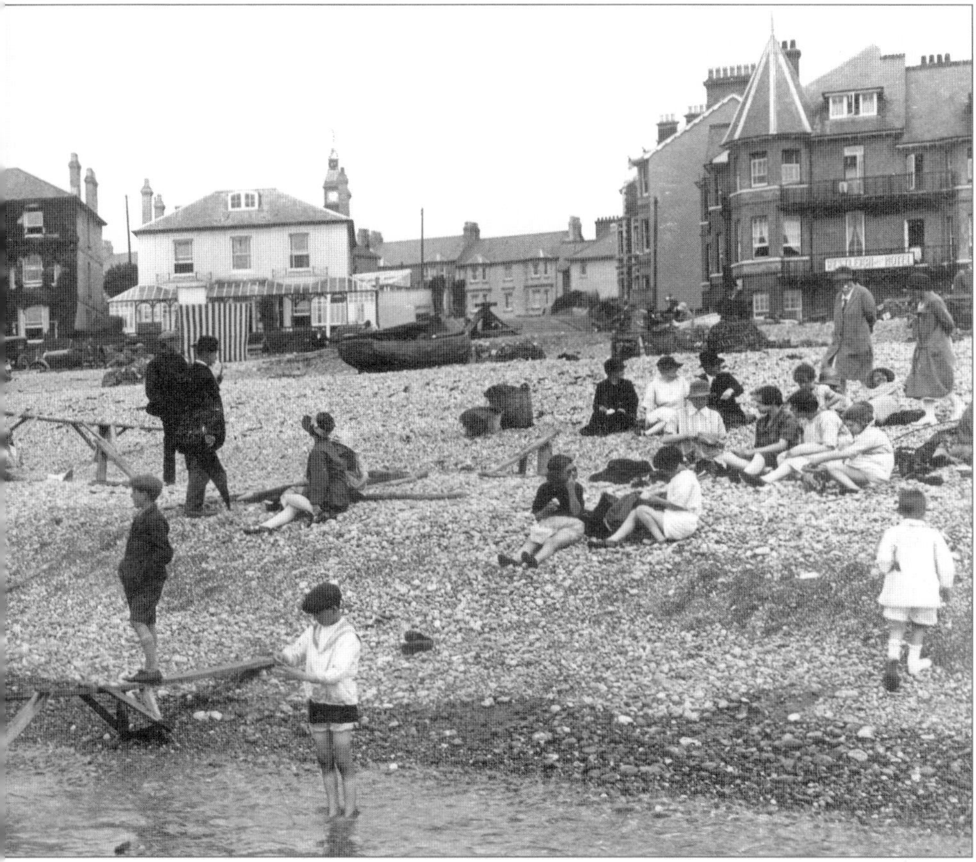

SEATON
From the Sea 1927
79830

Seaton's herring fishing industry had all but died by 1927, and local fishermen were having to supplement their earnings by offering fishing expeditions and trips around the bay for tourists.

SEATON
White Cliff from Jubilee Gardens c1955 S84037

The beach below White Cliff has long been one of Seaton's favoured bathing places, recommended in many guidebooks, though a charge of 4d was made during the earlier decades of the last century.

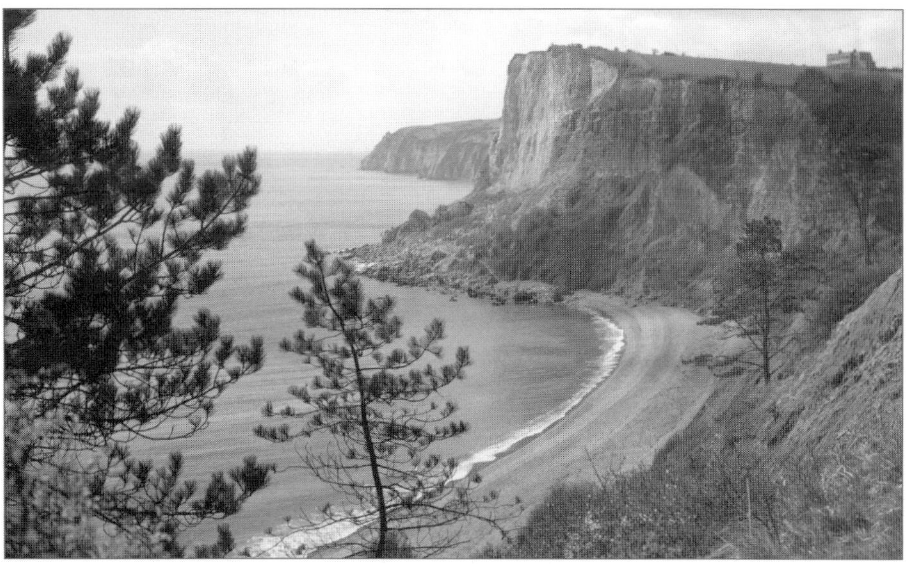

▶ **SEATON**
The Beach c1965
S84118

This view looks across the bay, with the chalk height of Beer Head in the far distance. Among the pebbles on Seaton's beach may be found jasper, beryl and garnet. Tourists are clambering aboard a local fishing boat for a voyage out into Lyme Bay.

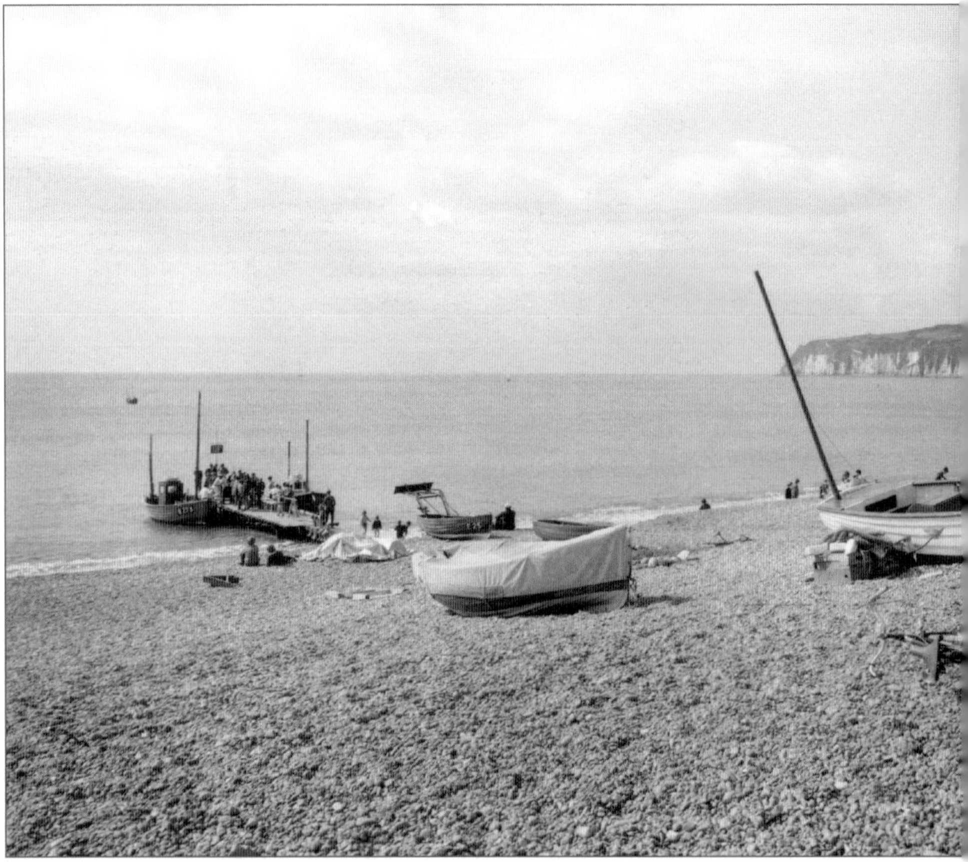

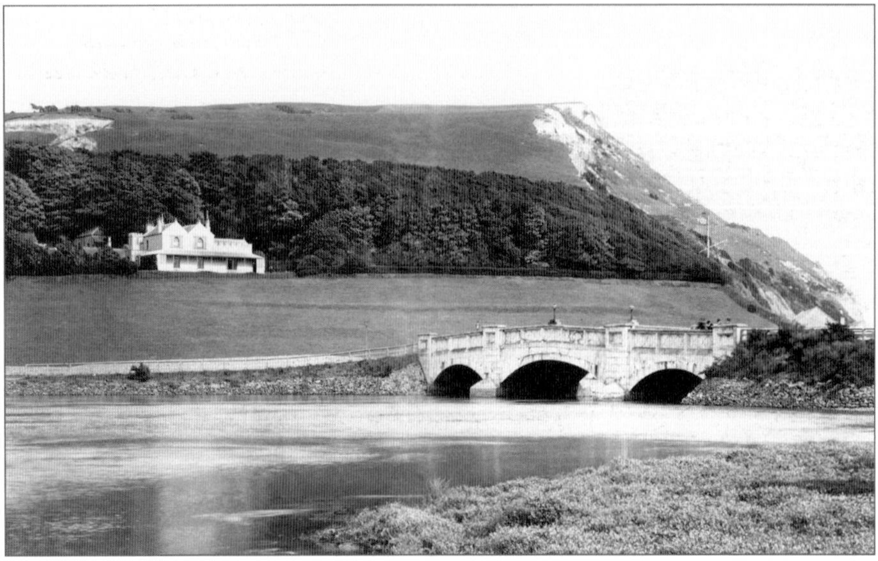

◀ **AXMOUTH**
The Bridge and Haven Cliff 1895
36082

Despite the masonry facings, this bridge across the Axe is made of concrete, built to the design of Philip Brannon in 1877. It is the oldest surviving concrete bridge in Britain and was scheduled as an ancient monument in the 1970s. In 1990 a new bridge was built to spare the older crossing the weight of today's traffic.

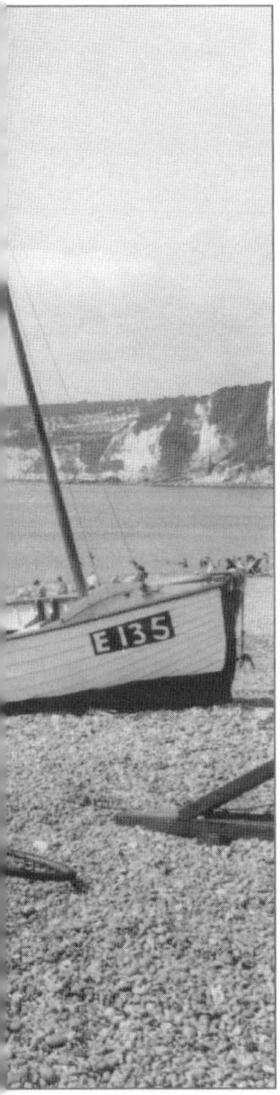

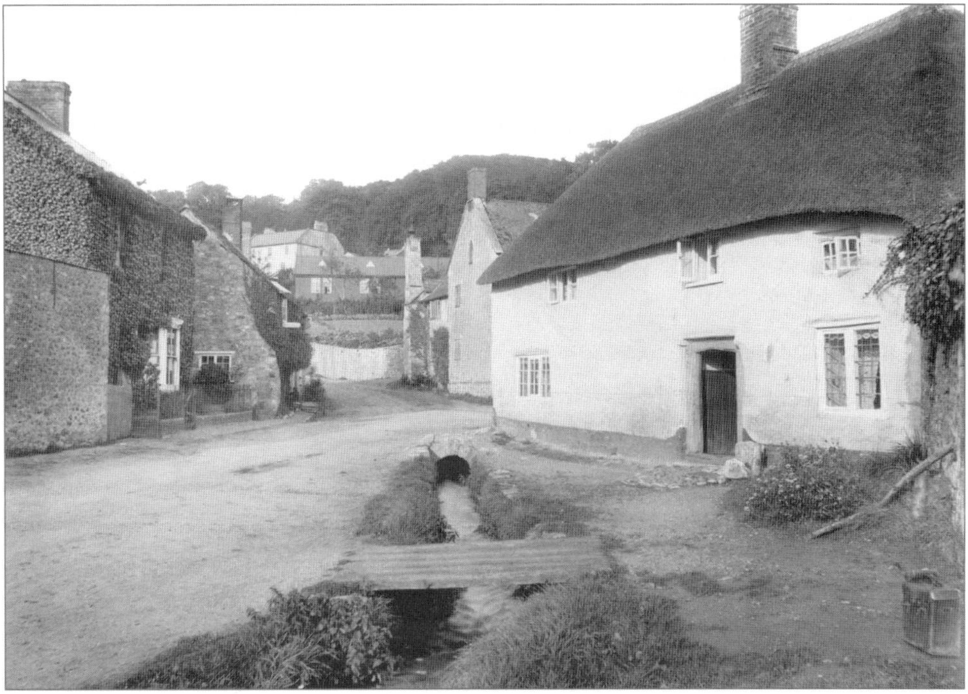

▲ **AXMOUTH,** *A Village Street 1918* 68694

Axmouth stands at the southern end of the Fosse Way, the great Roman road that strides across England from far-off Lincolnshire. The village probably dates from Saxon times, and it was a royal manor of King Athelstan, Edward the Confessor and William the Conqueror. In past centuries the village was much bigger than the Axmouth of today.

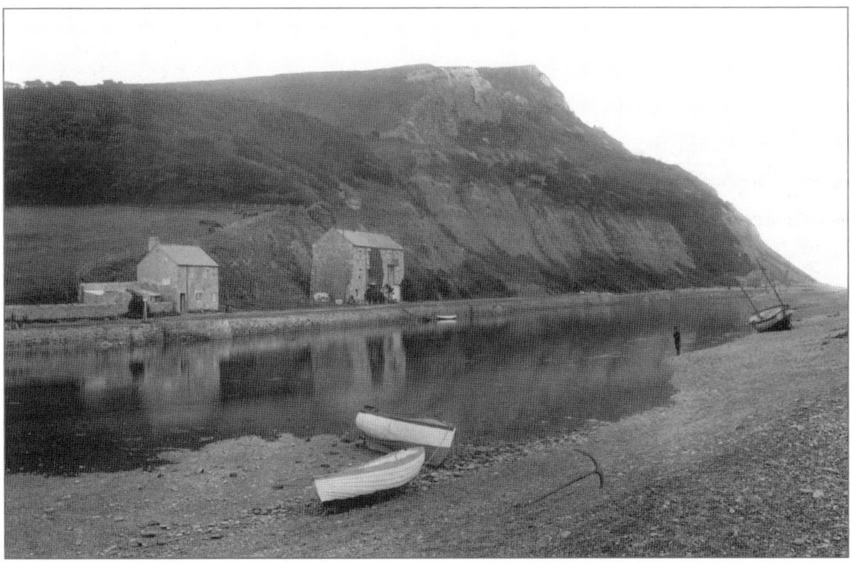

◄ **AXMOUTH** *The Harbour and Haven Cliff 1922* 72931

Axmouth was once a considerable port, and boats navigated the River Axe as far as Colyton. Certainly the Vikings, raiding this coast, used the Axe to seek plunder far inland. By the reign of Henry VIII, ridges of pebbles barred access to all but the smallest vessels - causing the creation of a new port at Lyme Regis.

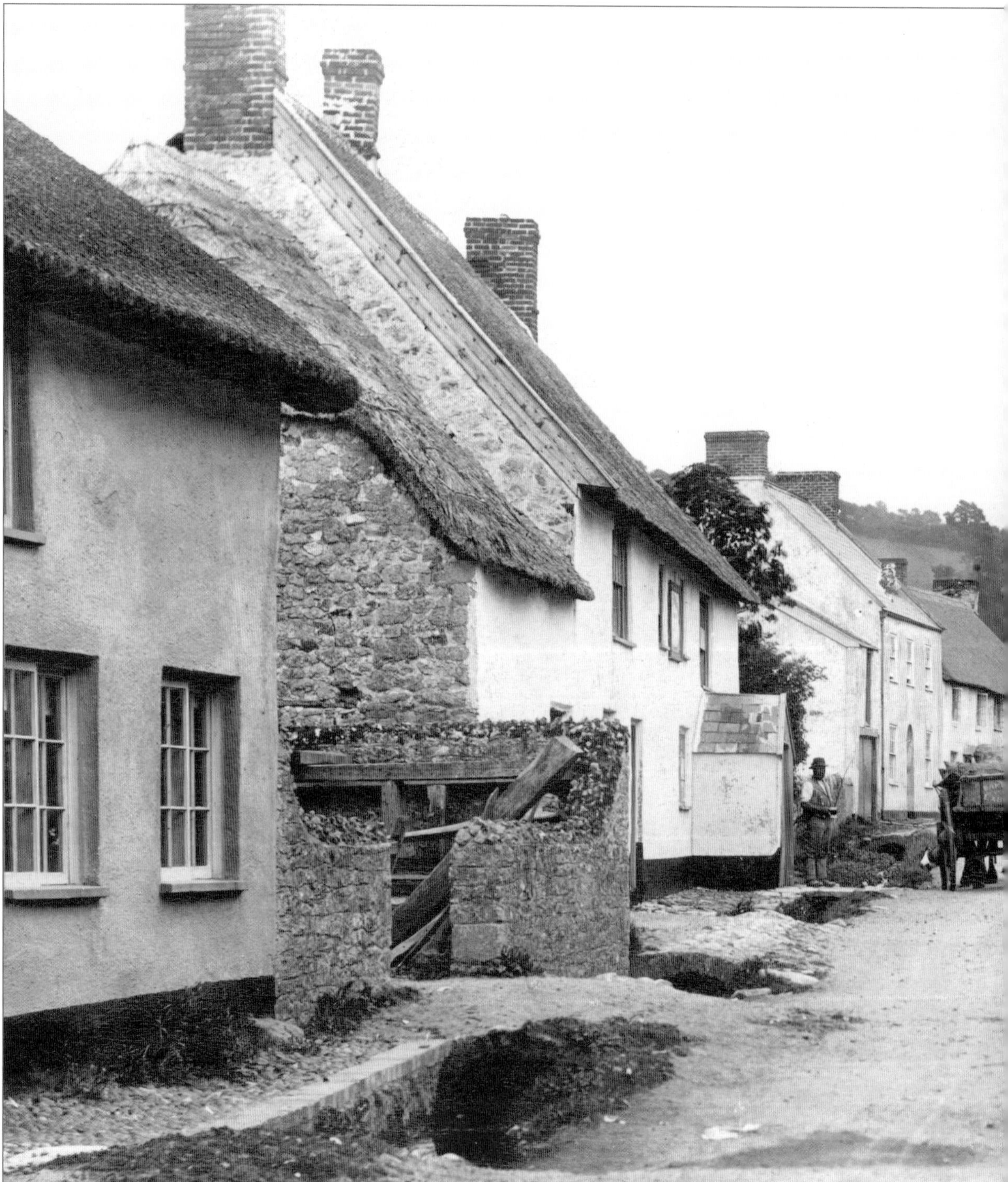

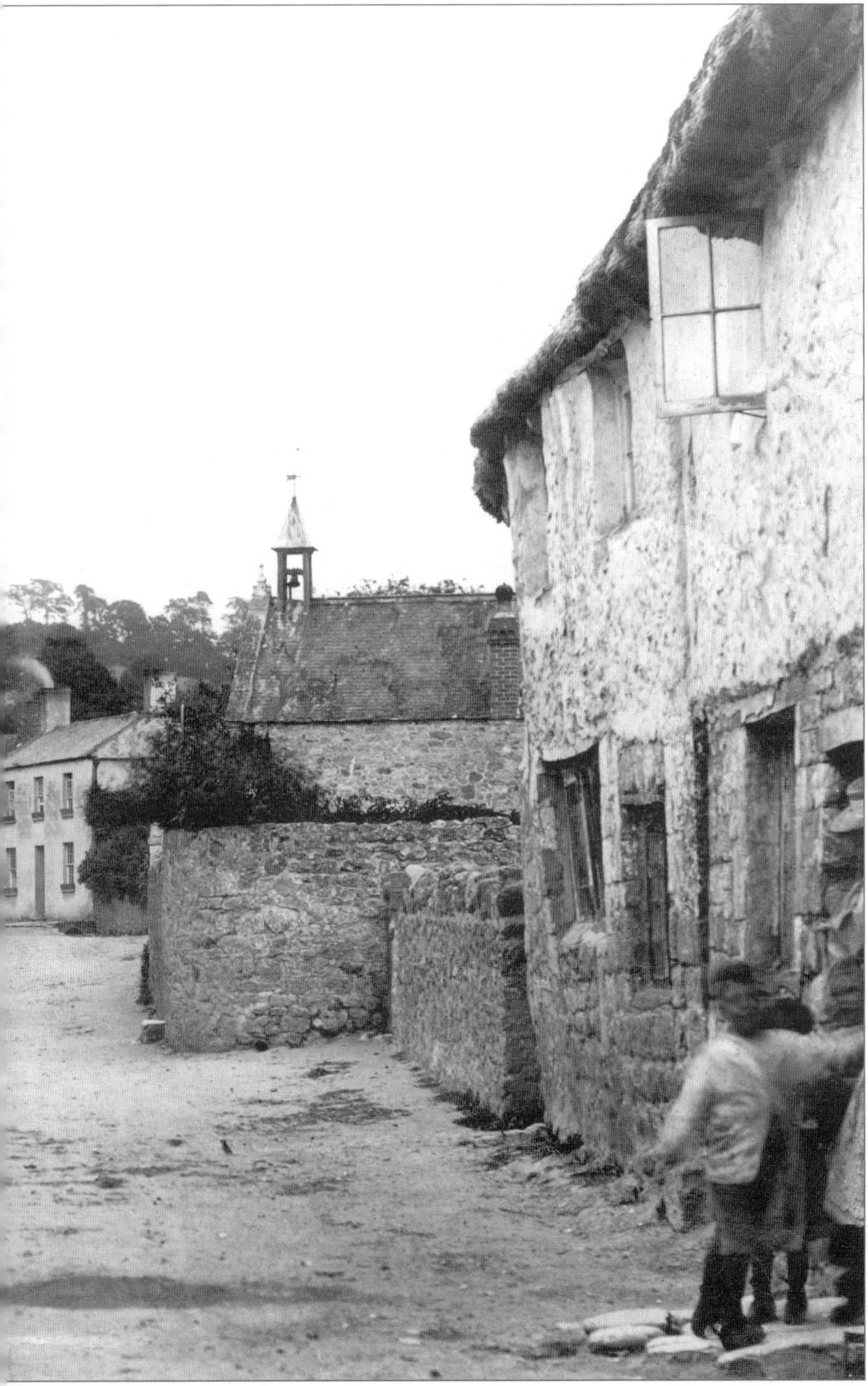

AXMOUTH
The Village 1898 42443

Axmouth is one of Devon's loveliest villages, and boasts one of Britain's finest and most unspoiled Norman churches. A farm cart waits outside the Harbour Inn (left) - perhaps as its owner seeks refreshment. The cottages where the children are gathered disappeared in the last half of the 20th century, and so did the bell on the Victorian chapel.

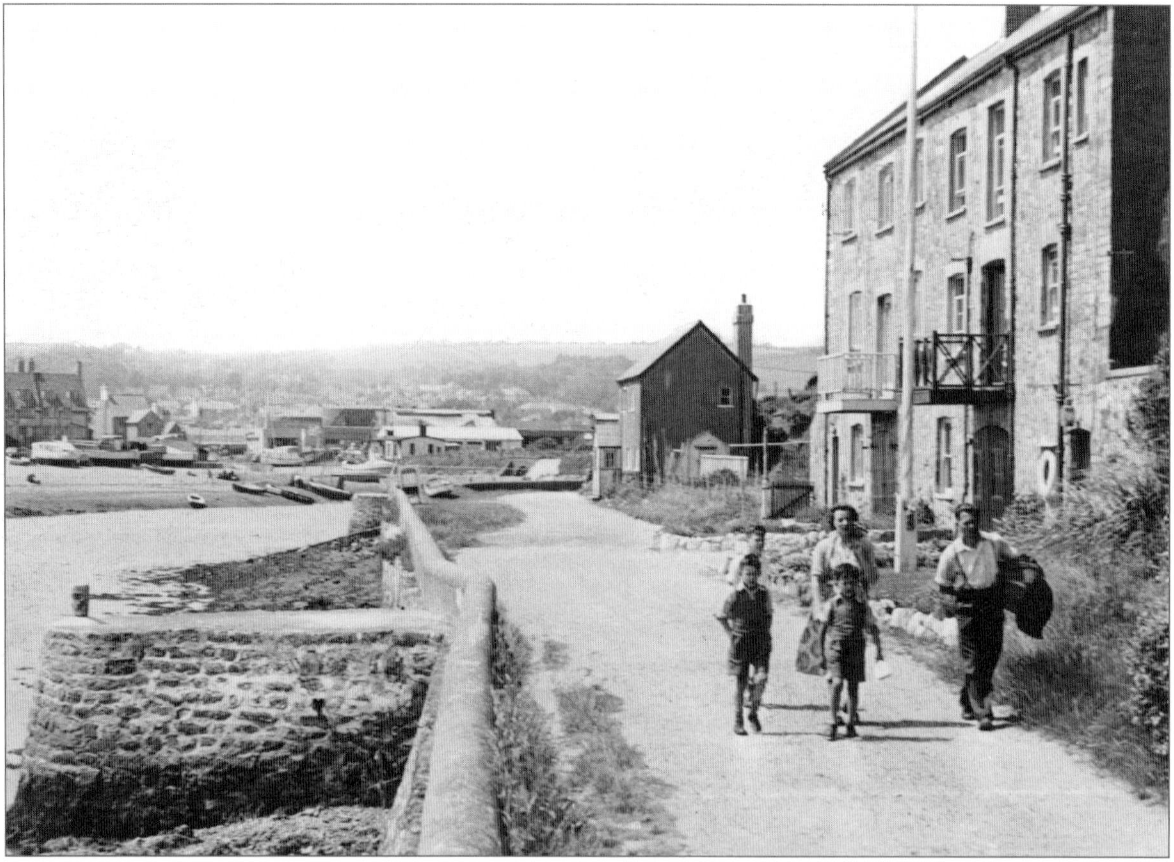

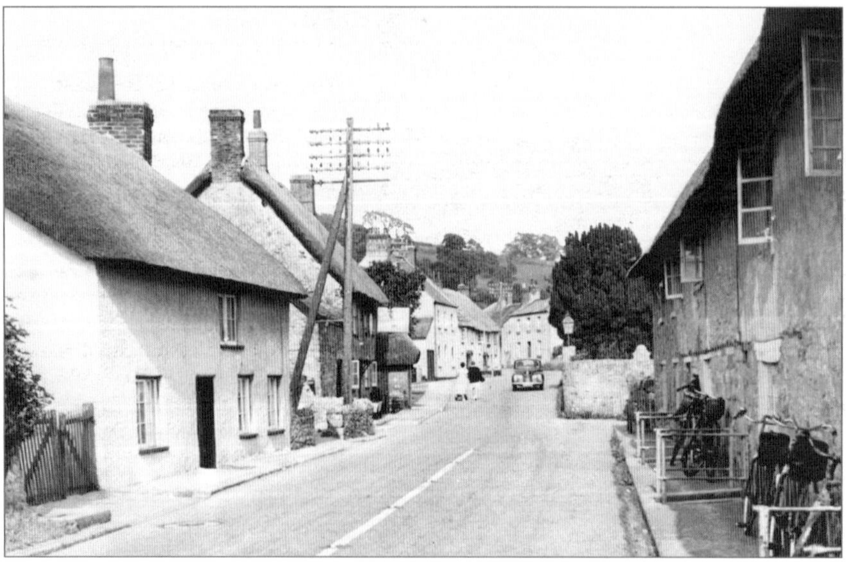

◄ **AXMOUTH**
The Village c1955
A83012

It is worth comparing this picture of Church Street with the similar view taken in 1898 (42443 on page 89) to see the changes wrought by the 20th century, particularly the need to cater for motor traffic. See how the road has been tarmacked, with the puddle-gathering culverts and uneven surfaces smoothed out and proper pavements provided. The delightfully unspoiled cottages on the right have been removed, sad to say.

◄ **AXMOUTH**
The Harbour Entrance c1955
A83019

Axmouth's harbour, a mile from the heart of the village, is as picturesque as when the Frith photographers took this series of photographs. The long stretch of the River Axe between Axmouth and Colyford is an excellent habitat for wildfowl, and birdwatchers often line the riverbank in the early months of the year. Across the river is the sprawling town of Seaton.

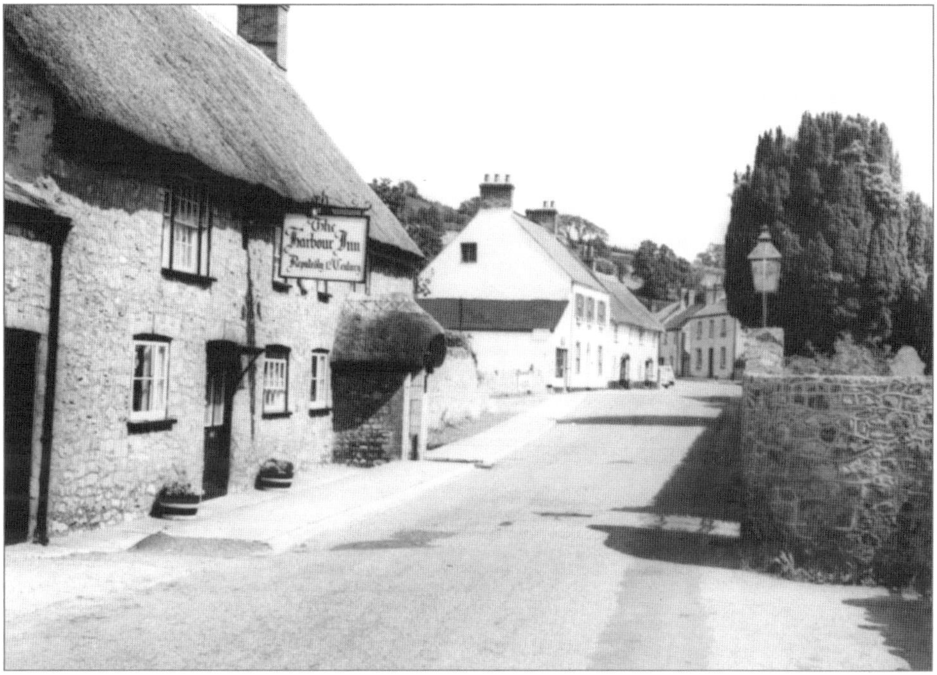

▲ **AXMOUTH,** *The Harbour Inn c1955* A83031

The Harbour Inn is at least 800 years old, and very popular with the many birdwatchers who come to see the wildfowl on the River Axe. A comparison with the previous photographs of Church Street will show how little it changed in the half century following Victoria's reign, though in the 1898 photograph (42443, page 89) it is whitewashed, its stonework hidden, and the roof cheap and functional.

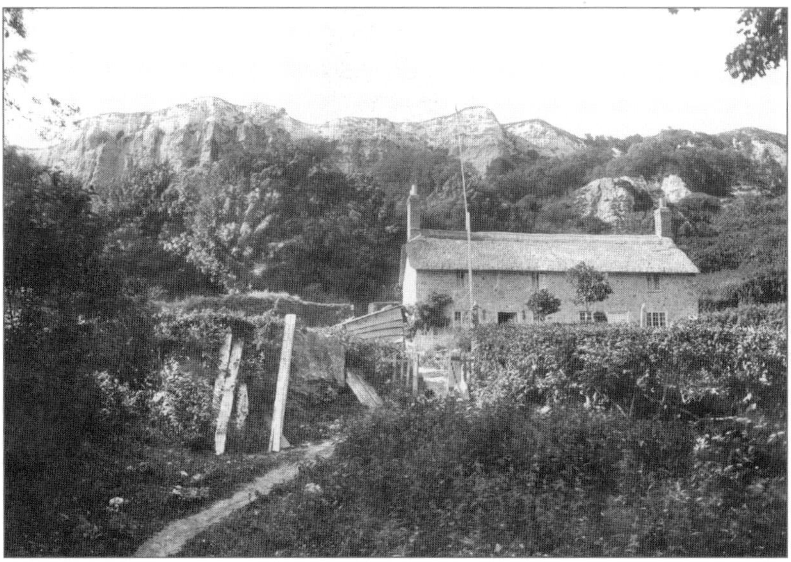

◄ **ROUSDON**
Landslip Cottage 1900 45263

The great landslip of the coast between Axmouth and Lyme Regis took place on Christmas Day 1839, when a chasm nearly a mile in length was created when the existing cliffs fell towards the sea - carrying some cottages with them, though no one was hurt. In the decades that followed there were a number of minor landslips, forming the wild and jumbled wood and cliff that we see today. It is a hard walk between Axmouth and Lyme, and there are no exits, so use public transport to return home or retrace your steps. The landslip is now a National Nature Reserve.

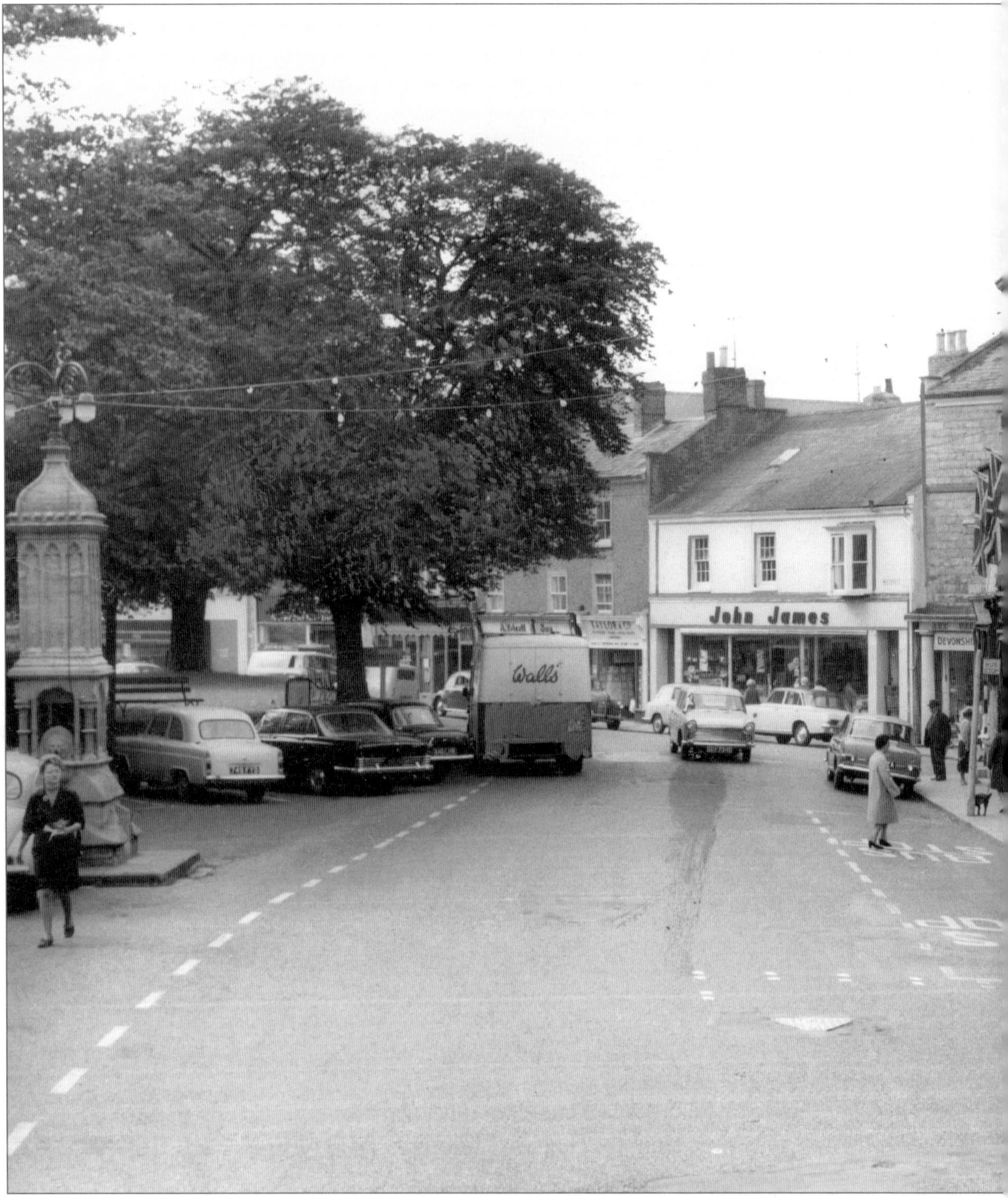
John James
Wall's

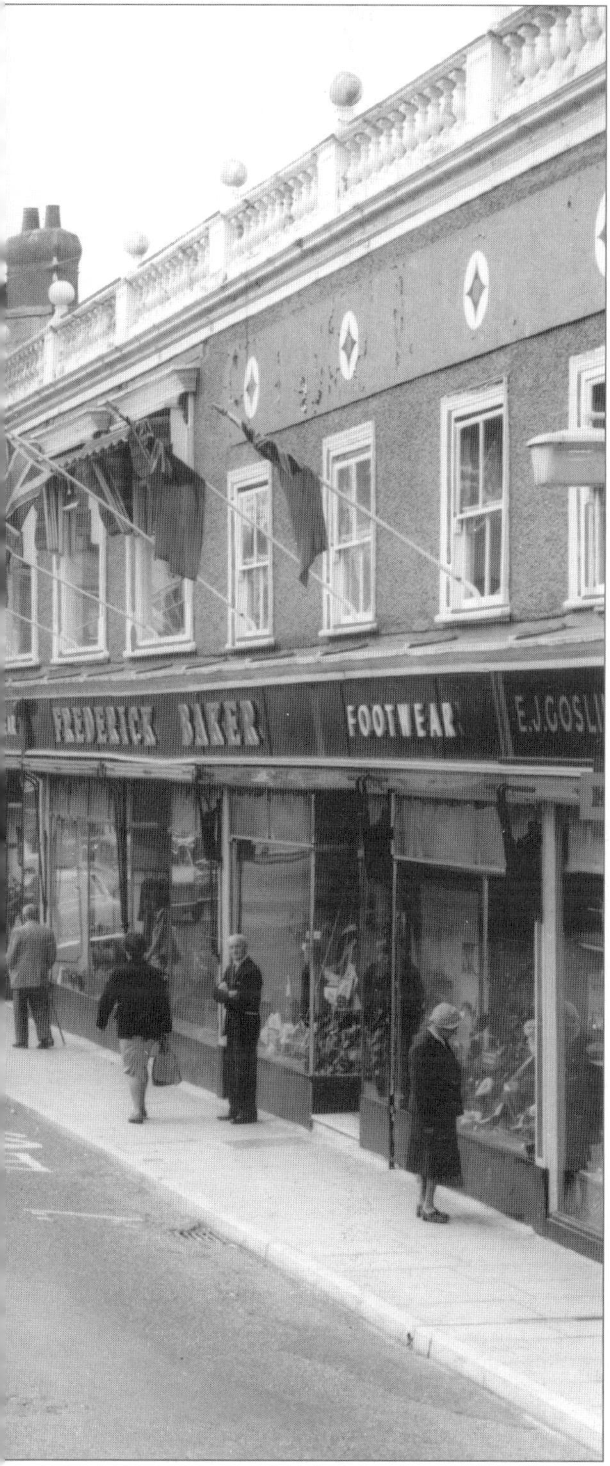

A PASTORAL LAND

AMID the meadows and ridges of East Devon are some of England's most delightful villages and small market towns. In this selection of photographs we see these habitations before the dominance of motor traffic, when it was still possible for people to walk down a street heedless of danger. Here we see the village inns in the days when they catered mostly for local people rather than visitors, and the churches when religion still held a powerful sway over people's lives.

Axminster and Colyton are two of the larger settlements, but they are still quite small towns known for their markets, places where residents and village folk came together - and still do - on market days. The surrounding villages might be slightly bigger now than in the days when these photographs were taken, but there is little of the housing sprawl that has so badly urbanised other English counties.

The countryside is stunningly beautiful, its high ridges offering rural views for fifty miles; tiny rivers gurgle along across water meadows where you might only see a solitary heron in an hour's walk. Its woodlands are deep - for this is still a very wooded part of the county - and at their best in springtime, when the bluebells carpet the shaded hillsides. Little has changed since these photographs were taken, so leave the car behind and explore.

AXMINSTER, *Trinity Square c1965* A88092

Axminster is a busy little market town within hailing distance of the Dorset border. The market, held here in Trinity Square, dates to the 12th century. On the left is the memorial to Queen Victoria's Golden Jubilee around which the market stalls are erected. Beyond Boots the Chemist (right) - still on the same site - is the shop of E J Gosling, then Frederick Baker's, and in the distance are John James and Taylor & Company.

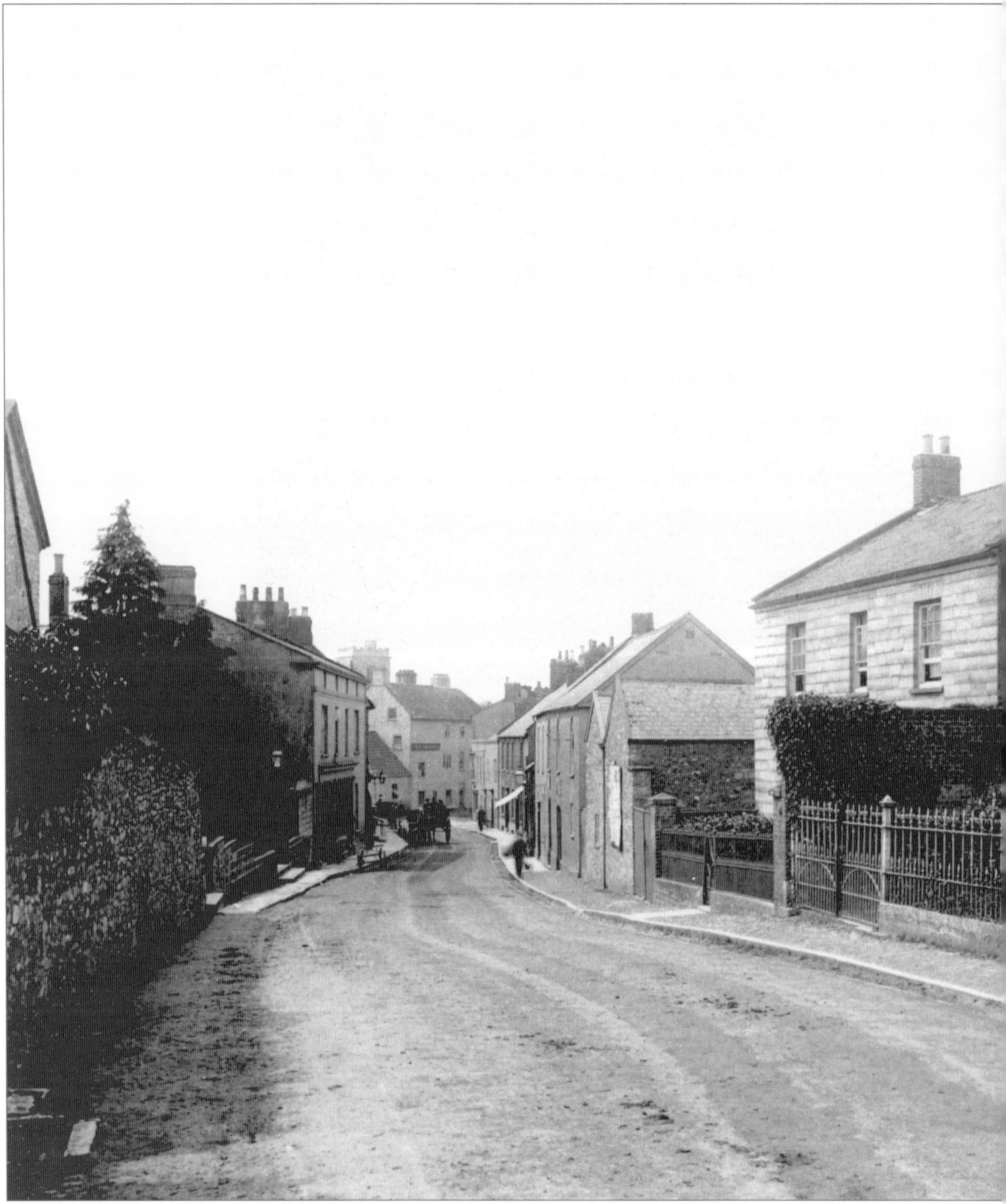

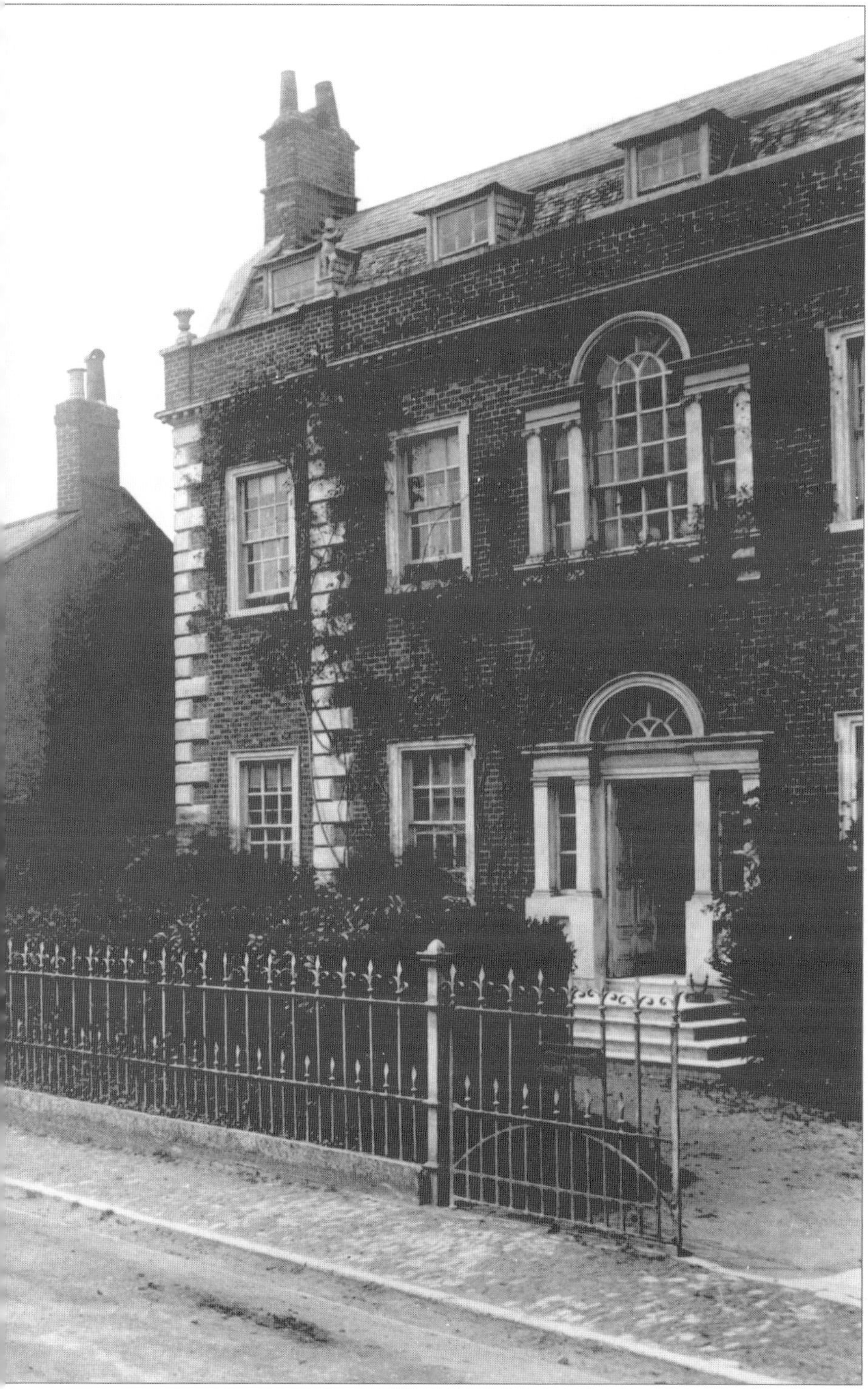

AXMINSTER
Chard Street 1902 48455

Axminster was once famous for the manufacture of carpets, though the industry relocated to Wilton after 1835. On the left is the United Reformed church, where rests Thomas Whitty, who founded the Axminster carpet industry in the 18th century. The imposing residence on the right is Oak House, built for local lawyer Simon Bunter in the 1750s. In the far distance is the George Hotel, a coaching inn dating to 1594.

▼ **AXMINSTER,** *Castle Hill 1902* 48459

Castle Hill was one of Axminster's earliest residential streets, though always mixed with trade. The cottages on the right have survived, although they are much altered. A little way down is the Gospel Hall, and three doors down a tiny hardware shop. The thatched cottages beyond have been demolished and replaced. The factory at the foot of the hill is The Old Brush Works.

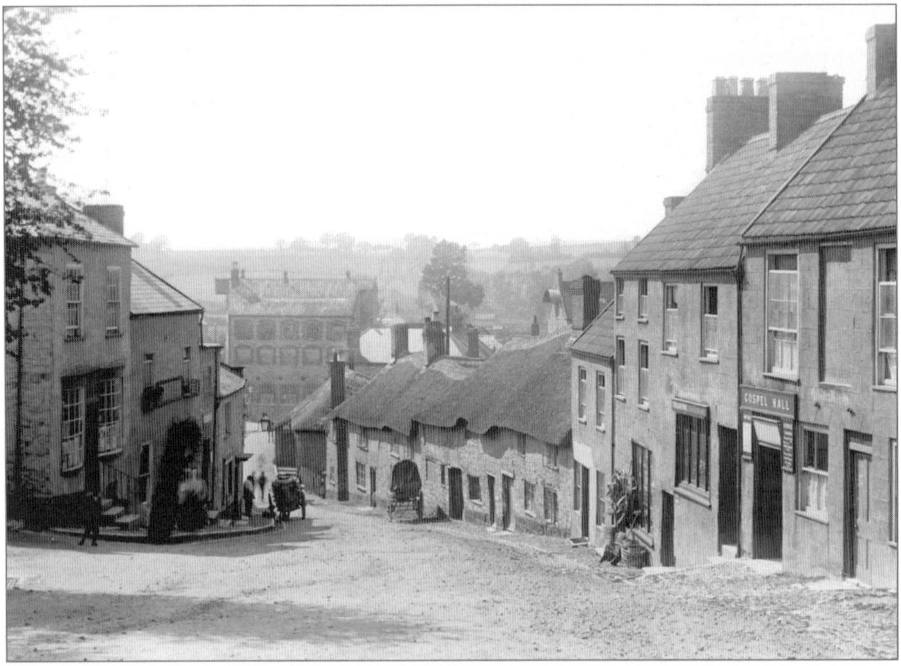

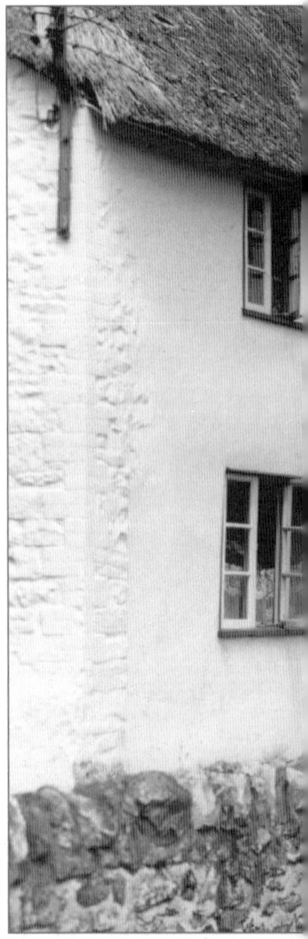

► **AXMINSTER**
St Mary's Church c1960 A88030

Axminster's parish church is Saxon in origin - tradition relates that King Athelstan founded a college for priests here in 937. Much of what remains is Norman and Early English; the mighty tower was rebuilt in the 13th century. A piece of original Axminster carpet hangs within.

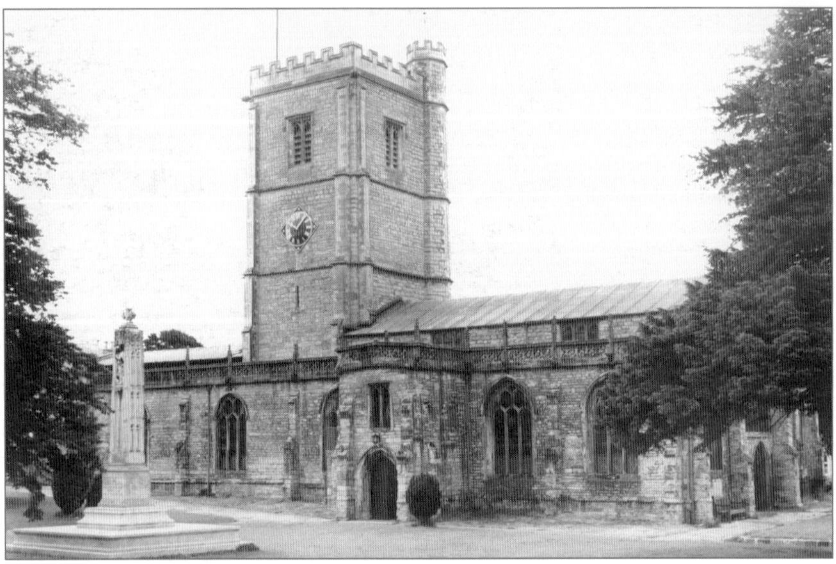

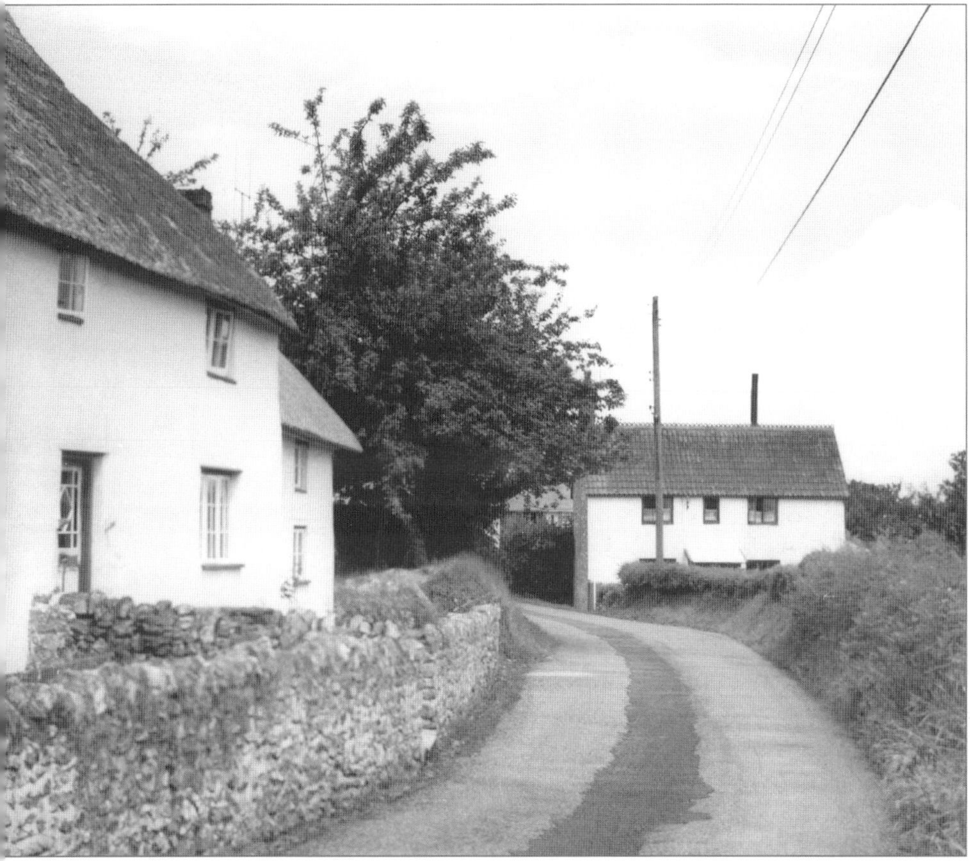

◄ **CHARDSTOCK**
Holy City c1960
C302006

Chardstock was a Dorset village until 1886, when it was 'moved' across into Devon. The county border is not far away. Many of the farms in the parish date back over 800 years, and there are a number of picturesque cottages.

► **COLYFORD**
Swan Hill 1907
58048

Colyford was established by Thomas Basset as a new borough in the 1200s. A town grew up around this ford over the River Coly, a mayor was elected, and a cattle fair was held. Such prosperity did not last, and Colyford had declined by the 18th century. It remains a village of beautiful cottages on the high road between Exeter and Dorchester.

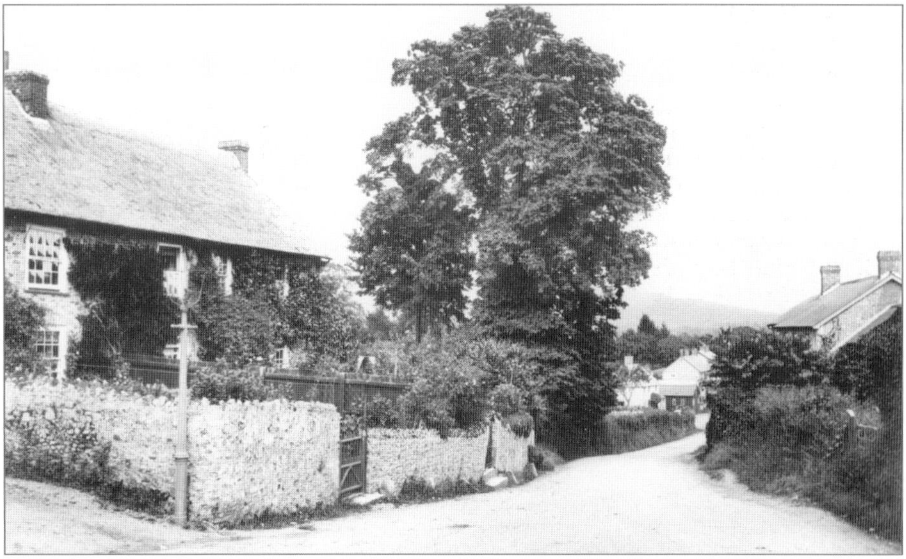

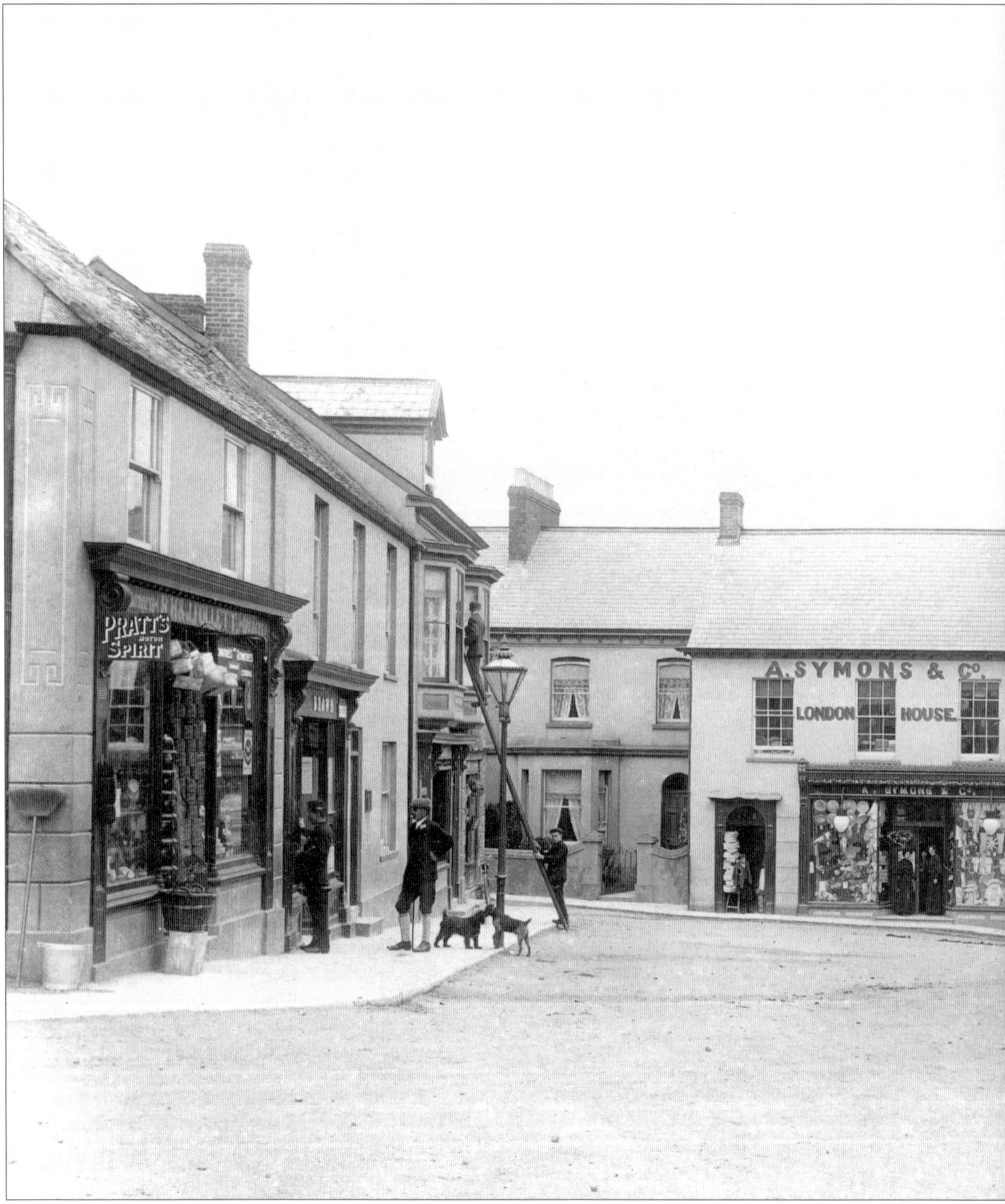
PRATT'S
SPIRIT
A. SYMONS & Co.
LONDON HOUSE.

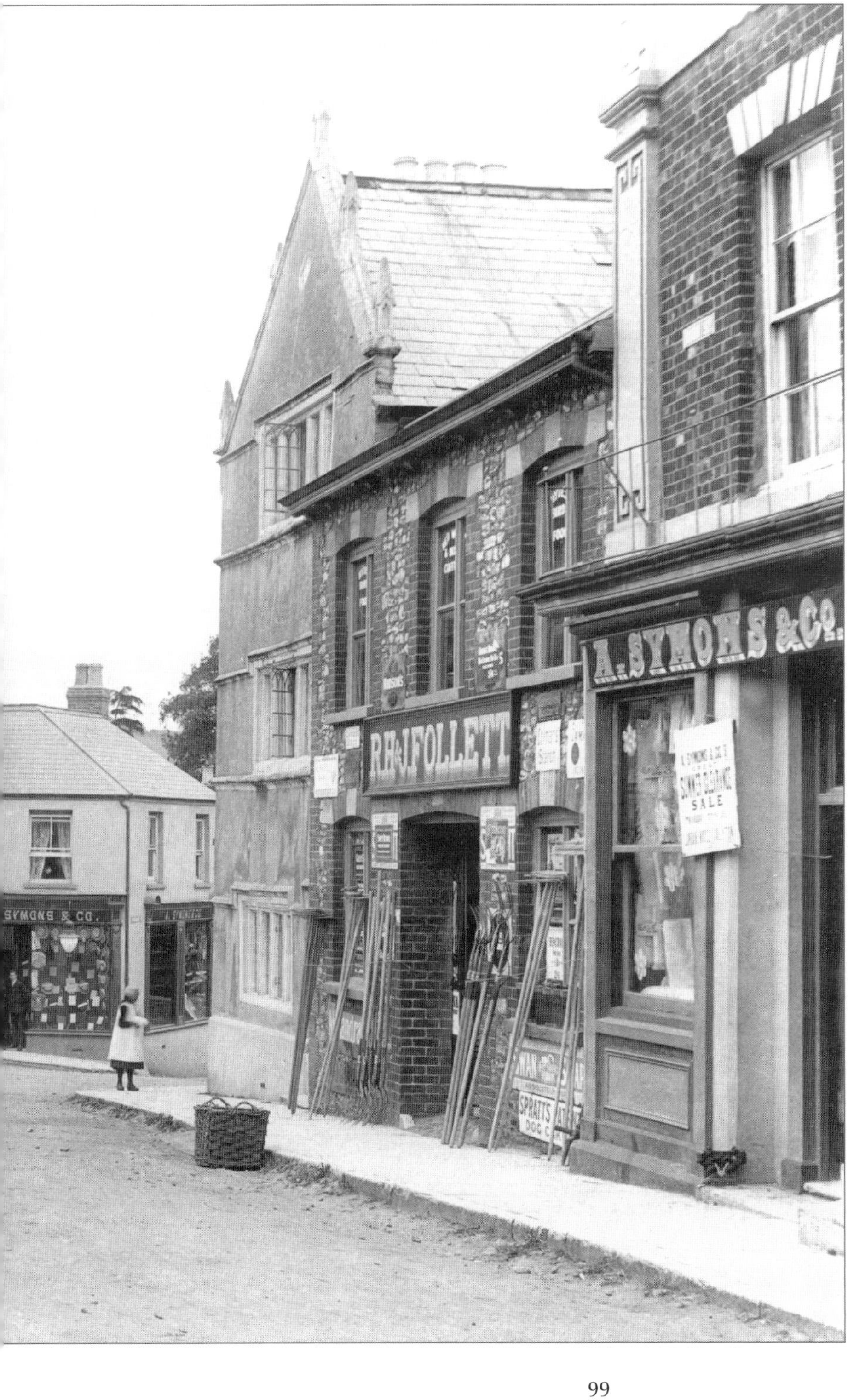

COLYTON
Market Place 1907 58043

On the left of this scene we see R H and J Follett, a grocer's, and then Messrs Brown - notice the man in the plus-fours with his two dogs, and the window cleaner up the ladder. On the far side of the square is A Symons & Co, with three smiling shop assistants posing in the doorway. Their shop stocked ladies' wear, with the menswear shop next door. On the right is Follett's hardware shop with a selection of tools displayed outside, with Symons' other shop selling household linen and advertising its 'Great Summer Clearance Sale'. Follett's still trades as a general merchant in Colyton.

COLYTON
Church Path c1955
C110007

Colyton's street pattern bears the marks of its Saxon founders, for this is a town with a long history. A number of skirmishes were fought in the parish's fields during the Civil War, and many local men fought in the Duke of Monmouth's ill-fated rebellion in 1685.

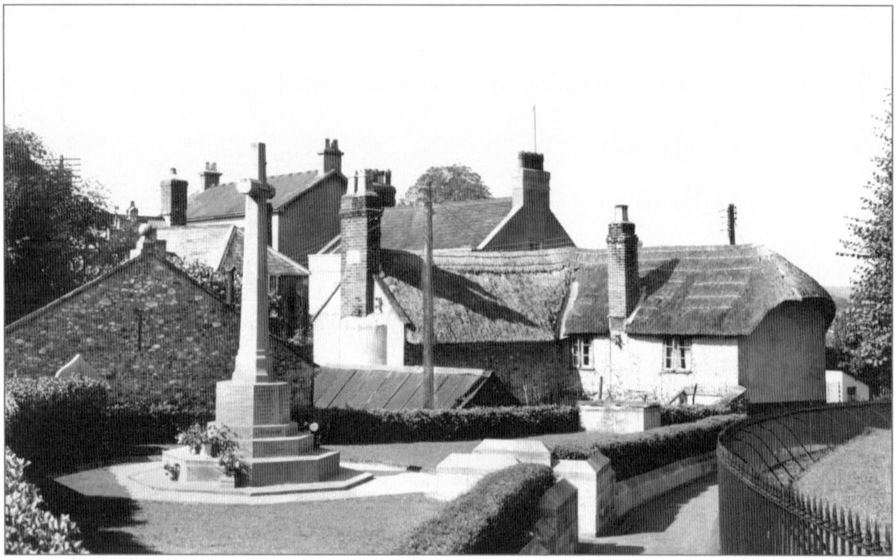

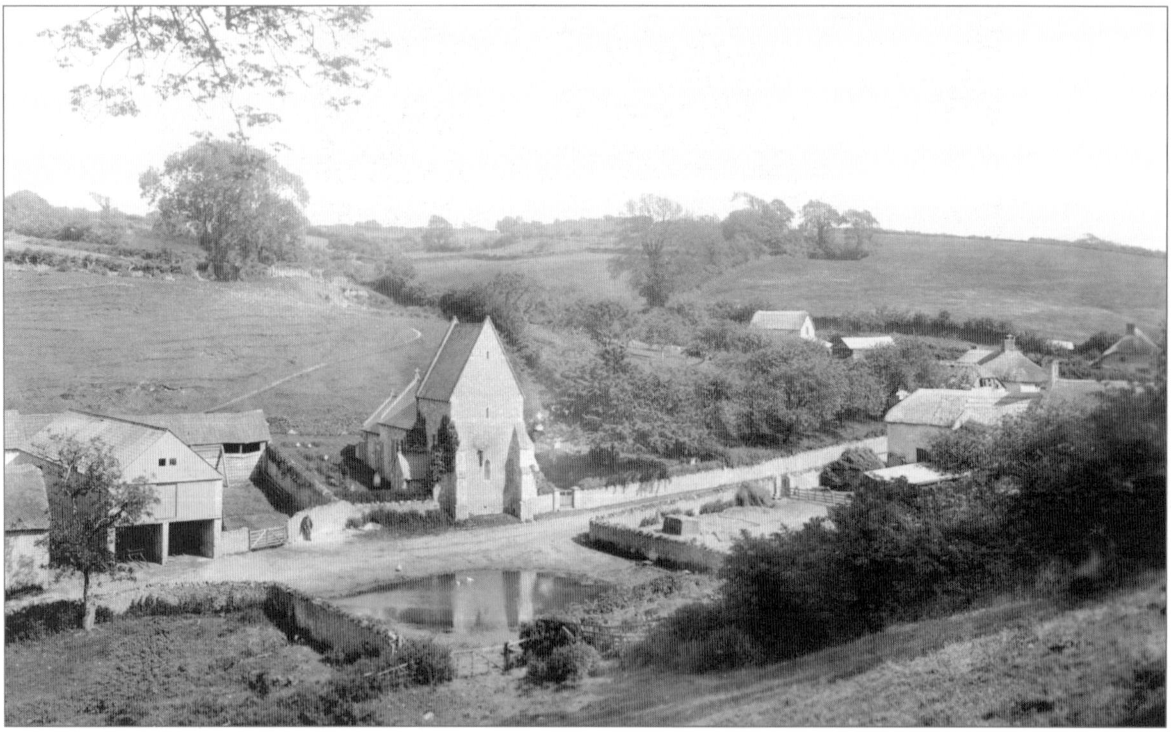

COMBPYNE, *The Church 1900* 45261

Combpyne's parish church with its unusual saddleback tower dates to the 13th century. Despite some Victorian restoration, this little church remains unspoiled.

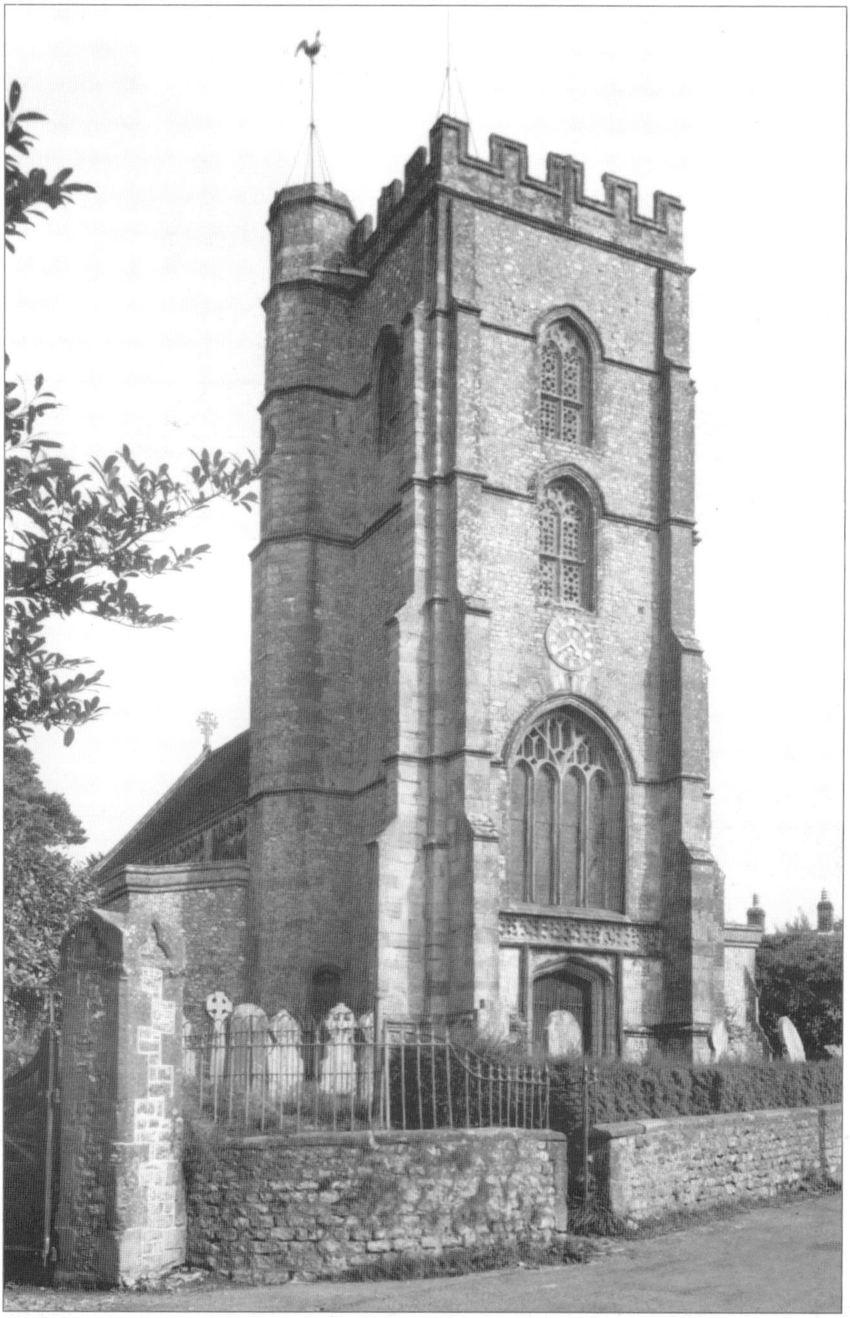

HAWKCHURCH, *The Church Tower c1955* H46013

Hawkchurch is situated in wild and wooded country, close to where Devon slips imperceptibly into Dorset. A church has stood here since Saxon times, and its fine Norman interior has somehow survived the worst excesses of the Victorian restorers.

KILMINGTON
The Village c1960
K23012

Kilmington sprawls across the hillside along the line of a Roman road to Exeter. Not far away is Coryton Park, rebuilt in 1754-56 by Benedictus Mawood Tucker, afterwards Sheriff of Devon.

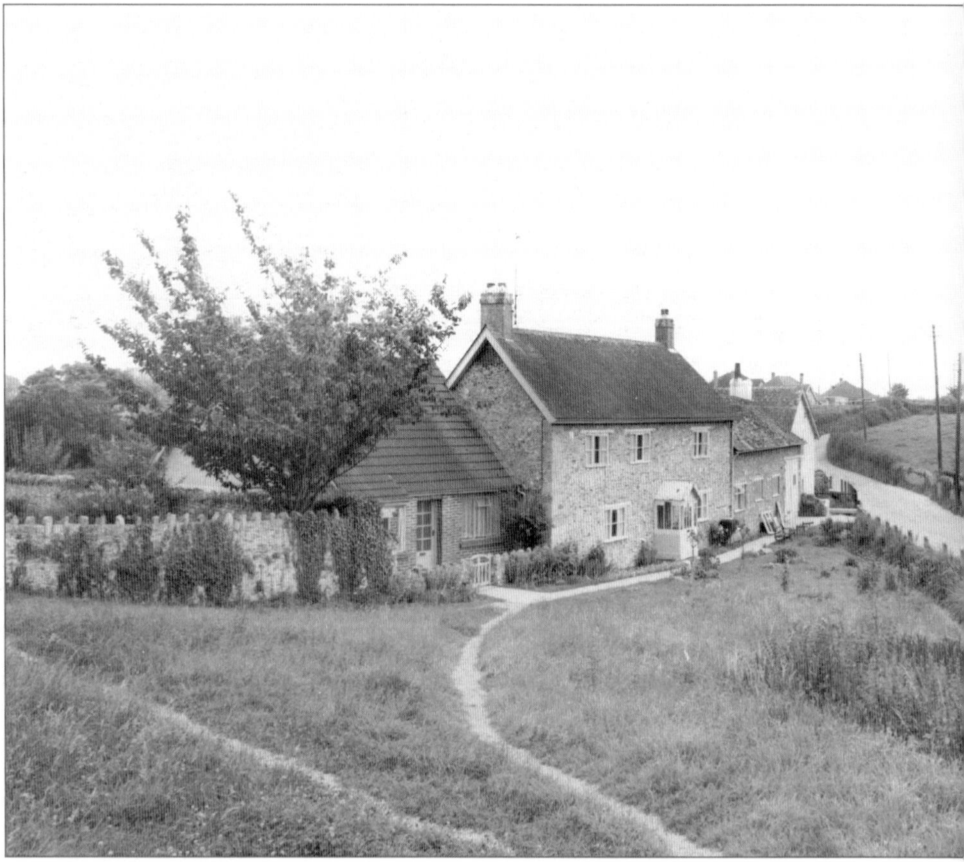

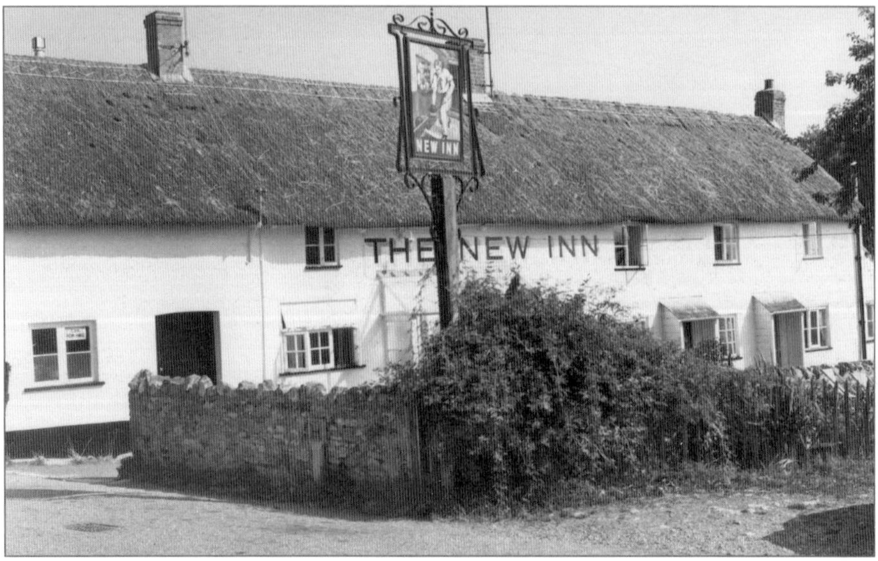

KILMINGTON
The New Inn c1960
K23005

Most of East Devon's public houses are extremely ancient, and have served as places of refreshment for centuries. Travellers on the high road between Dorchester and Exeter would have turned off the trail to seek shelter in the New Inn, which is older than its name suggests. Notice the 'car for hire' sign in the window (left).

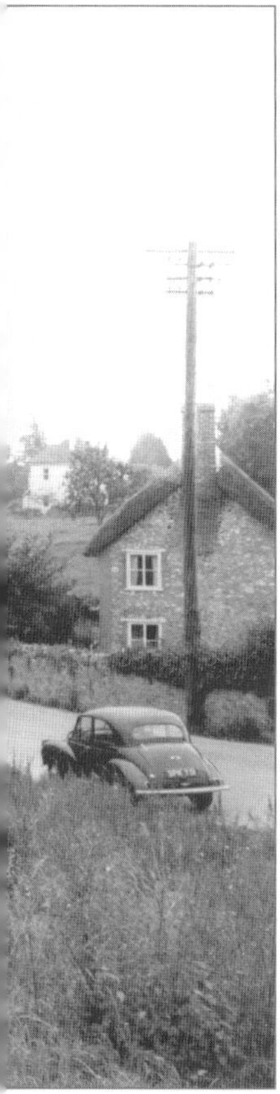

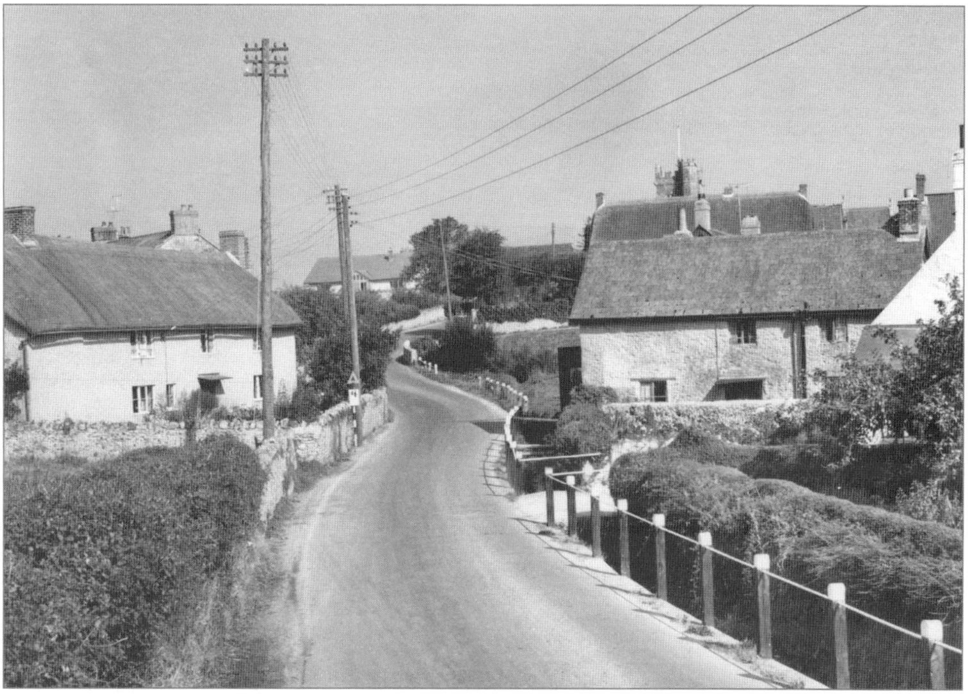

▲ **KILMINGTON,** *Whitford Road c1960* K23002

The Edwardian guidebook writer Francis Bickley described Kilmington thus: 'its branching streets, its old cottages with their bright gardens, the clear waters of its streamlet, all these go to the making of a gem among villages, a place where one could linger long were it not for the call of the road'.

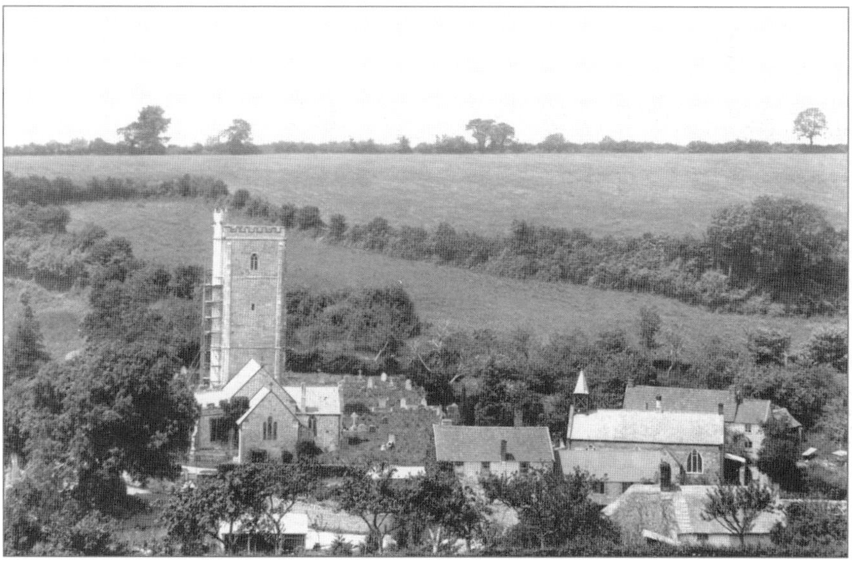

◄ **MEMBURY**
The Church and the Schools 1902 48478

The hillsides and vales of Membury have been farmed since at least the Iron Age. In the chancel of this parish church is the tomb of Sir Shilston Calmady, killed nearby whilst fighting for Parliament in the Civil War. Not far away is another of East Devon's prehistoric hill-forts.

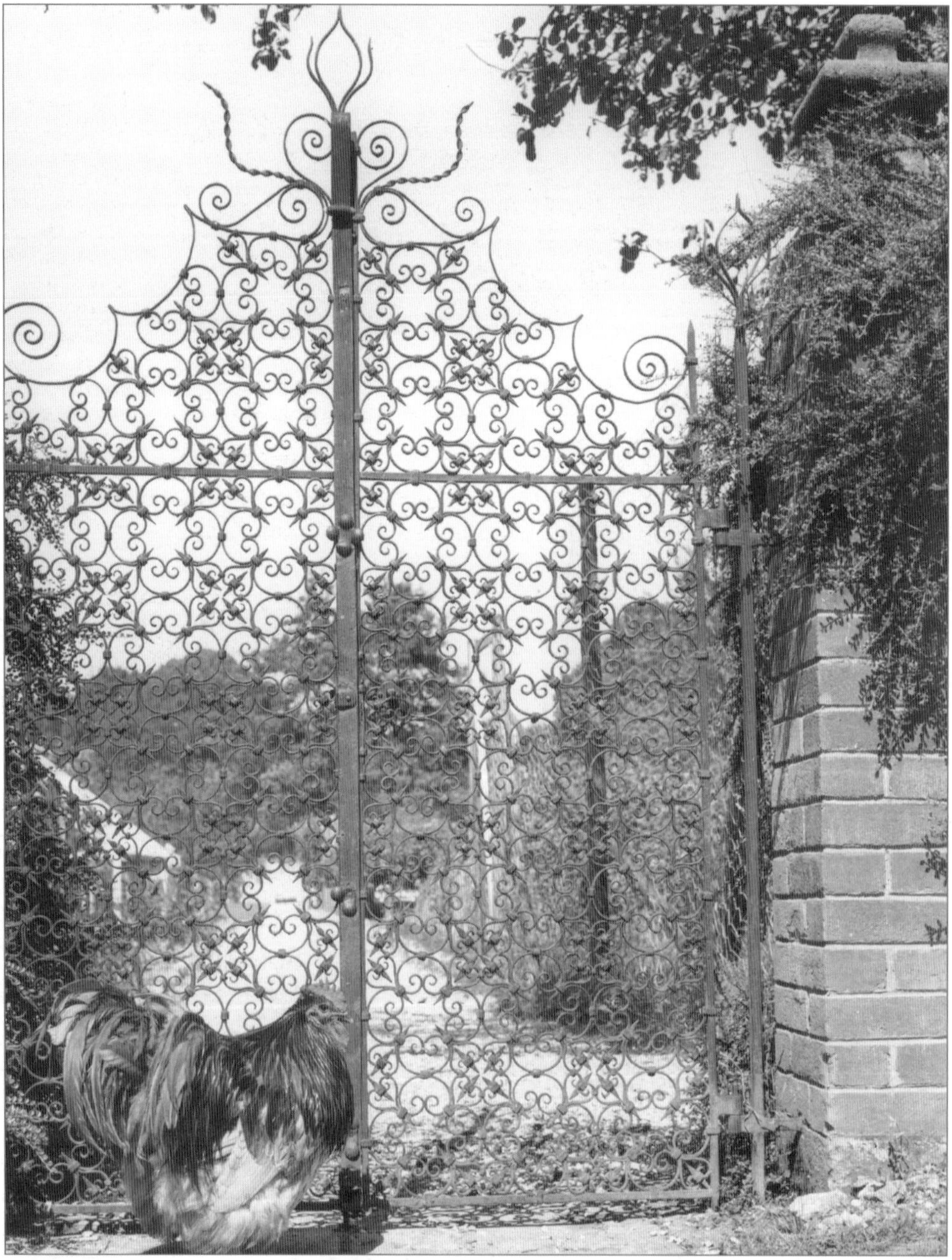

MUSBURY, *Ashe House, the Italian Gate c1960* M174040

John Churchill, the future Duke of Marlborough, victor of Blenheim and Ramillies, and ancestor of Sir Winston Churchill, may have been born at Ashe House in 1650. Axminster's church records note that 'John, the sonne of Mr Winstone Churchill, was baptised at Ash the 12th Daye of June in the year of our lord god'. The parson clearly forgot to put the year of birth in the register, though it was added to the margin some time later.

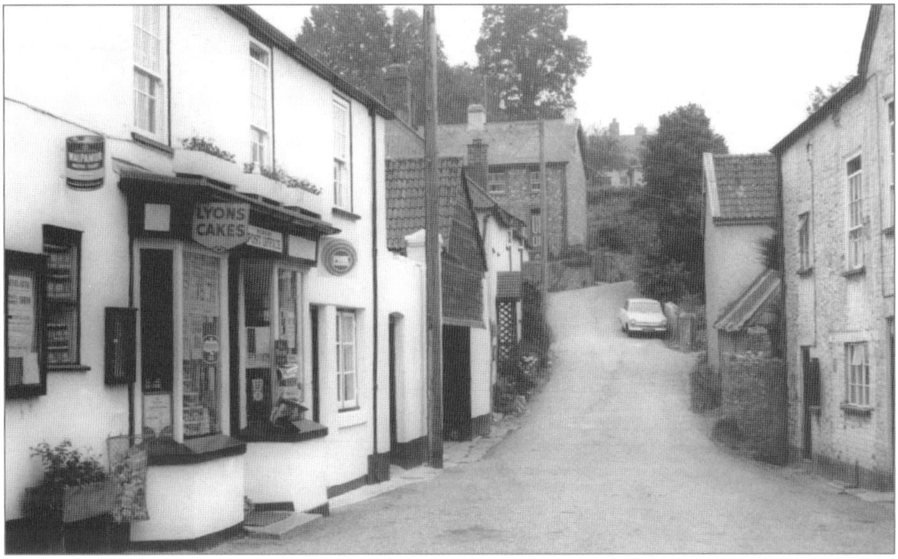

MUSBURY
The Post Office c1965 M174055

On a windswept hillside above Musbury is an Iron Age hill-fort, for this was the borderland between two Iron Age tribes. The River Axe, far below, was once navigable as far as the meadows below Musbury. Legend claims this to be the site of the great battle of Brunanburgh, where King Athelstan's Saxons defeated a combined army of Danes, Picts and Scots.

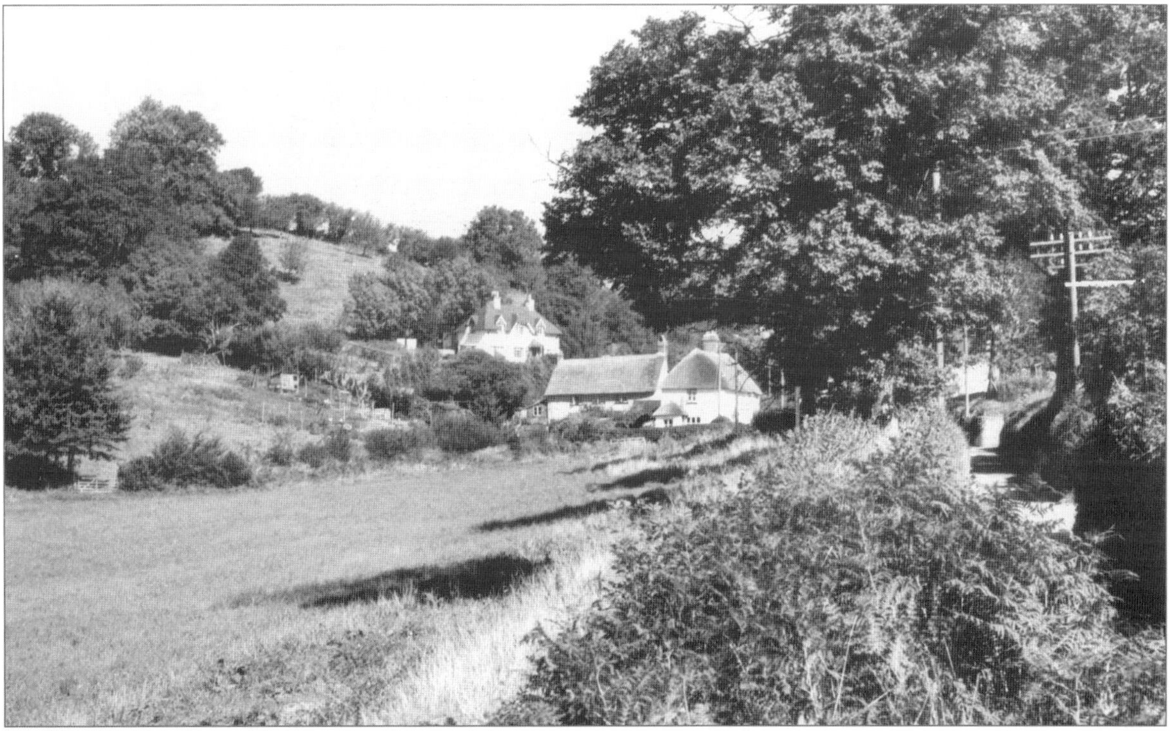

OFFWELL, *The Lower Village c1960* O60016A

Offwell hides in the hills to the south-west of Honiton, half-forgotten by time and well off the tourist trail. A network of footpath and bridleways offers excellent views across East Devon's pastoral landscape.

▼ **ROUSDON,** *The Church 1900* 46053

Rousdon, now part of Combpyne civil parish, nestles above the great coastal landslip between Axmouth and Lyme Regis. When Sir H W Peek acquired the Rousdon estate, he found the old parish church of St Pancras in ruins. He had it rebuilt with this pagoda-like tower in 1872.

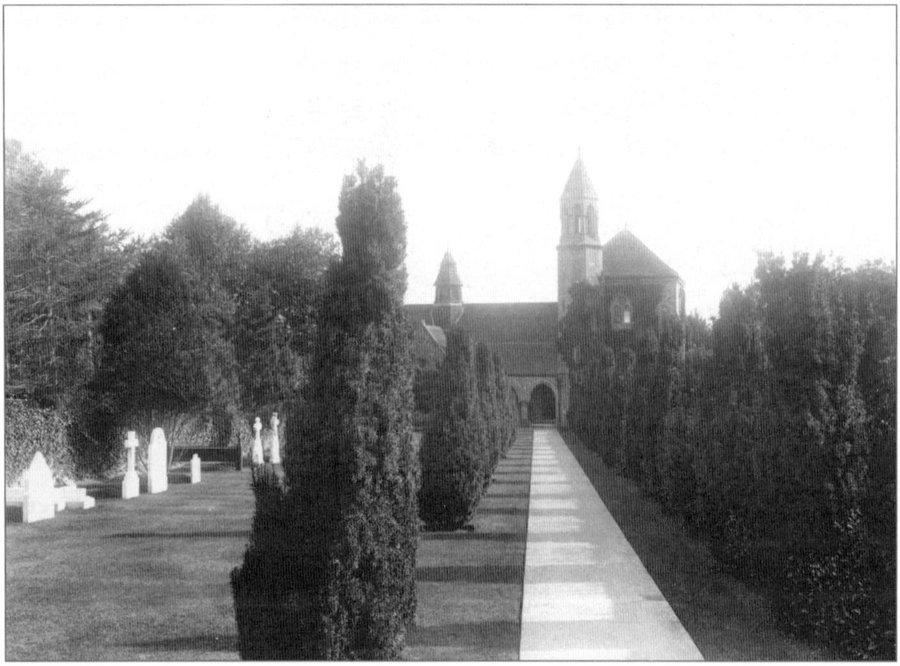

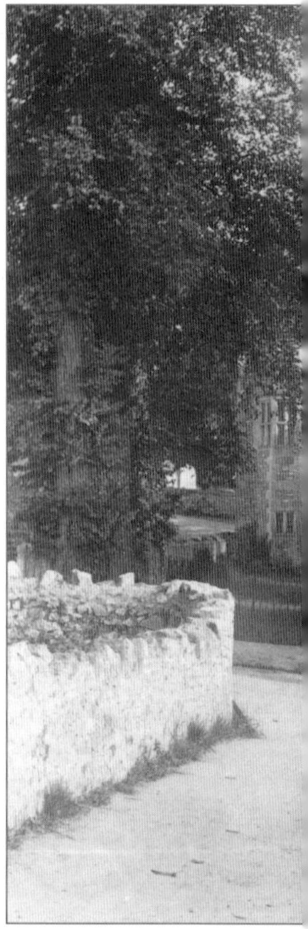

► **ROUSDON**
Rousdon House 1900
46050

Rousdon House was built for Sir H W Peek in the 19th century in an extraordinary mixture of architectural styles. The marble used throughout the building was retrieved from a ship that had been wrecked on the coast nearby. From 1938 until 1998 Rousdon housed Allhallows School, which relocated here from Honiton.

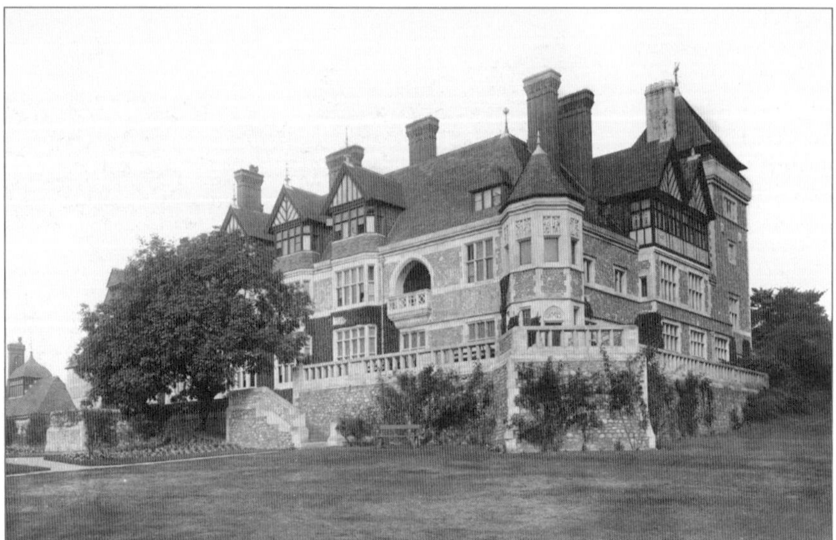

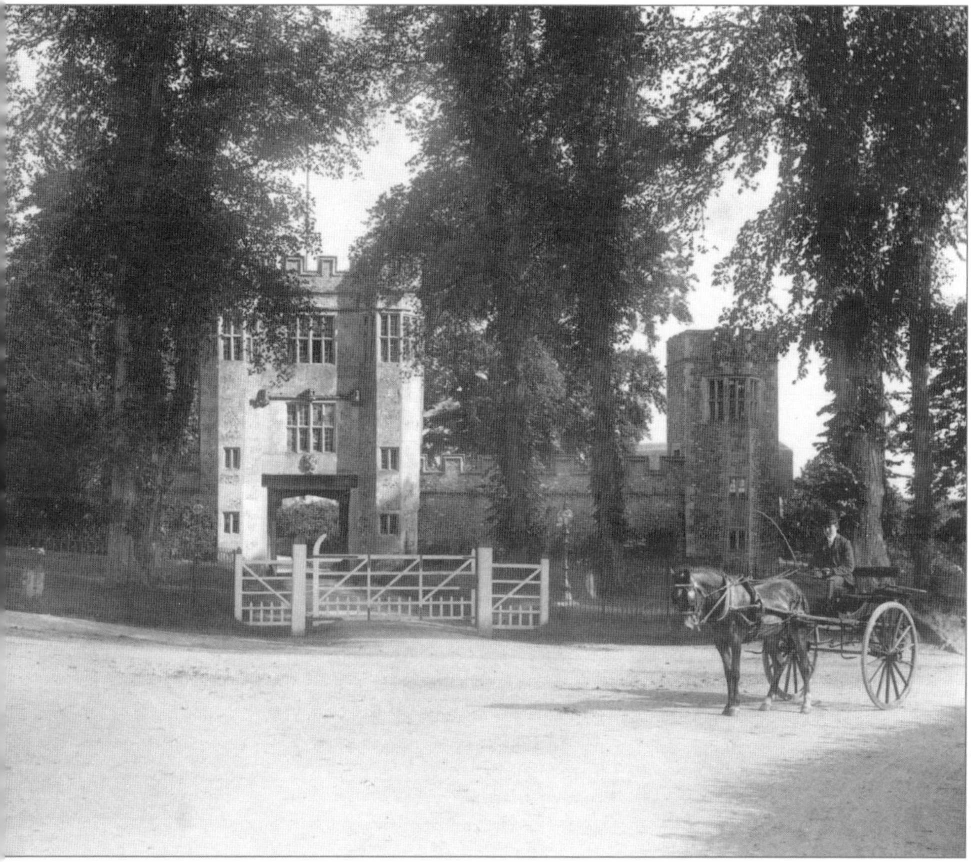

SHUTE
The Old Gateway 1902 48474

Shute was the home of the Bonville family until their fortunes declined after the Wars of the Roses. The estate, with its extensive and very beautiful deer park, passed into the hands of the Pole family, who built a Georgian mansion in the grounds of the old house. The trees and fences have since been removed.

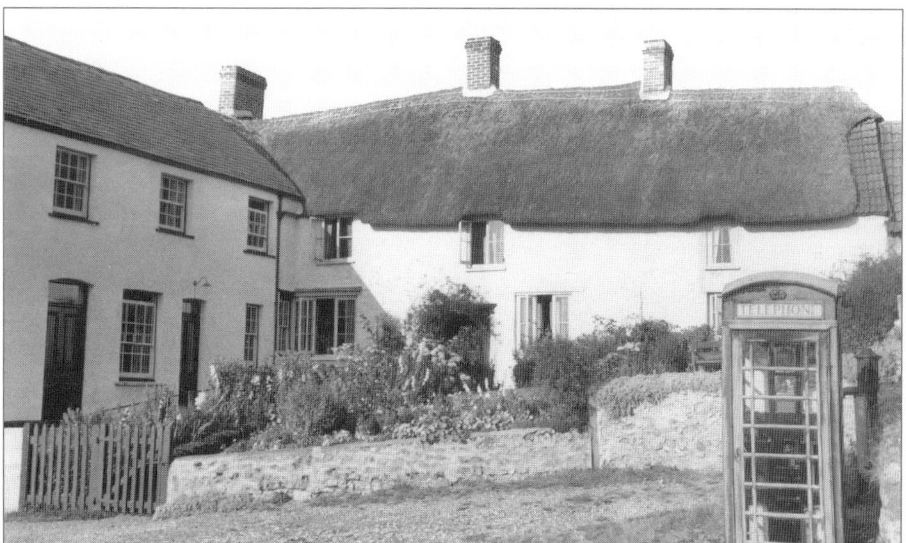

SHUTE
The Beagles c1955
S358006

Shute is a collection of scattered hamlets on a hillside offering wonderful views. Its cottages consist of a wide variety of architectural styles. Just to one side of the telephone kiosk is the original water pump for these buildings.

SIDBURY
The Village 1906
53821

Sidbury offers real evidence of Saxon occupation, for work on the church chancel in 1898 revealed a tiny Saxon crypt below the church, which is now open to the public on some summer afternoons. Opposite the church are the Red Lion and the Royal Oak public houses.

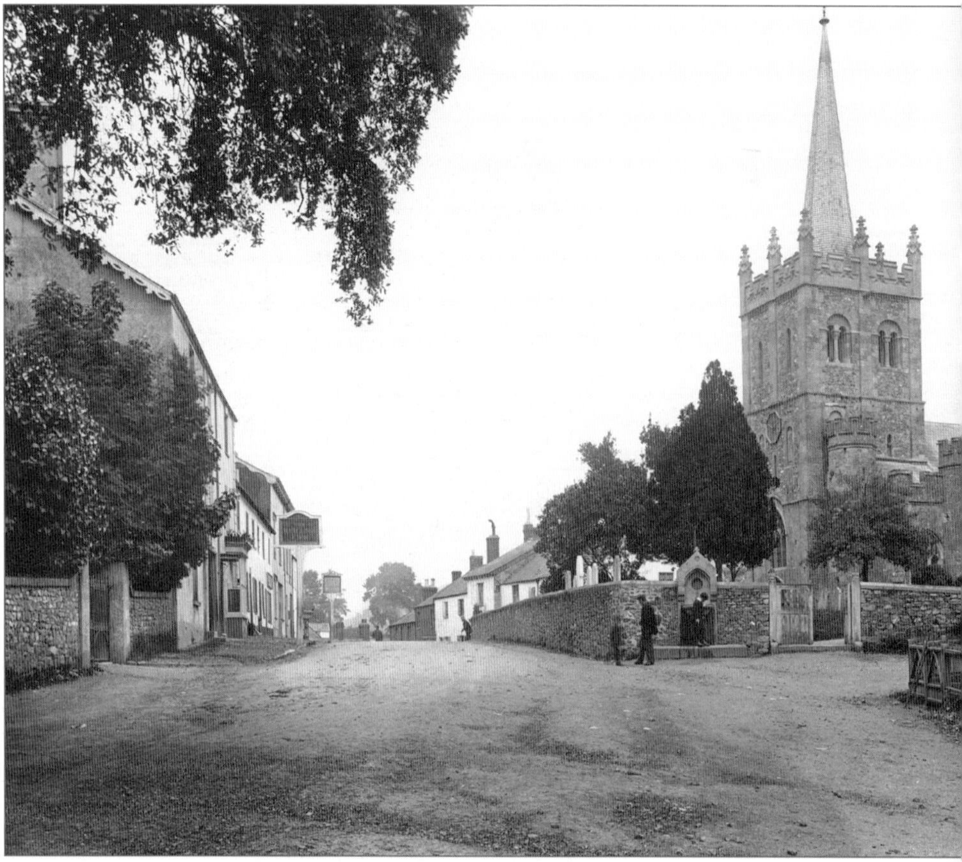

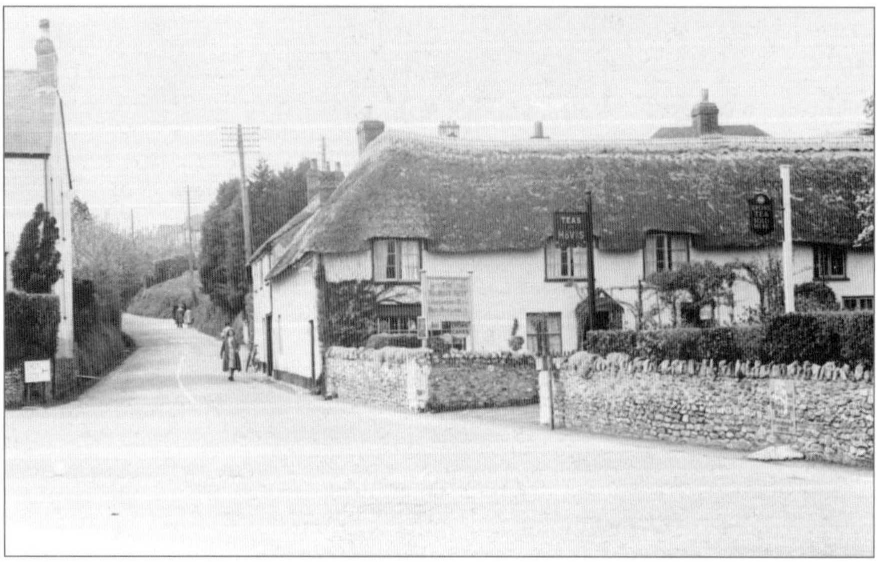

SIDFORD
The View from the Crossroads c1955
S128011

And how this view has changed in the half century since this photograph was taken! What was a quiet semi-rural turning has become a busy road junction, complete with road widening and traffic lights. A petrol filling station has been built on the right-hand side of the road.

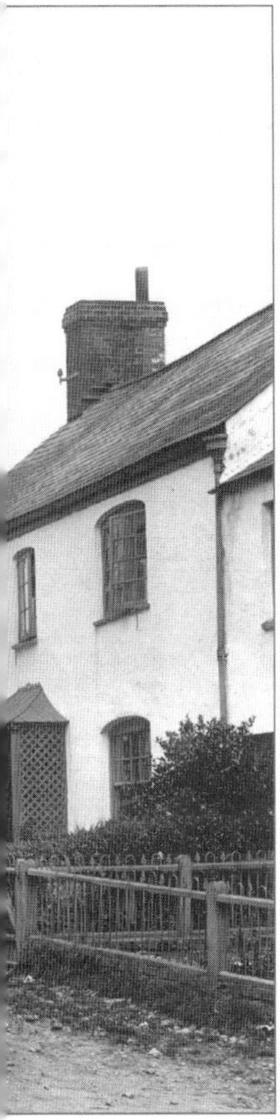

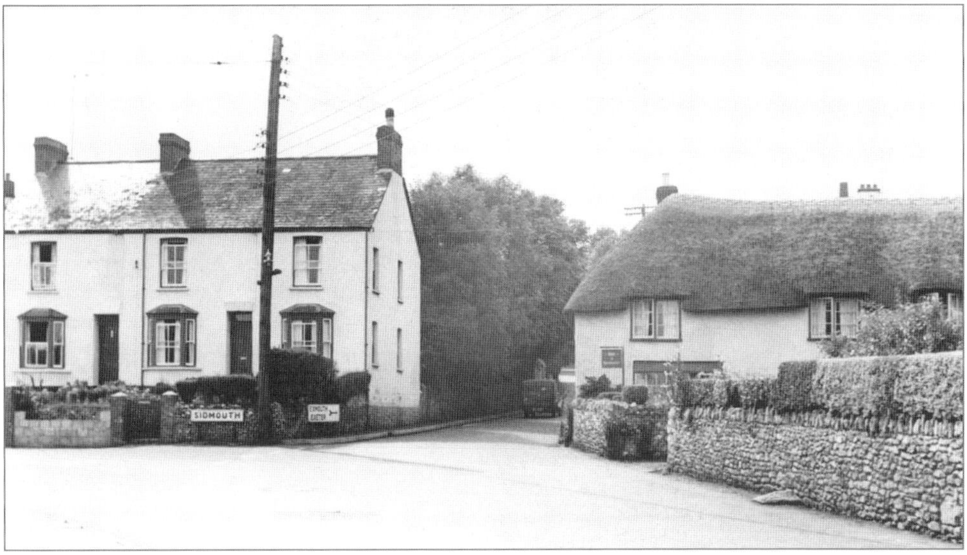

▲ **SIDFORD,** *The Exeter and Sidmouth Roads c1955* S128018

Too many tourists see Sidford only as a very busy road junction on their way to Sidmouth - a great pity, for despite its constant flow of traffic, Sidford has some delightful buildings and a rather beautiful setting.

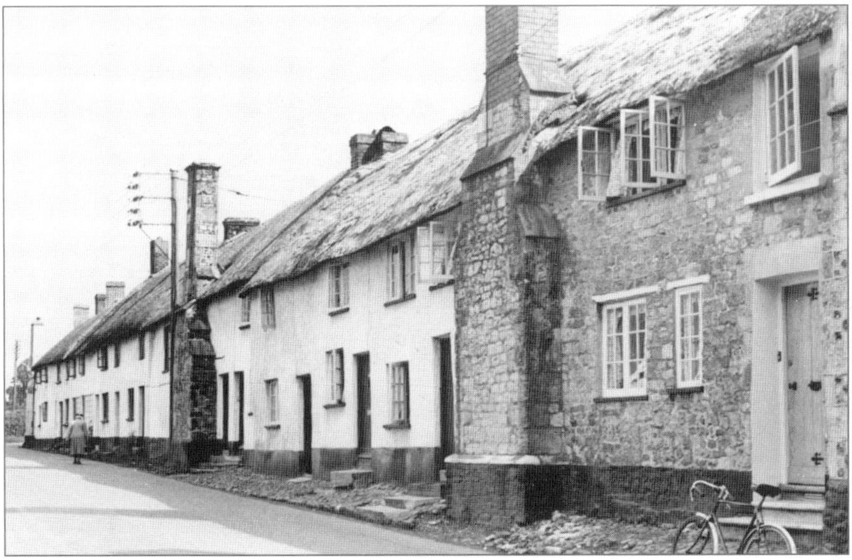

◄ **SIDFORD**
Old Cottages, School Street c1955
S128019

In the 1950s, most of Sidford's cottages were owned by villagers who worked locally. Today's residents are more likely to commute to Sidmouth or Exeter. The rural dwellers of past times would have been amazed at the price of a property in Sidford in the 21st century.

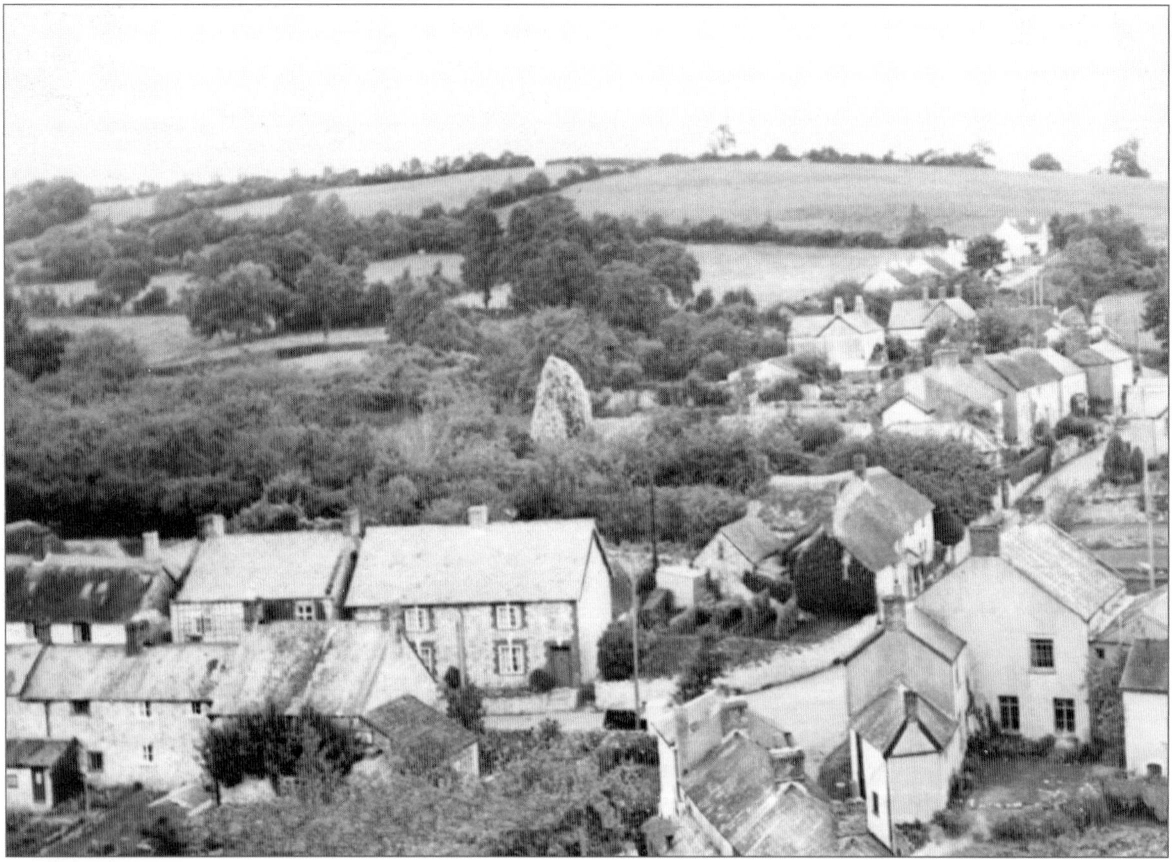

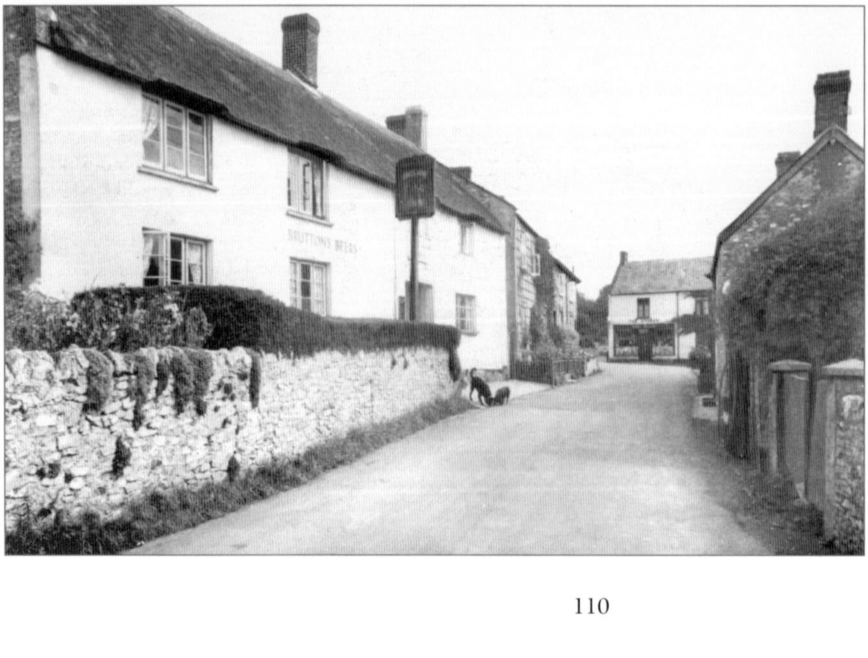

◄ **STOCKLAND**
The King's Arms
c1955 S365013

In the 1950s the majority of village inns in this pastoral land would have catered almost entirely for locals and the occasional passing tourist. In the years since, public houses such as the King's Arms have had to attract a clientele form further afield in order to survive.

◄ **STOCKLAND** *The View from the Church Tower c1955* S365002

Stockland huddles on a long ridge to the west of the River Yarty, its surrounding hilltops offering fine views over East Devon. Guarding the western edge of the ridge is Stockland Great Camp, a boundary fortification of the Dumnonii, the Iron Age inhabitants of Devon.

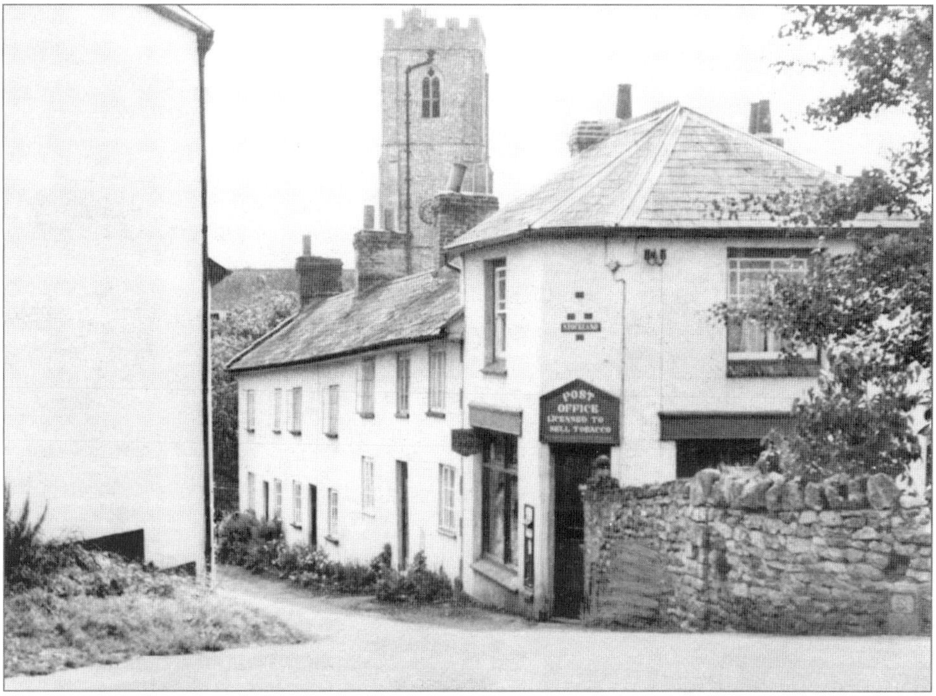

▲ **STOCKLAND,** *The Post Office c1955* S365012

The parish church of St Michael dates to the 14th century, but it was considerably enlarged over the following century. Its impressive tower stands high above the surrounding village, which has changed little since this photograph was taken.

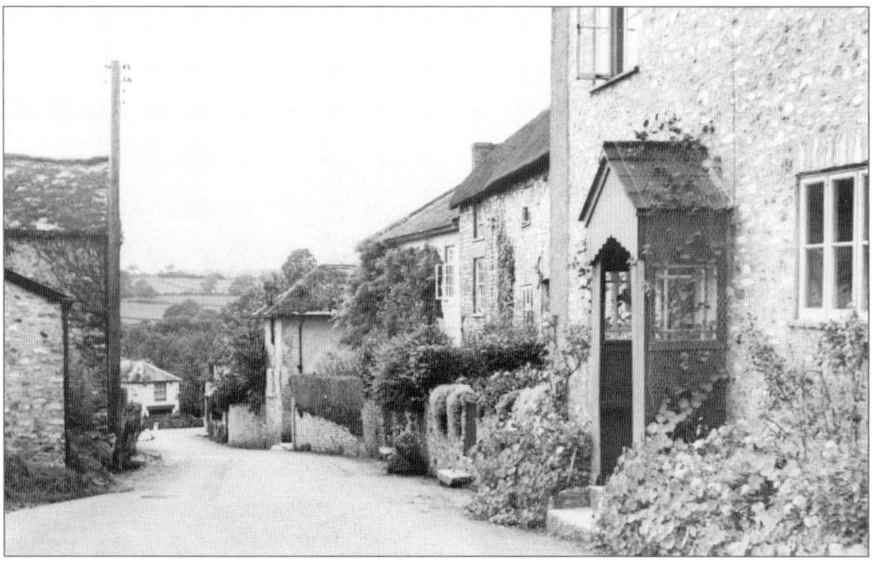

◄ **STOCKLAND** *The Village c1955* S365008

If the Frith photographer from the 1950s were to walk around Stockland now, he would find little had changed, though he would have to step aside a little more often for passing motor cars.

▼ **UPLYME,** *Yawl Bottom 1900* 45264

A walk through the countryside around Uplyme often takes you as much into Dorset as Devon, for the county border weaves around the ridges, woods and tiny brooks of the locality. Yawl is a dramatic deep combe which gives a real taste of East Devon's pastoral land.

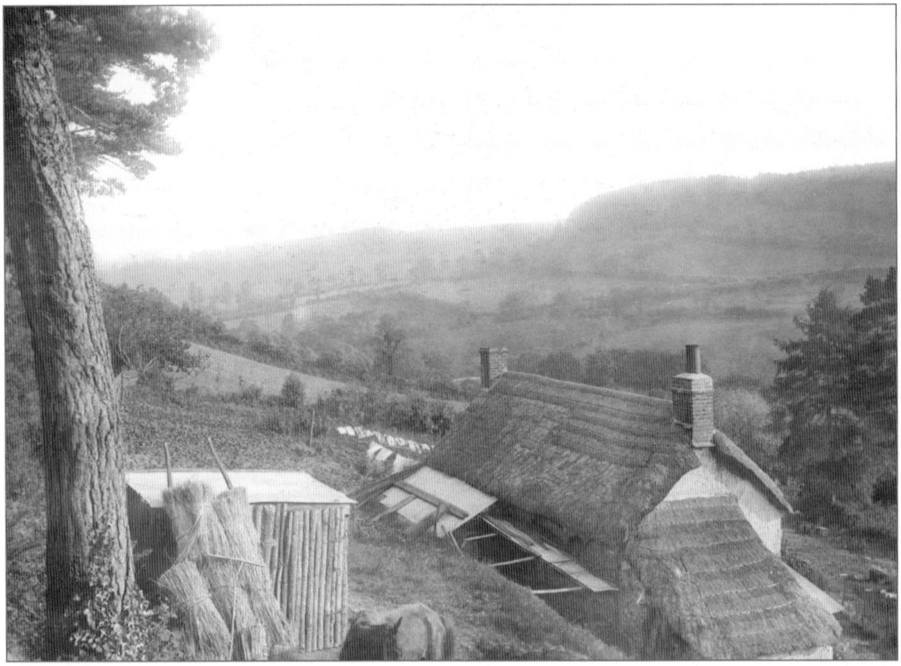

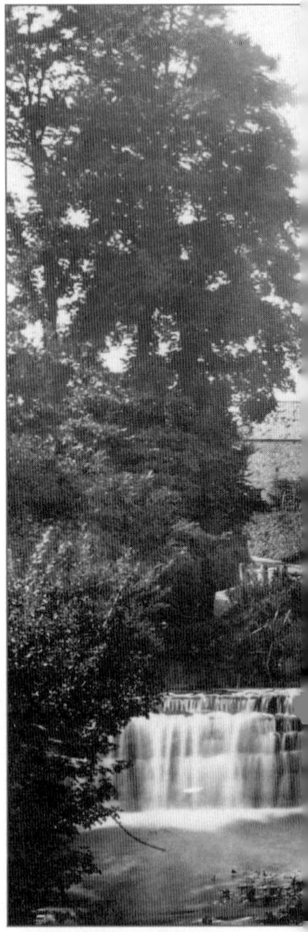

► **UPLYME**
Harcombe House 1925
76745

Harcombe runs roughly parallel to Yawl; it is another long combe running north from the main valley of the River Lim. In the quieter hours of the day, the careful walker might well see deer feeding in the wood-bounded pastures. Harcombe House is a good example of the many fine properties here.

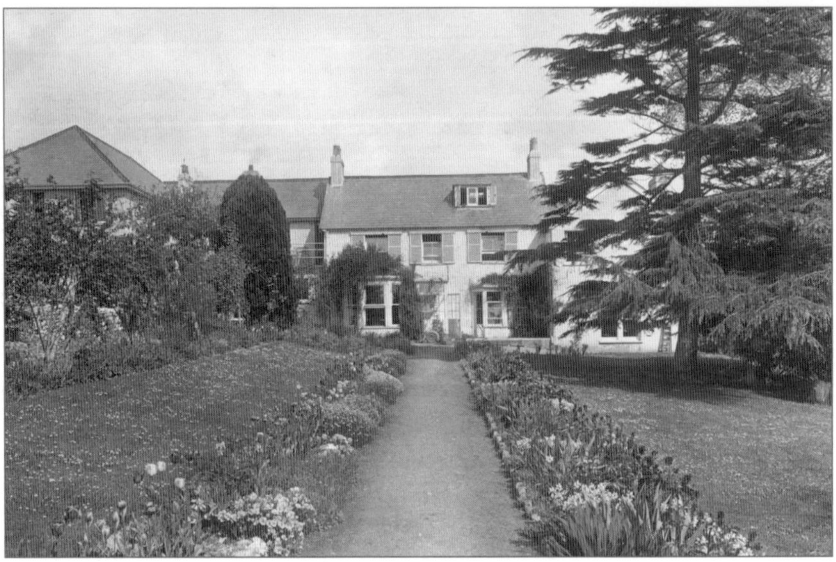

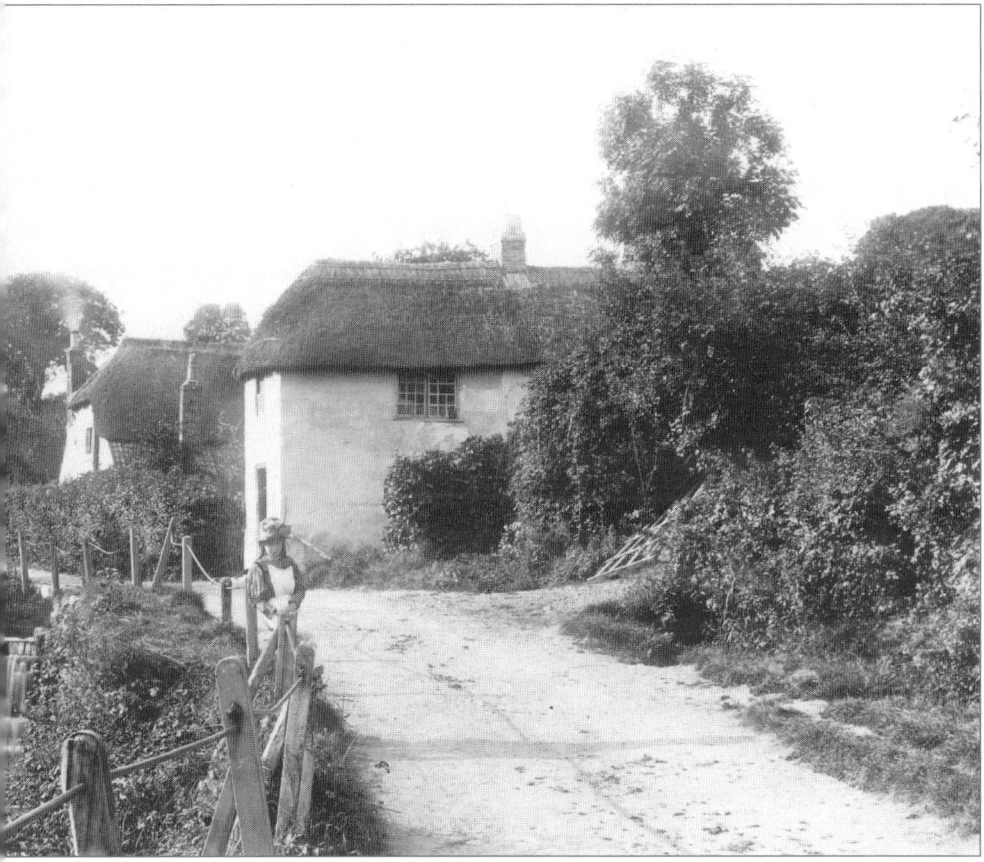

UPLYME
The Mill 1892
31315

Uplyme tends to be overshadowed by its famous Dorset neighbour Lyme Regis, though in past times the latter was known as Nether Lyme to distinguish it from the village higher up the valley of the Lim. A walk to Uplyme has always been a favourite excursion for visitors to Lyme. Jane Austen, who loved the locality, wrote of 'the woody varieties of the cheerful village of Uplyme.'

UPLYME
The Church c1960
U7004

Uplyme's church tower is 47 feet high and a prominent landmark, once used a triangulation station by mapmakers. The medieval church has some particularly grotesque gargoyles - one depicts Judas Iscariot being eaten by a demon. The walls we see here lining the churchyard path have since been removed.

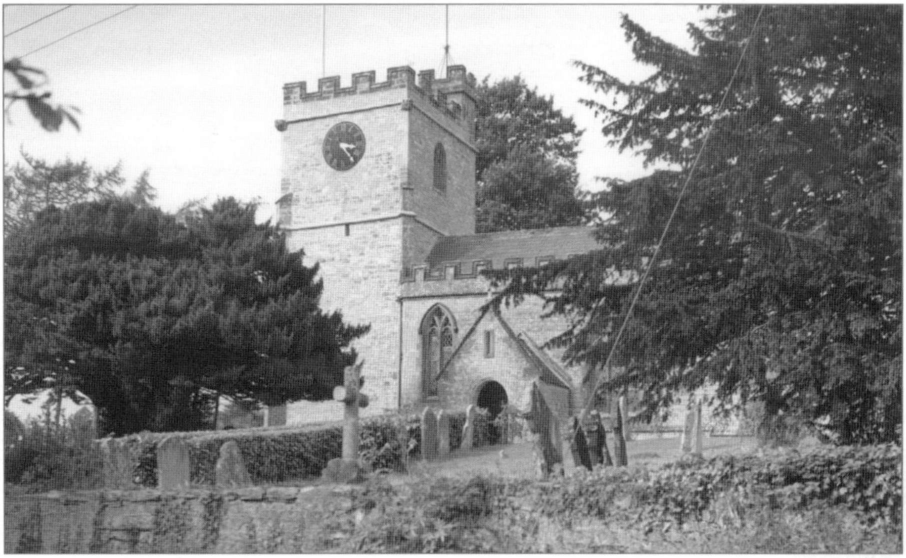

YARCOMBE
The Yarcombe Inn c1955 Y19037

This beautiful old inn started out as part of a monastery in the 9th century, and it remained a Church House, accommodating visiting clergy, during later centuries. In 1582 it was acquired by Sir Francis Drake, whose descendants have lived in the village in the years since.

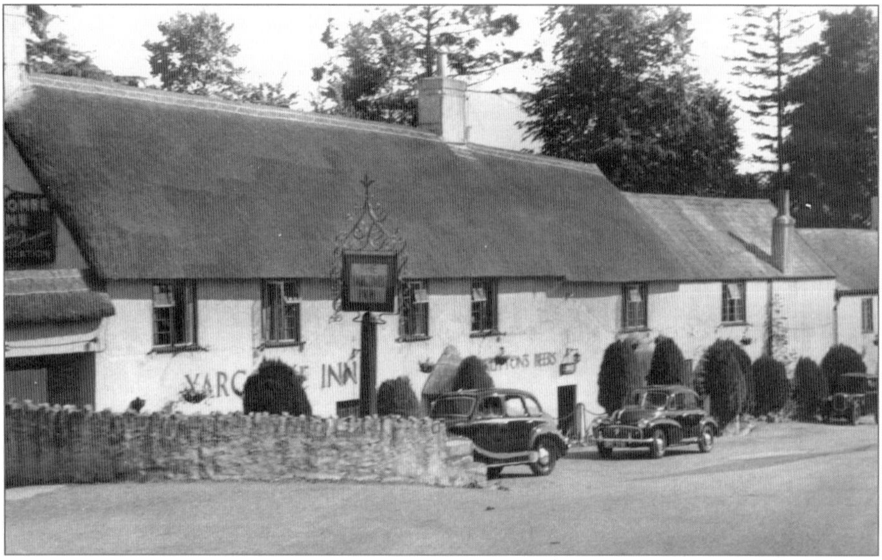

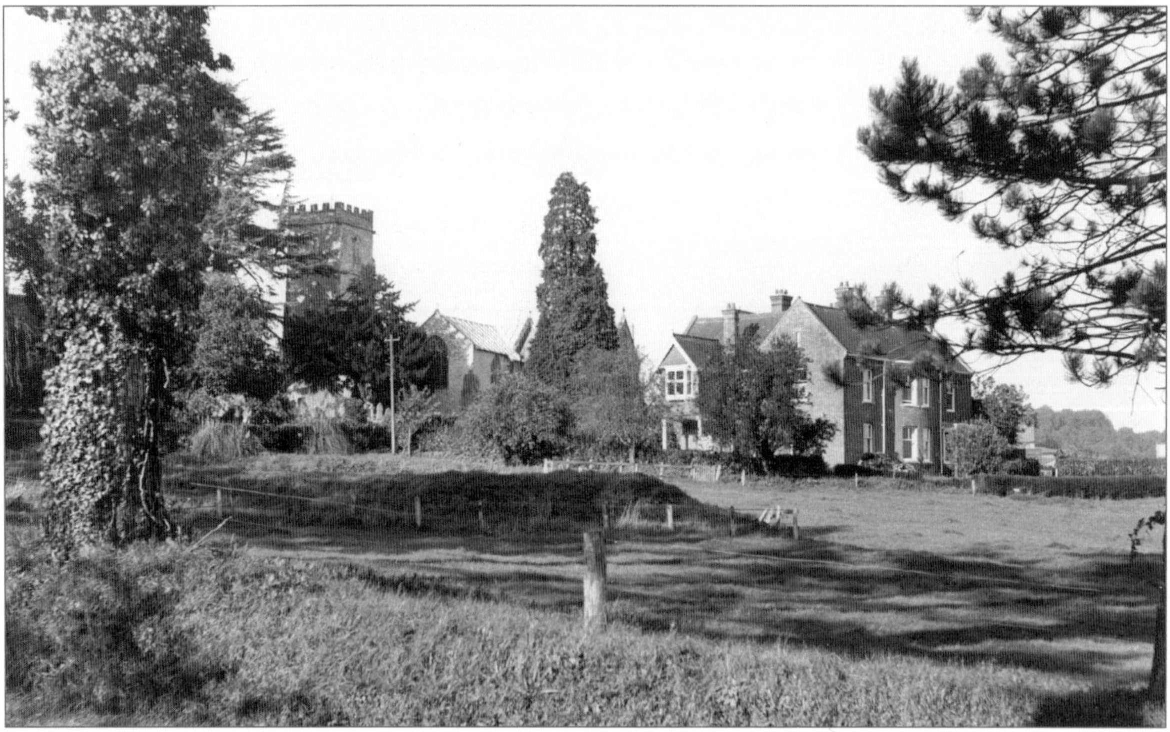

YARCOMBE, *The Church and the Vicarage c1960* Y19023

Yarcombe is situated in a beautiful fold of the Blackdown Hills, one of the least spoiled parts of East Devon. Its parish church of St John the Baptist dates from the 15th century, but it has suffered a great deal of Victorian restoration.

INDEX

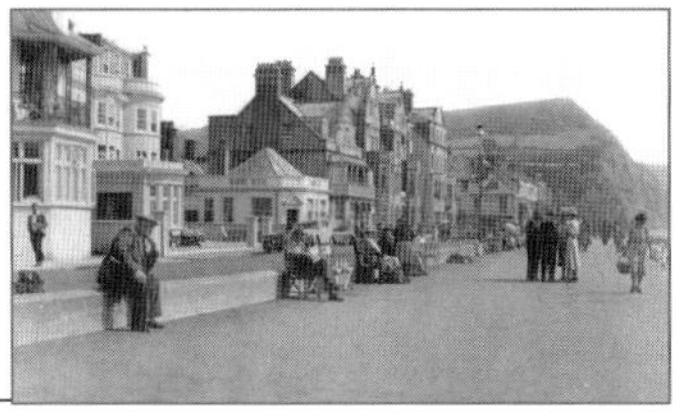

Axminster 92-93, 94-95, 96
Axmouth 86, 87, 88-89, 90, 91
Beer 13, 75, 76-77, 78-79, 80
Branscombe 73, 74-75
Budleigh Salterton 24, 25, 26, 27, 28-29, 40-41
Chardstock 96-97
Colaton Raleigh 46-47
Colyford 97
Colyton 98-99, 100
Combpyne 100
East Budleigh 42-43
Exmouth 14-15, 16-17, 18-19, 20-21, 22
Feniton 56-57
Gittisham 56-57
Harpford 49
Hawkchurch 101
Hayes Barton 44
Honiton 57, 58, 59, 60-61
Kilmington 102-103
Ladram Bay 62-63, 64-65
Littleham 22, 23, 24-25
Lympstone 28, 29, 30-31
Membury 103
Musbury 104, 105
Newton Poppleford 47, 48-49
Offwell 105
Otterton 44, 45, 46
Ottery St Mary 49, 50-51, 52-53, 54, 55
Rockbeare 34-35
Rousdon 106
Salcombe Regis 73
Seaton 80-81, 82-83, 84-85, 86-87
Shute 106-107
Sidbury 108-109
Sidford 108, 109
Sidmouth 11, 65, 66, 67, 68-69, 70-71, 72
Stockland 110, 111
Talaton 35
Topsham 31, 32, 33
Uplyme 112-113
Woodbury 36, 37, 38-39
Yarcombe 114

Frith Book Co Titles

www.francisfrith.co.uk

The Frith Book Company publishes over 100 new titles each year. A selection of those currently available is listed below. For latest catalogue please contact Frith Book Co.
Town Books 96 pages, approximately 100 photos. ***County and Themed Books*** 128 pages, approximately 150 photos (unless specified). All titles hardback with laminated case and jacket, except those indicated pb (paperback)

Title	ISBN	Price
Amersham, Chesham & Rickmansworth (pb)	1-85937-340-2	£9.99
Andover (pb)	1-85937-292-9	£9.99
Aylesbury (pb)	1-85937-227-9	£9.99
Barnstaple (pb)	1-85937-300-3	£9.99
Basildon Living Memories (pb)	1-85937-515-4	£9.99
Bath (pb)	1-85937-419-0	£9.99
Bedford (pb)	1-85937-205-8	£9.99
Bedfordshire Living Memories	1-85937-513-8	£14.99
Belfast (pb)	1-85937-303-8	£9.99
Berkshire (pb)	1-85937-191-4	£9.99
Berkshire Churches	1-85937-170-1	£17.99
Berkshire Living Memories	1-85937-332-1	£14.99
Black Country	1-85937-497-2	£12.99
Blackpool (pb)	1-85937-393-3	£9.99
Bognor Regis (pb)	1-85937-431-x	£9.99
Bournemouth (pb)	1-85937-545-6	£9.99
Bradford (pb)	1-85937-204-x	£9.99
Bridgend (pb)	1-85937-386-0	£7.99
Bridgwater (pb)	1-85937-305-4	£9.99
Bridport (pb)	1-85937-327-5	£9.99
Brighton (pb)	1-85937-192-2	£8.99
Bristol (pb)	1-85937-264-3	£9.99
British Life A Century Ago (pb)	1-85937-213-9	£9.99
Buckinghamshire (pb)	1-85937-200-7	£9.99
Camberley (pb)	1-85937-222-8	£9.99
Cambridge (pb)	1-85937-422-0	£9.99
Cambridgeshire (pb)	1-85937-420-4	£9.99
Cambridgeshire Villages	1-85937-523-5	£14.99
Canals And Waterways (pb)	1-85937-291-0	£9.99
Canterbury Cathedral (pb)	1-85937-179-5	£9.99
Cardiff (pb)	1-85937-093-4	£9.99
Carmarthenshire (pb)	1-85937-604-5	£9.99
Chelmsford (pb)	1-85937-310-0	£9.99
Cheltenham (pb)	1-85937-095-0	£9.99
Cheshire (pb)	1-85937-271-6	£9.99
Chester (pb)	1-85937-382 8	£9.99
Chesterfield (pb)	1-85937-378-x	£9.99
Chichester (pb)	1-85937-228-7	£9.99
Churches of East Cornwall (pb)	1-85937-249-x	£9.99
Churches of Hampshire (pb)	1-85937-207-4	£9.99
Cinque Ports & Two Ancient Towns	1-85937-492-1	£14.99
Colchester (pb)	1-85937-188-4	£8.99
Cornwall (pb)	1-85937-229-5	£9.99
Cornwall Living Memories	1-85937-248-1	£14.99
Cotswolds (pb)	1-85937-230-9	£9.99
Cotswolds Living Memories	1-85937-255-4	£14.99
County Durham (pb)	1-85937-398-4	£9.99
Croydon Living Memories (pb)	1-85937-162-0	£9.99
Cumbria (pb)	1-85937-621-5	£9.99
Derby (pb)	1-85937-367-4	£9.99
Derbyshire (pb)	1-85937-196-5	£9.99
Derbyshire Living Memories	1-85937-330-5	£14.99
Devon (pb)	1-85937-297-x	£9.99
Devon Churches (pb)	1-85937-250-3	£9.99
Dorchester (pb)	1-85937-307-0	£9.99
Dorset (pb)	1-85937-269-4	£9.99
Dorset Coast (pb)	1-85937-299-6	£9.99
Dorset Living Memories (pb)	1-85937-584-7	£9.99
Down the Severn (pb)	1-85937-560-x	£9.99
Down The Thames (pb)	1-85937-278-3	£9.99
Down the Trent	1-85937-311-9	£14.99
East Anglia (pb)	1-85937-265-1	£9.99
East Grinstead (pb)	1-85937-138-8	£9.99
East London	1-85937-080-2	£14.99
East Sussex (pb)	1-85937-606-1	£9.99
Eastbourne (pb)	1-85937-399-2	£9.99
Edinburgh (pb)	1-85937-193-0	£8.99
England In The 1880s	1-85937-331-3	£17.99
Essex - Second Selection	1-85937-456-5	£14.99
Essex (pb)	1-85937-270-8	£9.99
Essex Coast	1-85937-342-9	£14.99
Essex Living Memories	1-85937-490-5	£14.99
Exeter	1-85937-539-1	£9.99
Exmoor (pb)	1-85937-608-8	£9.99
Falmouth (pb)	1-85937-594-4	£9.99
Folkestone (pb)	1-85937-124-8	£9.99
Frome (pb)	1-85937-317-8	£9.99
Glamorgan	1-85937-488-3	£14.99
Glasgow (pb)	1-85937-190-6	£9.99
Glastonbury (pb)	1-85937-338-0	£7.99
Gloucester (pb)	1-85937-232-5	£9.99
Gloucestershire (pb)	1-85937-561-8	£9.99
Great Yarmouth (pb)	1-85937-426-3	£9.99
Greater Manchester (pb)	1-85937-266-x	£9.99
Guildford (pb)	1-85937-410-7	£9.99
Hampshire (pb)	1-85937-279-1	£9.99
Harrogate (pb)	1-85937-423-9	£9.99
Hastings and Bexhill (pb)	1-85937-131-0	£9.99
Heart of Lancashire (pb)	1-85937-197-3	£9.99
Helston (pb)	1-85937-214-7	£9.99
Hereford (pb)	1-85937-175-2	£9.99
Herefordshire (pb)	1-85937-567-7	£9.99
Herefordshire Living Memories	1-85937-514-6	£14.99
Hertfordshire (pb)	1-85937-247-3	£9.99
Horsham (pb)	1-85937-432-8	£9.99
Humberside (pb)	1-85937-605-3	£9.99
Hythe, Romney Marsh, Ashford (pb)	1-85937-256-2	£9.99
Ipswich (pb)	1-85937-424-7	£9.99
Isle of Man (pb)	1-85937-268-6	£9.99
Isle of Wight (pb)	1-85937-429-8	£9.99
Isle of Wight Living Memories	1-85937-304-6	£14.99
Kent (pb)	1-85937-189-2	£9.99
Kent Living Memories(pb)	1-85937-401-8	£9.99
Kings Lynn (pb)	1-85937-334-8	£9.99

Available from your local bookshop or from the publisher

Frith Book Co Titles (continued)

Title	ISBN	Price
Lake District (pb)	1-85937-275-9	£9.99
Lancashire Living Memories	1-85937-335-6	£14.99
Lancaster, Morecambe, Heysham (pb)	1-85937-233-3	£9.99
Leeds (pb)	1-85937-202-3	£9.99
Leicester (pb)	1-85937-381-x	£9.99
Leicestershire & Rutland Living Memories	1-85937-500-6	£12.99
Leicestershire (pb)	1-85937-185-x	£9.99
Lighthouses	1-85937-257-0	£9.99
Lincoln (pb)	1-85937-380-1	£9.99
Lincolnshire (pb)	1-85937-433-6	£9.99
Liverpool and Merseyside (pb)	1-85937-234-1	£9.99
London (pb)	1-85937-183-3	£9.99
London Living Memories	1-85937-454-9	£14.99
Ludlow (pb)	1-85937-176-0	£9.99
Luton (pb)	1-85937-235-x	£9.99
Maidenhead (pb)	1-85937-339-9	£9.99
Maidstone (pb)	1-85937-391-7	£9.99
Manchester (pb)	1-85937-198-1	£9.99
Marlborough (pb)	1-85937-336-4	£9.99
Middlesex	1-85937-158-2	£14.99
Monmouthshire	1-85937-532-4	£14.99
New Forest (pb)	1-85937-390-9	£9.99
Newark (pb)	1-85937-366-6	£9.99
Newport, Wales (pb)	1-85937-258-9	£9.99
Newquay (pb)	1-85937-421-2	£9.99
Norfolk (pb)	1-85937-195-7	£9.99
Norfolk Broads	1-85937-486-7	£14.99
Norfolk Living Memories (pb)	1-85937-402-6	£9.99
North Buckinghamshire	1-85937-626-6	£14.99
North Devon Living Memories	1-85937-261-9	£14.99
North Hertfordshire	1-85937-547-2	£14.99
North London (pb)	1-85937-403-4	£9.99
North Somerset	1-85937-302-x	£14.99
North Wales (pb)	1-85937-298-8	£9.99
North Yorkshire (pb)	1-85937-236-8	£9.99
Northamptonshire Living Memories	1-85937-529-4	£14.99
Northamptonshire	1-85937-150-7	£14.99
Northumberland Tyne & Wear (pb)	1-85937-281-3	£9.99
Northumberland	1-85937-522-7	£14.99
Norwich (pb)	1-85937-194-9	£8.99
Nottingham (pb)	1-85937-324-0	£9.99
Nottinghamshire (pb)	1-85937-187-6	£9.99
Oxford (pb)	1-85937-411-5	£9.99
Oxfordshire (pb)	1-85937-430-1	£9.99
Oxfordshire Living Memories	1-85937-525-1	£14.99
Paignton (pb)	1-85937-374-7	£7.99
Peak District (pb)	1-85937-280-5	£9.99
Pembrokeshire	1-85937-262-7	£14.99
Penzance (pb)	1-85937-595-2	£9.99
Peterborough (pb)	1-85937-219-8	£9.99
Picturesque Harbours	1-85937-208-2	£14.99
Piers	1-85937-237-6	£17.99
Plymouth (pb)	1-85937-389-5	£9.99
Poole & Sandbanks (pb)	1-85937-251-1	£9.99
Preston (pb)	1-85937-212-0	£9.99
Reading (pb)	1-85937-238-4	£9.99
Redhill to Reigate (pb)	1-85937-596-0	£9.99
Ringwood (pb)	1-85937-384-4	£7.99
Romford (pb)	1-85937-319-4	£9.99
Royal Tunbridge Wells (pb)	1-85937-504-9	£9.99
Salisbury (pb)	1-85937-239-2	£9.99
Scarborough (pb)	1-85937-379-8	£9.99
Sevenoaks and Tonbridge (pb)	1-85937-392-5	£9.99
Sheffield & South Yorks (pb)	1-85937-267-8	£9.99
Sherborne (pb)	1-85937-301-1	£9.99
Shrewsbury (pb)	1-85937-325-9	£9.99
Shropshire (pb)	1-85937-326-7	£9.99
Shropshire Living Memories	1-85937-643-6	£14.99
Somerset	1-85937-153-1	£14.99
South Devon Coast	1-85937-107-8	£14.99
South Devon Living Memories (pb)	1-85937-609-6	£9.99
South East London (pb)	1-85937-263-5	£9.99
South Somerset	1-85937-318-6	£14.99
South Wales	1-85937-519-7	£14.99
Southampton (pb)	1-85937-427-1	£9.99
Southend (pb)	1-85937-313-5	£9.99
Southport (pb)	1-85937-425-5	£9.99
St Albans (pb)	1-85937-341-0	£9.99
St Ives (pb)	1-85937-415-8	£9.99
Stafford Living Memories (pb)	1-85937-503-0	£9.99
Staffordshire (pb)	1-85937-308-9	£9.99
Stourbridge (pb)	1-85937-530-8	£9.99
Stratford upon Avon (pb)	1-85937-388-7	£9.99
Suffolk (pb)	1-85937-221-x	£9.99
Suffolk Coast (pb)	1-85937-610-x	£9.99
Surrey (pb)	1-85937-240-6	£9.99
Surrey Living Memories	1-85937-328-3	£14.99
Sussex (pb)	1-85937-184-1	£9.99
Sutton (pb)	1-85937-337-2	£9.99
Swansea (pb)	1-85937-167-1	£9.99
Taunton (pb)	1-85937-314-3	£9.99
Tees Valley & Cleveland (pb)	1-85937-623-1	£9.99
Teignmouth (pb)	1-85937-370-4	£7.99
Thanet (pb)	1-85937-116-7	£9.99
Tiverton (pb)	1-85937-178-7	£9.99
Torbay (pb)	1-85937-597-9	£9.99
Truro (pb)	1-85937-598-7	£9.99
Victorian & Edwardian Dorset	1-85937-254-6	£14.99
Victorian & Edwardian Kent (pb)	1-85937-624-X	£9.99
Victorian & Edwardian Maritime Album (pb)	1-85937-622-3	£9.99
Victorian and Edwardian Sussex (pb)	1-85937-625-8	£9.99
Villages of Devon (pb)	1-85937-293-7	£9.99
Villages of Kent (pb)	1-85937-294-5	£9.99
Villages of Sussex (pb)	1-85937-295-3	£9.99
Warrington (pb)	1-85937-507-3	£9.99
Warwick (pb)	1-85937-518-9	£9.99
Warwickshire (pb)	1-85937-203-1	£9.99
Welsh Castles (pb)	1-85937-322-4	£9.99
West Midlands (pb)	1-85937-289-9	£9.99
West Sussex (pb)	1-85937-607-x	£9.99
West Yorkshire (pb)	1-85937-201-5	£9.99
Weston Super Mare (pb)	1-85937-306-2	£9.99
Weymouth (pb)	1-85937-209-0	£9.99
Wiltshire (pb)	1-85937-277-5	£9.99
Wiltshire Churches (pb)	1-85937-171-x	£9.99
Wiltshire Living Memories (pb)	1-85937-396-8	£9.99
Winchester (pb)	1-85937-428-x	£9.99
Windsor (pb)	1-85937-333-x	£9.99
Wokingham & Bracknell (pb)	1-85937-329-1	£9.99
Woodbridge (pb)	1-85937-498-0	£9.99
Worcester (pb)	1-85937-165-5	£9.99
Worcestershire Living Memories	1-85937-489-1	£14.99
Worcestershire	1-85937-152-3	£14.99
York (pb)	1-85937-199-x	£9.99
Yorkshire (pb)	1-85937-186-8	£9.99
Yorkshire Coastal Memories	1-85937-506-5	£14.99
Yorkshire Dales	1-85937-502-2	£14.99
Yorkshire Living Memories (pb)	1-85937-397-6	£9.99

Frith Products & Services

Francis Frith would doubtless be pleased to know that the pioneering publishing venture he started in 1860 still continues today. Over a hundred and forty years later, The Francis Frith Collection continues in the same innovative tradition and is now one of the foremost publishers of vintage photographs in the world. Some of the current activities include:

Interior Decoration

Today Frith's photographs can be seen framed and as giant wall murals in thousands of pubs, restaurants, hotels, banks, retail stores and other public buildings throughout the country. In every case they enhance the unique local atmosphere of the places they depict and provide reminders of gentler days in an increasingly busy and frenetic world.

Product Promotions

Frith products are used by many major companies to promote the sales of their own products or to reinforce their own history and heritage. Frith promotions have been used by Hovis bread, Courage beers, Scots Porage Oats, Colman's mustard, Cadbury's foods, Mellow Birds coffee, Dunhill pipe tobacco, Guinness, and Bulmer's Cider.

Genealogy and Family History

As the interest in family history and roots grows world-wide, more and more people are turning to Frith's photographs of Great Britain for images of the towns, villages and streets where their ancestors lived; and, of course, photographs of the churches and chapels where their ancestors were christened, married and buried are an essential part of every genealogy tree and family album.

Frith Products

All Frith photographs are available Framed or just as Mounted Prints and Posters (size 23 x 16 inches). These may be ordered from the address below. From time to time other products - Address Books, Calendars, Table Mats, etc - are available.

The Internet

Already fifty thousand Frith photographs can be viewed and purchased on the internet through the Frith websites and a myriad of partner sites.

For more detailed information on Frith companies and products, look at these sites:

www.francisfrith.co.uk
www.francisfrith.com
(for North American visitors)

See the complete list of Frith Books at:

www.francisfrith.co.uk

This web site is regularly updated with the latest list of publications from the Frith Book Company. If you wish to buy books relating to another part of the country that your local bookshop does not stock, you may purchase on-line.

For further information, trade, or author enquiries please contact us at the address below:

The Francis Frith Collection, Frith's Barn, Teffont, Salisbury, Wiltshire, England SP3 5QP.
Tel: +44 (0)1722 716 376 Fax: +44 (0)1722 716 881 Email: sales@francisfrith.co.uk

See Frith books on the internet at www.francisfrith.co.uk

FREE MOUNTED PRINT

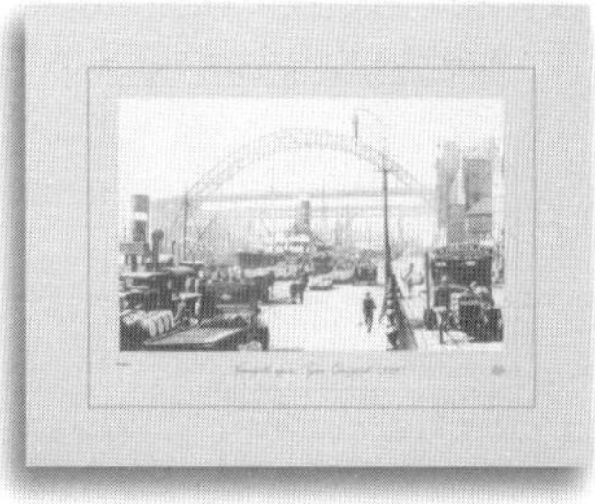

Mounted Print
Overall size 14 x 11 inches

Fill in and cut out this voucher and return *it with your remittance for £2.25 (to cover postage and handling). Offer valid for delivery to UK addresses only.*

Choose any photograph included in this book. *Your SEPIA print will be A4 in size. It will be mounted in a cream mount with a burgundy rule line (overall size 14 x 11 inches).*

Order additional Mounted Prints at HALF PRICE (only £7.49 each*)
If you would like to order more Frith prints from this book, possibly as gifts for friends and family, you can buy them at half price (with no additional postage and handling costs).

Have your Mounted Prints framed
For an extra £14.95 per print* you can have your mounted print(s) framed in an elegant polished wood and gilt moulding, overall size 16 x 13 inches (no additional postage and handling required).

*** IMPORTANT!**

These special prices are only available if you order at the same time as you order your free mounted print. You must use the ORIGINAL VOUCHER on this page (no copies permitted). We can only despatch to one address.

Send completed Voucher form to:
The Francis Frith Collection, Frith's Barn, Teffont, Salisbury, Wiltshire SP3 5QP

CHOOSE ANY IMAGE FROM THIS BOOK

Voucher *for **FREE** and Reduced Price Frith Prints*

Please do not photocopy this voucher. Only the original is valid, so please fill it in, cut it out and return it to us with your order.

Picture ref no	Page no	Qty	Mounted @ £7.49	Framed + £14.95	Total Cost
		1	Free of charge*	£	£
			£7.49	£	£
			£7.49	£	£
			£7.49	£	£
			£7.49	£	£
			£7.49	£	£
Please allow 28 days for delivery			* Post & handling (UK)		£2.25
			Total Order Cost		£

Title of this book ....
I enclose a cheque/postal order for £ ....
made payable to 'The Francis Frith Collection'

OR please debit my Mastercard / Visa / Switch / Amex card
(credit cards please on all overseas orders), details below

Card Number

Issue No (Switch only) Valid from (Amex/Switch)

Expires Signature

Name Mr/Mrs/Ms ....
Address ....
....
....
.... Postcode ....
Daytime Tel No ....
Email ....

Valid to 31/12/05

Free Print - see overleaf

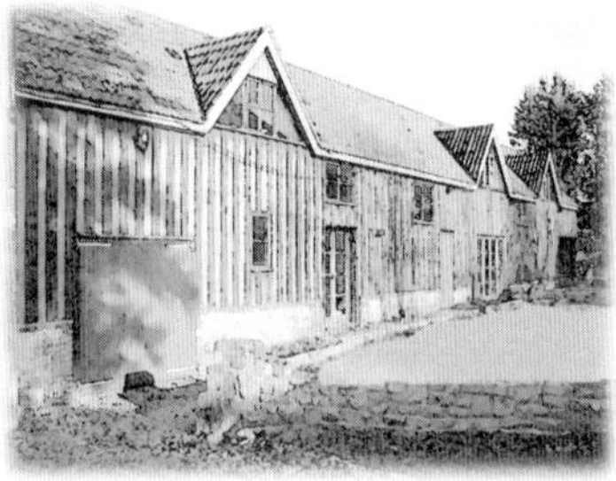

Would you like to find out more about Francis Frith?

We have recently recruited some entertaining speakers who are happy to visit local groups, clubs and societies to give an illustrated talk documenting Frith's travels and photographs. If you are a member of such a group and are interested in hosting a presentation, we would love to hear from you.

Our speakers bring with them a small selection of our local town and county books, together with sample prints. They are happy to take orders. A small proportion of the order value is donated to the group who have hosted the presentation. The talks are therefore an excellent way of fundraising for small groups and societies.

Can you help us with information about any of the Frith photographs in this book?

We are gradually compiling an historical record for each of the photographs in the Frith archive. It is always fascinating to find out the names of the people shown in the pictures, as well as insights into the shops, buildings and other features depicted.

If you recognize anyone in the photographs in this book, or if you have information not already included in the author's caption, do let us know. We would love to hear from you, and will try to publish it in future books or articles.

Our production team

Frith books are produced by a small dedicated team at offices in the converted Grade II listed 18th-century barn at Teffont near Salisbury, illustrated above. Most have worked with the Frith Collection for many years. All have in common one quality: they have a passion for the Frith Collection. The team is constantly expanding, but currently includes:

Jason Buck, John Buck, Ruth Butler, Heather Crisp, David Davies, Isobel Hall, Julian Hight, Peter Horne, James Kinnear, Karen Kinnear, Tina Leary, Stuart Login, Amanda Lowe, David Marsh, Sue Molloy, Kate Rotondetto, Dean Scource, Eliza Sackett, Terence Sackett, Sandra Sampson, Adrian Sanders, Sandra Sanger, Julia Skinner, Claire Tarrier, Lewis Taylor, Shelley Tolcher and Lorraine Tuck.